MODERN
HOUSE 2

CLARE MELHUISH

DOMESTIC ARCHITECTURE & CULTURAL VALUES IN THE 1990s

This book comprises a survey of privately commissioned, architect-designed houses across the world, most of which have been featured in the pages of international architecture magazines. Many of them have been designed, in consultation with their clients, by architects who are well known within a global architectural community, sustained both by the media and by the physical circulation of people carrying current ideas around the architectural schools and offices of the world. The transnational reputations enjoyed by these architects are built largely through the agency of the magazines, publishing built work, competition projects and exhibition reviews. These reveal, and sustain, a commonality of language across the work, even though much of it may appear visually distinct, and be physically located in far-removed places with highly contrasting, even conflicting, environmental characteristics and cultural histories. This commonality resides in an affirmation of a relationship with the recent architectural history of Europe, notably the ideology and technology developed by the architects and theorists of the Modern Movement, which undoubtedly underpins advanced architectural education throughout the world – modelled as that is on the precedents established by the major western European educational institutions.

Strictly speaking, the term 'modern' embraces the whole of history after medieval times. But it is commonly used to describe the conditions of the historical era brought into being by industrialization and capitalism, perceived as synonymous with technological and material progress, and inseparable from the concept of 'Westernization' to those societies outside the American/European economic and political axis. The Modern Movement in architecture and design aspired to give those conditions physical expression, by applying the newly available industrial technologies to the processes of construction and fabrication, and, in so doing, radically altering the historical physical environment of buildings and objects. This ambition went hand in hand with an egalitarian moral and political programme dedicated to improving the quality of life and expectations of ordinary people, particularly in the cities, through a rationalization of domestic and working lives, and the adequate provision of living space, light and sanitary facilities for everybody. It was firmly linked with the rise of Socialism, most explicitly perhaps in pre-Stalinist Soviet Russia, where the modernist agenda highlighted the need to free people from the material clutter and physical drudgery of traditional homes so that they might instead help build the new political order;[1] but equally in Clement Attlee's Welfare State Britain, where post-war reconstruction produced the highest proportion of council housing in western Europe.

The goal of being 'modern' is still highly prized by political regimes everywhere and the societies they govern, particularly in those countries still undergoing industrialization. In the West, however, the environmental and social impact of the modernizing process has taken a terrible toll, encouraging the growth of doubts and insecurities about the very nature of modernity. Once the energy of post-war reconstruction, fed by utopian dreams and a commitment of government resources, had died away, considerable disillusion set in: people had to confront the material evidence for the success of modernization. By the 1980s, a full-scale rejection of the Modern Movement design programme, understood as a vehicle of expression for the modernizing impulse, had erupted, and a whole set of assumptions about the validity of that programme was challenged.

In the precursor to this volume, Modern House, John Welsh traced the roots of the contemporary phenomenon of the privately commissioned house back to the tradition of the modernist villa established in the early decades of the twentieth century. According to Welsh, the flourishing of the phenomenon during the 1980s and early 90s owed much to the similarity of economic conditions in the two periods: boom and bust cycles creating

1   Buchli, Victor,
An Archaeology of
Socialism, (Oxford: Berg
Publishers Ltd, 1999)
2   Brindley, Tim,
The Modern House
in England, in Ideal
Homes?: Social Change
and Domestic Life,
ed Tony Chapman and
Jenny Hockey (London:
Routledge, 1999)

small economic elites of millionaires through precisely the same processes that cast millionaires onto, and beyond, the poverty line. For this type of client, the commissioning of a modern house from an architect provided an advertisement of economic success and social status defined by money and fashion, as opposed to ancestral lineage. Welsh suggests that the parallels in the conditions of patronage are reflected by the dominant influence of Modern Movement architectural imagery in the private domestic architecture of the 1980s.

However, many architects of the last two decades, even those serving rich private clients, have exercized a more critical relationship with the Modern Movement, in terms of both image and content. The new private houses of the 1990s represent a manifestation of essentially forward-looking impulses that have emerged from tremendous ideological and aesthetic battles fought during the 1980s. It is impossible to launch a discussion of private house design entirely divorced from an understanding of developments in housing design during the same period. And, as far as this is concerned, the overwhelming factor determining design policy was the unremitting condemnation of every aspect of the modernist approach – culminating in the first wholesale demolitions of, mainly high-rise, modernist housing developments. The major points of criticism

were the deterioration of the material fabric, the negative psychological effect of the industrial appearance of the buildings, and the problematic relationship between private and public space. Weighed against these negative aspects is the discovery through user surveys, cited by Tim Brindley (1999), of levels of 'strong satisfaction with the internal qualities of their homes' on the part of tenants of Modern council housing in Britain.[2] Good space standards, large windows, views of skies and open space outside, and compact, modern kitchens and bathrooms, provided most residents with considerably better standards of material comfort than were offered by the working-class housing of the previous century.

Nevertheless, housing providers embarked on a programme of reinvention of a product which looked increasingly to that model as its point of reference, as well as that of the garden city, or colonial bungalow, style of semi-detached suburban dwelling constructed earlier in the twentieth century. The collapse of Ronan Point in Britain (1968) and the demolition of the high-rise Pruitt-Igoe block in the United States (1972), are often cited as dramatic events which symbolically wiped out the certainties of the Modern Movement design programme, but a radical revision of the concept of the future of architecture was already underway. At the same time, a climate of public censorship was

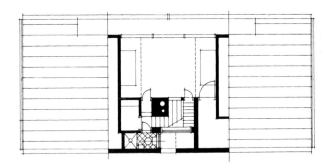

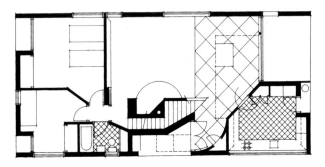

3 Herbert, Gilbert
The Dream of the Factory
Made House (Cambridge,
MA: MIT Press, 1984)

developing in Europe and America, and especially in Britain, of any interest in Modern Movement design principles, both in the domestic sphere and in that of civic and commercial buildings. This was efficiently monitored by planning authorities and by the emerging historic conservation bodies, while in Britain in the 1980s it was even given the royal seal of approval through the intervention of the Prince of Wales.

During this difficult period of radical rethinking, in which the personal desires of clients had also to be mediated by the extensive aesthetic restrictions imposed by the authorities, one of the most influential private houses was that designed by Robert Venturi for his mother: the Vanna Venturi house in Philadelphia, completed in 1964. The flat, cut-out appearance of the front facade, giving no hint of what lay behind it, represented a dramatic break with the modernist villa, in which the clarity of the form, and its streamlined, transparent three-dimensionality was of primary importance. The Vanna Venturi house presented to the world a strange ensemble of pseudo-historical features, including a dominating chimney-stack, pitched roof and gable-end front facade, split pediment motif over the front door and Diocletian window on the rear facade. Internally, the simple, orthogonal ground plan is extruded to form a complex volume and section in which the influence of

the American Shingle Style and British Arts and Crafts Movement – pre-Modern Movement developments – is evident.

If the intentions of the building itself were not immediately clear in its material realization, Venturi made them so in his book, Complexity and Contradiction in Architecture, published in 1966. This theoretical treatise was to provide the basis for an essentially anti-modernist – or 'post-modernist' – stance in architecture developed during the subsequent decade and on into the 1980s. In his preface of 1977, Venturi himself described its contents as an attack on 'the limitations of orthodox Modern architecture and city planning, in particular, the platitudinous architects who invoke integrity, technology, or electronic programming as ends in architecture … and suppress those complexities and contradictions inherent in art and experience'. Thus the Vanna Venturi house, as Venturi's first building commission, became very much the crucible for the development of an extremely influential fresh direction in architectural thinking pervading much of the architecture of the 1980s – probably quite as much as the Modern Movement itself. Certainly, the critics of Modernism, including planners and conservationists, latched on to Venturi's message, without necessarily having a proper understanding of his sophisticated intellectual agenda, and used it to underpin

The industrialized appearance of the AEG
turbine factory in Berlin (right), 1908–9, by
Peter Behrens, is symbolic of the Deutscher
Werkbund's attitudes towards the collaboration between mechanization and the arts.
    Robert Venturi's mother's house (opposite),
completed in 1964 in Chestnut Hill,
Philadelphia, was one of the most influential
private house designs to emerge since the
Modern Movement. The house represents
a break with the modernist villa approach –
a classic example of the way in which
the domestic building commission was used
as a laboratory for developing innovative
architectural concepts and technologies

their censorship of Modern Movement ideas
in the realm of construction.

The Vanna Venturi house is a classic
example of the way in which the domestic
building commission has been significantly
used by architects as a laboratory for
developing innovative architectural concepts
and technologies, meaning that private
houses have a tremendous importance in the
history of architecture. The architect-
designed private house is very rarely simply
the expression of the personal whim of a rich
individual client, largely determined by
fashion, or an advertisement for his or her
social and economic success. More often than
not the dialogue with the client represents
the framework – offering both constraint and
liberation – within which avant-garde ideas
can be explored. This was certainly the case
with the best known Modern Movement
houses, such as the Schröder House,
designed by Gerrit Thomas Rietveld for Alice
Schröder (1923–4), or the Farnsworth
House by Mies van der Rohe for Edith
Farnsworth (1945–50) – even when, as in
the latter case, the relationship between
architect and client became so strained as
finally to break down completely in a court
of law. During the 1980s and 1990s, when
the worldwide recession in the construction
industry prevented larger-scale building, the
private house became an important focus
for the development of space, form, social

relationships and construction technology, in
a climate of disillusion and suspicion about
the legacy of Modernism.

Construction

The fundamental weakness of the neo-
historical backlash in architecture was the
impossibility of reversing the revolution
which had transformed the processes of
traditional building into what had become a
'construction industry'. Mechanization and
mass production had produced far-reaching
changes in construction technology which
were inherent to the evolution of building
form and spatial organization away from
traditional models, and domestic architecture
had, since the nineteenth century, been a
crucial field of research and development in
this area. The continuation of this tradition
by the architects of the modern houses of
the 1980s and 1990s, influenced by acute
concerns about the relationship between
industry and environmental sustainability,
and also by the legacy of colonialism,
provides one of the major themes of
this survey.

The leading figures in the Modern
Movement acknowledged the implications of
the industrial revolution for architecture as
inevitable, and set out to explore the new
formal and spatial possibilities it offered.
By 1907, when the Deutscher Werkbund
was founded by Peter Behrens to promote

collaboration between industry and
architects, mechanization had already had
a far-reaching effect on construction. The
mechanized cutting of bricks, the factory
production of glass (so that it was no
longer a luxury item) and of wire nails,
revolutionizing timber construction, plus the
increasing availability of standardized,
factory-made components ready for
installation such as sanitary fittings, lights
and radiators, amounted to what Gilbert
Herbert has described as a 'creeping
industrialization' of construction.[3] There had
also been considerable progress in the
development of prefabrication technology,
which reached a high point in 1905, with the
construction by JA Brody in Liverpool of a
three-storey block of flats using panels of
reinforced concrete.

The principles of prefabricated
construction largely underlie modern
construction technology and its development
into the future. They established the primacy
of frame and infill structure over the load-
bearing masonry wall – the two fundamental
procedures of building craft classified by the
nineteenth-century architectural theorist
Gottfried Semper. Semper's work is
discussed by Kenneth Frampton in his
significant recent study of constructional
technique (and materials) as part of
the essence of architectural form and
expression, a thesis which aims to 'mediate

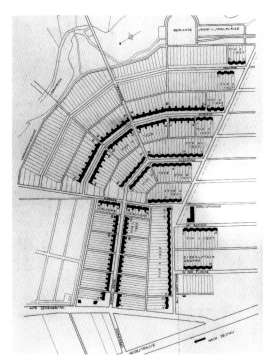

4 Frampton, Kenneth
Studies in Tectonic
Culture: the Poetics
of Construction in
Nineteenth and Twentieth
Century Architecture
(Cambridge, MA
MIT Press/Graham
Foundation, 1998)
5 Buckminster Fuller,
1972, as quoted
in Russell, Barry
Building Systems,
Industrialization and
Architecture (John Wiley
and Sons, 1981)
6 Brindley, Tim
The Modern House
in England, op cit

In response the demand for low-cost, post-war housing, the Bauhaus erected the radical prefabricated Muche-Paulick prototype steel house (left below) at the Siedlung Dessau-Törten (building exhibition) of 1926 (left). The house was made of steel plates with an insulating lining of Torfoleum board.
  Richard Buckminster Fuller's Dymaxion House (opposite) was designed in 1927, but at that time the technology to execute such a design simply did not exist. It can be regarded as a vital precursor of a visionary, 'futuristic' architectural tradition exploring new technologies and materials.

and enrich the priority given to space' as the driving principle of architectural form.[4] This is extremely relevant to an understanding of the way in which prefabrication, resulting in a general reduction in sheer material mass and weight combined with a whole new vocabulary of detailing, impinged on the nature of architecture, particularly domestic architecture, in the twentieth century.

Between 1905 and 1945, stimulated by the catastrophic destruction of homes, towns and cities brought about by the two world wars and the need for rapid reconstruction, technology advanced rapidly. After World War I, the British government approved 110 systems of industrialized construction for application in the design of houses, embracing a range of industrially produced materials and components. These included rolled-steel frames, sheet-steel panels, precast concrete units, felt insulation and asbestos-cement inner lining. In 1926, the Bauhaus (established in 1918 by Walter Gropius after his resignation from Behrens' office to explore the relationship between art and industry) erected the Muche-Paulick prototype steel house at Törten, made of steel plates with an insulating lining of Torfoleum board: wood-wool on a peat fibre base. Gropius subsequently worked extensively on the refinement of the Hirsch Copper House system, producing one of the prototype designs exhibited at the Growing House

Exhibition (Wachsende Haus) in Berlin, in 1932. The system was shown alongside several others using modular structural and panel systems designed by architects including Otto Bartning, Erich Mendelsohn, Max and Bruno Taut and Hans Poelzig. After his exile to the United States, Gropius dedicated his architectural career to the development and refinement of industrial construction systems, including the famous Packaged House, with Konrad Wachsmann, of 1943, a system comprising load-bearing wood-framed panels which was used by Richard Neutra in California.

The contribution of the Modern Movement architects in Germany to the revolution in ideas about construction, using the house as a laboratory for experimentation and development, is a fundamental influence on the work of architects today. But, in terms of the imagery of prefabricated construction, the single project which has had perhaps the most enduring impact on the imagination of architects in the latter half of the twentieth century is the futuristic Dymaxion House, designed as early as 1927 by Richard Buckminster Fuller in California. Its primary structural element was a central mast made of Duralamin and anchored in a solid base containing septic and fuel tanks. The two floors were laid on pneumatic bladders supported by perimeter tubes suspended from the mast by tensile cables. The external

walls were to be made of transparent plastic, with curtains of aluminium sheeting. Light and air were to be distributed by ceiling units, and the doors were to be operated by photoelectric cells. The futuristic character of the house was extended to a pneumatic bed, and the suggestion that clothing and bed covering would be unnecessary, because optimum environmental conditions could be maintained inside the structure.

At the time, the technology to execute such a design simply did not exist, and its visionary nature explains why it has been of such enduring interest to subsequent generations of architects, each with new technological and material resources at its disposal. In the 1960s and 70s there was a great flowering of architectural ideas and imagery which can be characterized as part of a tradition in which the Dymaxion House was a vital precursor, although other important contemporary influences, such as Pop art and high-tech, were also involved. Some of the most significant work was produced by the Archigram group in Britain, highlighting the possible uses of tensile and pneumatic structures in building construction, soft fabrics in place of the rigid materials used in both traditional and the newer prefabricated architecture, and technological gadgetry inside the home. These proposals went hand-in-hand with current ideals of social liberation and freedom of movement, emphasizing the dissolution, or reinvention, of the traditional family unit as the key to the transformation of society. In this context, the implications of radically redesigning the traditional typology of the house-home, as the

material embodiment and representation of the family unit, were particularly significant and politically provocative.

These avenues of enquiry remain vital today, less so, perhaps, in connection with a radical social manifesto (more of which later), but increasingly so in the light of ecological concerns. It is interesting to remember that Buckminster Fuller himself was promoting a highly developed ecological agenda in the 1930s, both as editor of Shelter magazine, and in his architectural work. He even went so far as to propose that architecture should be renamed 'environmental designing'. The sheer visual impact of the Dymaxion House design has tended to obscure the significance of his collaboration with his father-in-law in the immediately preceding years on the Stockade Building System, using light blocks of fibrous material such as straw bonded with cement. This concept, which was eventually bought by a large-scale commercial building operation, encapsulated Fuller's belief that the industrialization of building construction held the key to 'solving total humanity's evolutionary shelter problems', while respecting the Earth's resources.[5]

Today, the principle of lightweight, prefabricated, recyclable construction, that can be carried out quickly and simply, and does not have an irreversible impact on the earth, is central to the environmental agenda in architecture. One of the more positive effects of colonialism, in the post-colonial era, has been its introduction of Western architects to non-European building traditions which make use of locally available, replaceable

materials, and particular forms of spatial organization which enhance the interaction between structure, environment and climatic conditions. That particular history resulted most directly in the curious, but now classic, hybrid form of the colonial bungalow, but also opened up a world of sophisticated timber, mud and tent structures which embody the ideals of Buckminster Fuller, Gropius and the other pioneers of industrialized construction. Kenneth Frampton cites the instance of the late Dutch architect Aldo van Eyck, for example, whose 'anthropological approach to the primitive building cultures of North Africa' led him to use a combination of two kinds of shallow concrete dome in the orphanage he designed in Amsterdam in 1960.[6]

But advances in the production of materials, such as thermal glass and sophisticated plastics, combined with refinements in structural engineering and the massively enhanced power and scope of computer technology, have had a significant impact on the conception and design of the modern building envelope. Subsequently, a wide range of experiments have been made in the layering of thin enclosing skins made out of various substances, with the capacity to respond to varying environmental stimuli through the operation of sensors and computer programming. These technological advances are making it possible to develop construction systems which are highly sensitive and responsive to the environment; but, even more significantly, it is also suggested that the dramatic advances recently made in the new biotechnologies and nanotechnology may

7 Spiller, Neil.
Digital Dreams,
Architecture and the New
Alchemic Technologies
(London: Ellipsis, 1998).
8 Carsten, Janet and
Hugh-Jones, Stephen
About the House
(Cambridge, MA: CUP,
1995). See also an
extract from the
introduction of
Architecture and
Anthropology, AD Profile
124, ed Melhuish, Clare
(London: Academy
Editions, 1996).
9 Friedman, Alice T.
Women and the Making of
the Modern House (New
York: Harry N. Abrams,
1998).
10 Le Corbusier, Plan
of the Modern House,
lecture 1929.
11 Ravetz, Alison and
Turkington, David. English
Domestic Environments
1914–2000
(E & F N Spon, 1995).
12 Buchli, Victor.
An Archaeology of
Socialism, op cit.

even enable us to 'grow' all-natural building materials in the foreseeable future. The architect Neil Spiller proposes that nanotechnology will make it possible 'to design materials that can change their innate qualities and topologies', going far beyond the current concept of the 'smart' building embodied in the addition of 'simple prosthetics such as light sensors and small electric motors.' These developments mean that: 'Technology is at a cathartic moment: its relationship to the natural world is on the verge of becoming less parasitic and more symbiotic', and therefore 'it seems short-sighted to suggest that high technology is a danger to our ecosystem'. Spiller is emphatic that the future of architecture should not be about a '"back-to-basics" puritanism and inert, natural, hand-crafted, slow and labour-intensive manufacturing processes', but about 'an ecology of reuse and bioreconfiguration'.[7] These are all factors that will reinforce the the role of the domestic dwelling in the early twenty-first century as a laboratory for some of the interesting developments in architectural thought.

Spatial Organization

The anthropologist Claude Lévi-Strauss was the first person to put forward a theoretical understanding of the house as a form of social organization, having been inspired to consider the subject by an interest in the noble houses of medieval Europe. The significance of his work has been more recently clarified by anthropologists Carsten and Hugh-Jones,[8] who state that, despite the lack of 'any detailed attention to the most obvious feature of houses: their physical characteristics', his focus is important because 'it brings together aspects of social life which have previously been ignored or treated separately.' Carsten and Hugh-Jones suggest that architectural studies of the house have tended to 'focus on the more material aspects of dwellings … but … often say relatively little about the social organization of the people who live inside'. Clearly, the two must be fundamentally related, and a discussion of the former can only be incomplete without the latter. Carsten and Hugh-Jones put it succinctly: 'The house … is an ordinary group of people concerned with their day-to-day affairs, sharing consumption and living in the shared space of a domestic dwelling. It is out of these everyday activities, carried on without ritual, reflection or fuss and, significantly, often by women, that the house is built.'

In the context of the modern house as essentially a Western phenomenon, this definition serves to highlight the all-important role in the conception and development of an architectural idea of the dialogue between the architect and client – as future occupant of the house – and the wider social context in which that takes place. With regard to the stress on the role of women, it is interesting to note that a significant number of the key Modern Movement houses were designed for female clients, as has been documented in the fascinating book edited by Alice T Friedman, biographer of the Farnsworth House.[9]

The architects of the Modern Movement pursued ideas about the reorganization of internal domestic space which were radical for their time, but which can also be shown to be part of an inevitable historical evolution of the European and American domestic interior reflecting the process of social change and its effect on living patterns inside the home. When Le Corbusier notoriously redefined the house as 'a machine for living in', he justified the analogy in terms that were perfectly reasonable in the light of the developments and expectations of the time, and provided a more or less accurate judgement of the way things would go in the future. 'What is a house for?' he asked in 1929. 'One enters, one carries on methodical functions … Circulation is everything. One can line up the functional elements of a house in a circuit, these being dimensioned and the indispensable contiguities determined.'[10] These ideas were particularly interesting to women, whose lives were still, and remain today, very bound up with the running of the

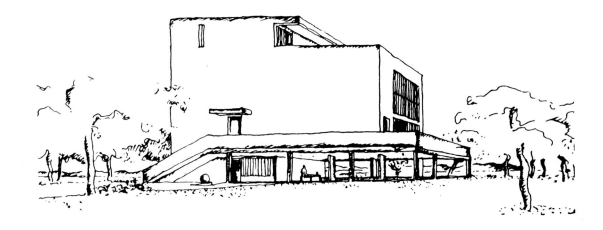

The Farnsworth House by Ludwig Mies van der Rohe in Plano, Illinois, 1945–51 (opposite), a key house of the Modern Movement, and an example of the importance of dialogue between the architect and the client, Edith Farnsworth, in the development of the brief.

Les Maisons Citrohan, 1920–2 (right). A concept for standardized housing by Le Corbusier, which established the principle of open-plan living space. The building is half-raised on pilotis, suggesting a functional stratification of the house as 'a machine for living in'.

Plan for interlocking duplex flats in the Soviet Union, 1927 (right). The development and implementation in Soviet Russia of ideas closely related to those of Le Corbusier and others in the West was explicitly intended to release women from the burdens of household labour so that they might be involved in the new political order.

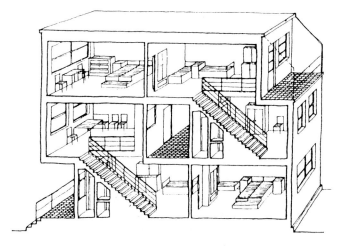

home, but whose perspective on the possibilities of life outside the home had been dramatically altered by the economic and social impact of the First World War.

David Turkington and Alison Ravetz have produced a valuable study of the evolution of the English domestic interior which clarifies change and development in spatial organization as normative, as opposed to a sustained status quo modelled on some 'traditional' ideal.[11] By the beginning of the twentieth century, the house had more or less ceased to accommodate both 'primary production (home-based and backyard industries … were scoured out by slum clearance)' and 'religious observances – the only vestige of this once important function … was in the parlour, with its hearth, family photographs and family Bible'. This represented a significant historical reinvention of the house, although the internal divisions of the home remained important in constituting particular codes of use – for instance, the location of bedrooms upstairs, the differentiation between 'public' front rooms and more private back rooms, the importance of a formal entrance hall and the separation of wet work (in a scullery), cooking and eating. But by the 1920s, this was also beginning to change, as women started to voice resentment of the extra work and isolation that such segregation entailed, especially as the incidence of servants

declined, and new, labour-saving domestic gadgetry gradually came onto the market. In this context, Le Corbusier's recommendations were not essentially revolutionary, although the development and implementation of closely related ideas in the Soviet Union was given an explicitly political dimension by the proponents of socialism – who wanted to see women released from the burdens of household labour in order to take up their responsibilities in building the new political order, and promoted the modernist concepts of the open-plan, uncluttered, labour-saving home to achieve that aim.[12]

The breakdown of internal divisions, which is exemplified in the key Modern Movement houses, and corresponding development of the larger, more open, multi-purpose space accommodating relaxation, eating, informal entertainment of guests, and even cooking, has had a fundamental influence on the way that houses are designed today. It reflects a form of social organization in which the family unit is smaller and therefore more homogeneous, and the home is used for exclusively domestic purposes, comprising activities in which the family operates as an integrated group, and which run sequentially rather than in parallel. This is very much the nuclear family group embodied in 1950s advertising images, revealing a keen emphasis on hygiene, health and efficiency, a fascination with the

13 Livingstone, Sonia:
The Meaning of Domestic
Techologies, from
Consuming Technologies:
Media and Information in
Domestic Spaces, ed.
Silverstone, Roger and
Hirsch, Eric (London:
Routledge, 1992)
14 Ravetz, Alison and
Turkington, David: English
Domestic Environments,
op.cit.
15 Damluji, Salma
Samar: The Architecture
of the United Arab
Emirates (Reading:
Garnet, 2000)
16 Reed, Christopher:
Not at Home: the
Suppression of the
Domestic in Modern Art
and Architecture
(London: Thames and
Hudson, 1996), quoting
cultural historian Walter
Benjamin

emerging new labour-saving technologies, and a society in which the formality of traditional visiting rituals was gradually being eroded.

Already cited is Brindley's reference to user studies which have 'repeatedly found' tenants of modernist council housing to express high levels of satisfaction with the internal qualities of their homes. This suggests that the open-plan concept of internal space has accurately reflected developments in post-war social and family structure. The more recent flowering of the metropolitan 'loft' phenomenon in 1990s America and Britain particularly shows how value has been reinvested into the qualities of open-plan living to stimulate a lively commercial market – at least among younger people. At the same time, the emphasis on hygiene has become even more pronounced, with a family house in the West now boasting two bathrooms as standard, or even a combined bathroom and WC attached to each bedroom. This reflects a model common to the non-temperate parts of the world and, interestingly, is a precedent already well-established in the design of late nineteenth-century colonial houses and apartments in cities such as Bombay, where frequent washing is a matter of necessity rather than choice due to the extreme heat and humidity.

This development in itself has considerable implications for the spatial organization of the home, serving to generate clustered groupings of functions (washing and sleeping) in formations which provide clues, perhaps, to the future development of the domestic interior layout. If individuals are to be provided with private washing facilities, one might ask: why not cooking and entertainment facilities too? Social psychologist Sonia Livingstone points out that, since it has become the norm to heat all the rooms in a house, not just the main living room, the likelihood of family members dispersing to different rooms has increased, enhanced by the prevalence of multiple items of domestic technology, such as telephones, televisions, radios, hi-fis and computers.[13] Indeed, certain social tendencies in the Western world suggest that the reworking of the domestic interior as a loose federation of autonomous living zones might solve many problems for families at the beginning of the twenty-first century.

A great deal of commentary exists on the so-called breakdown of the 'traditional' nuclear family, stimulated by observation of high rates of divorce and remarriage. This phenomenon has led to the emergence of greater variables in family structure, such as the possibly discontinuous occupation of any particular dwelling by increased numbers of children from different unions – and even, potentially, continued inhabitation of the same building by separated partners living independently. At the same time, the impact on Western societies of immigration from the former colonies, and gradual acculturation, has aroused awareness of and interest in alternative household models. Most notable is that of the extended family, where three generations might live together. This has particular relevance in the context of modern dilemmas about both the care of an increasingly ageing population, and that of the youngest members of society, as mothers of small children become increasingly disenchanted with a suburban nuclear family concept leading to isolation, loneliness and lack of help. More generally, the extended family represents a model of a social unit comprising many individuals of different ages, having different needs and interests, who might live together sharing some degree of common life, but also have a level of privacy and autonomy. In the light of ecological concerns about land use, the drain on resources and energy, this model is, clearly, far more efficient. From an architectural point of view, it stimulates a continuing discussion about the way the domestic interior can be organized to allow family units to live both together and apart, paying heed to common problems such as disabled access and use of traditional upper-level bedrooms, teenage noise and desire for independence, and the typical problems associated with the continuous care and

attention needed for small babies and toddlers. Both the multi-purpose space, and the clustered grouping model, along with multiple and separate access points, seem to provide useful starting points in these considerations, but ideally the flexibility to adapt to and accommodate continuous change, expansion and reduction should also be built in.

Further dimensions of cultural pluralism may also have effects, at least in the long term, on new ideas about the organization of internal domestic space. Ravetz and Turkington point out that 'Muslim households needed separate accommodation for men and women; many cultures separated inmates and strangers; and many brought the sacred back into the home, needing shrines, special places for prayer, ritual washing and perhaps religious gatherings.'[14] Salma Samar Damluji's recent study is also relevant to this discussion, showing how government-sponsored housing programmes designed to promote urban dwelling in the United Arab Emirates, and highly influenced by Western domestic models, were the subject of consistent resistance and demands for alteration by the intended occupants. These mainly focused on the inadequate number of rooms provided compared to the size of the family unit, the need for a detached kitchen and reception room (majlis), for reasons of hygiene and to preserve the privacy of the

family from guests and servants, and the need for an external living space, such as a terrace or colonnade.[15]

It will be interesting to see if the effect of cultural pluralism in the West is to stimulate a rediscovery of aspects of the pre-modern house – such as the accommodation of religious observances – in the houses of the future. But even if that were not the case, the technological revolution has already established the basis for the biggest revolution in domestic life as we know it now, but not as it was known to the families of previous centuries. The increasing availability of computer technology and access to the Internet has ensured that, for many people in the capitalist economies of the twenty-first century, home will also be the primary place of work: a return to a state of affairs predating the Industrial Revolution, and the increasing prevalence of office and factory employment. This, for the first time, led to the creation of a distinction between the living space and the work space – and with it the invention of the very notion of domesticity. Christopher Reed defines domesticity as 'a specifically modern phenomenon, a product of the confluence of capitalist economics, breakthroughs in technology, and Enlightenment notions of individuality'.[16]

In architectural terms, the reinvention of the home as centre of production has many spatial implications relating to the provision

The Schröder House (right and opposite), designed by Gerrit Thomas Rietveld with Truus Schröder in 1923–4, provided open-plan living space designed to facilitate a 'real exchange of ideas'. The house was located on what was effectively a 'brownfield' site on the end of an existing terrace of houses at the edge of the town

The plans show the upper floor with the retractible wooden partitions closed (right) and open (left), to reveal a more open-plan interior

17. Mitchell, William, City of Bits (Cambridge, MA: MIT Press, 1995), and E-topia (MIT, 1999), as discussed in his lecture at the Architectural Association, 1999
18. Casciato, Maristella, Family Matters: the Schröder House by Gerrit Rietveld and Truus Schröder, from Women and the Making of the Modern House, op cit

of dedicated workspace, and the organization of circulation to serve that space and to mediate between work and domestic activities; from the mechanical engineering perspective, it involves the reinvention of the house as a 'wired' structure, with ready access permitting repeated maintenance operations and updating of electronic data services. These areas of domestic design became extremely significant to the architects of the new houses of the 1990s – at the same time, they signal a certain inevitability in important structural and social changes in the troubled urban and suburban environments of the West as it enters a new century. William Mitchell, whose 1995 publication City of Bits offered, in his own words, 'a first sketch for some of the questions we ought to be asking about the digital world', more recently proposed that the reintegration of living and working space will generate a 'reclustering' or 'renucleation' of small-scale, fine-grained neighbourhoods'.[17] This would ensure increased local services, strengthened community structures, and a concomitant decline in crime, both in the inner city and suburban environments. His view underlines the important role that the new urban dwellings of the last decade and into the future have to play in the process of social change.

The notion of the formerly 'private' house as an increasingly permeable, public forum in which many parallel activities may take place at one time without causing disharmony, and where there is a sustained level of interaction with the environment beyond the house, was investigated in an important exhibition curated by Terry Riley at the Museum of Modern Art in New York in 1999. Entitled 'The Un-Private House', the exhibition comprised mainly contemporary American examples, but it is worth remembering that, once again, it had its precedents in European Modern Movement thinking. The Schröder House in Utrecht is a case in point, as Maristella Casciato reveals.[18] It was designed by Gerrit Thomas Rietveld for, or with, Truus Schröder, a widow with three children, who did not conform to the conventional model of wife and mother that was held up to women at that time. Born in 1889 and trained as a pharmacist, Schröder had left her husband three times, before he died, over disagreements about their children's upbringing. Not only was she trained as a pharmacist, but she also held such forceful ideas about her children's upbringing. She was explicit in her desire for a house where she could live closely with her children, and there could be 'a real exchange of ideas'. The collaboration (and relationship) with Rietveld resulted in the creation of a great open living and dining area on the first floor, which saw a constant flow of visitors

and hosted lively discussions, with smaller bedrooms arranged around it, divided by retractable wooden partitions. On the ground floor was a series of more private workrooms, including a studio, darkroom, maid's room, library and kitchen.

Described as a 'loony house' at the time by schoolmates of Schröder's daughter, it still has the capacity to startle, particularly in terms of its architectural expression, and the agenda which governed its spatial organization seems to have a renewed relevance at the beginning of a new century – as, indeed, does the choice of what was effectively a 'brownfield' site for the house on the end of an existing terrace of houses at the edge of the town.

Identity

Publications of this sort, which develop the relatively recent tradition of the picture book, help to perpetuate a perception of buildings as abstracted two-dimensional images created by the lens of the photographer and the artistic eye of the architect for the enjoyment of anonymous consumers. The image of the house provokes yearning and desire not entirely dissimilar to the advertising experience. This is particularly so in the case of the private house, because of its unavoidable conveyance of subtle messages about its occupant's style and standard of living. At the same time, media

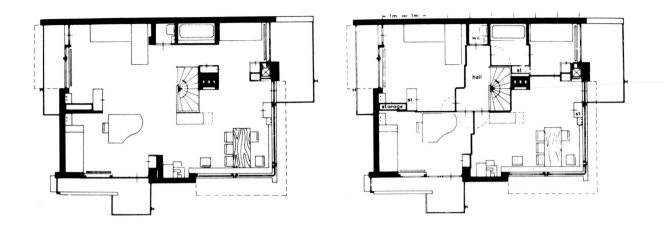

19 Tilley, Christopher Ethnography and Material culture, from The Sage Handbook of Ethnography, Atkinson, P et al (eds) (London: Sage 2000)

20 Bourdieu, Pierre Distinction: A Social Critique of the Judgement of Taste (London: Routledge, 1984)

21 Bourdieu, Pierre Outline of a Theory of Practice (Cambridge: CUP, 1977)

22 See the studies of shopping habits in north London, and customization of kitchens by council tenants on modernist estates, by anthropologist Danny Miller.

presentations of domestic architecture, in particular, are often criticized for showing houses as abstract architectural compositions, divested of all real human content and evidence of occupation. Indeed, the architecture itself may be accused of imposing an overly pure and rigid architectural order on the messy patterns of human life, failing to achieve an appropriate response to the programme of communal and individual activity which brings a house into being, and inhibiting flexibility of use, change and adaptation.

The image of a house conveys all sorts of information and triggers many cultural and individual associations in the mind of the viewer, but it is inevitably incomplete. The editing process of the camera lens effectively inhibits a proper understanding of the house as an element of material culture – that is, a multi-dimensional, synaesthetic (perceived through all five senses) material artefact which comes into its state of physical being as a result of complex social conditions, and consequently provides a focus for study and understanding of those processes. The client's motivation to commission an architect to design a house, and the architect's conception and development of a design, can thus be understood as mirrors of social and historical conditions. Furthermore, the continuous dialectic between constructions of things and persons which goes on in societies constitutes a dynamic relationship in which material artefacts themselves actively influence the developments of cultural and personal identities, and are mistakenly understood as passive.

It is important to remember that all material artefacts are polysemic, meaning that they can have a variety of different meanings depending on cultural and social context and time. And, the meaning of a house, fixed in one location, usually (but not always) forever, will always be comparatively stable compared to that of a portable material object. Nevertheless, new interpretations of the way a particular house embodies cultural and individual conscious-ness can always be constructed through time and in the minds of different commentators.[19]

The theorist Pierre Bourdieu defined a concept of habitus in the 1960s, which described everyday life as a series of micro-routines articulated by myriad forms of material culture, and establishing social status. In his book Distinction: A Social Critique of the Judgement of Taste[20], he presented and explained a detailed picture of French society and lifestyles across a broad spectrum through a survey and analysis of these forms. In an earlier study[21], he had shown how the traditional Kabyle House in Algeria displayed a structure and form which, analysed in terms of binary oppositions (for example: high/low, inside/outside, left/right, dark/light, wet/dry), reflected and sustained patterns of interaction in that society constructed around binary oppositions of youth and age, male and female and so on.

It is difficult when dealing with a global survey, as in this book, to do much more than underline the general principles driving the argument for a parallel understanding of the modern, architect-designed house as an essentially social construct rather than, say, an abstract, aestheticized product of an architect's imagination. However, one can begin to identify some aspects of the ways in which the modern houses of the 1990s have embodied cultural and individual identity defined by the conditions of post-industrial capitalism spreading throughout the world.

The major cultural forces during this period can arguably be identified as economic uncertainty, environmental anxiety and the revolution in electronic communications. The global recession at the end of the 1980s, from which only a slow recovery was made in the West during the first half of the 1990s, and which hit the Far East and former communist bloc states with even greater force in the second half of the decade, dashed the explosion of bold, ostentatious new design which celebrated the deregulation of the financial markets and conspicuous wealth of the Thatcher/Reagan years, accompanied by the slow disintegration of Eastern European and

Soviet communism. As the transition into the last decade of the century occurred, the popular pundits in the architecture and design media stressed the ascendance of new values of simplicity, understatement, and naturalness in design, reflecting a pervasive spirit of caution and a reaction against the material excesses of the 1980s. In architecture there was a marked movement away from exaggerated formal gestures, extravagant materials, and conspicuous detailing, and a return to the linear simplicity of orthogonal geometry, cheaper, renewable materials such as plywood, and unelaborated constructional detail, as the expression of a new aesthetic of the 'ordinary and the everyday'. Certainly, the post-modern emphasis on claddings, veneers, pseudo-historical detail taken from the classical canon of architecture, and loud colour virtually disappeared at this time, becoming synonymous with the brash corporate capitalism of a past era.

These tendencies in architecture were also in tune with the increasingly vocal message of environmental campaigners, aimed at an uneasy and receptive audience, and with the revolution in electronic communications, which in related ways have generated a reassessment of Western society's relationship with materiality. While it would be false to suggest that the consumer culture driven by the economic logic of capitalism went into retreat, convincing arguments have been put forward, for instance by the anthropologist Danny Miller, for the existence of more critical and discriminating relationships with the process of consumption than might be supposed.[22] The development of 'green awareness', embracing a conservationist attitude towards the consumption of material resources and things, and an awakening appreciation of the problem of accounting for the disposal of every artefact and substance in human use, must have a significant part to play in this shift. While this might be understood as a form of intensification of the engagement between humans and their material culture, there has at the same time been a heightening of interest in forms of material denial, or negation, aiming to undermine the relationship between humans and material things. This has been greatly stimulated by advances in computer technology since 1995, and the arrival of a world of virtual reality offering the potential for dissolving the material infrastructure of human life altogether. The anthropologist Victor Buchli has suggested that these developments simply represent a secular, latterday manifestation of a long, mainly religious, Western tradition of asceticism, providing a convincing rationale for the re-emergence of such an impulse in the wake of the material excesses of the 1980s.

These shifts in the dominant Western cultural value system must be read in conjunction with political events that included a general move to the left in the European and American power structures, with its implication of an enhanced sense of social responsibility and greater equality in the distribution of wealth, plus a remarkably swift indication of some disillusion – within ten years – on the part of the eastern European countries liberated, as it was thought, from communism to enjoy the material benefits of capitalism. This was especially the case in Russia itself where in 1998 the new free-market economy collapsed under the burden of corruption and gangsterism. In addition, an intensification of bad relations between the West and the new Islamic fundamentalist states succeeded in putting Western materialism and 'impiety' under a spotlight of sustained criticism.

The reassessment of material values is reflected in the new houses designed during the 1990s in all the aspects of materials, energy, and land use, and in the emergence of the concept of the pre-wired dwelling. With the Rio Summit of 1992, the statistics for consumption of natural resources made it clear that the industrialized construction industry needed to renegotiate its relationship with building materials as a matter of urgency. And with fifty per cent of the world's energy consumption attributed to

Levittown at Lake Success (left), Long Island, New York, of 1949, was one of the massive suburban estates built by the entrepreneurial developer William Levitt. It typifies the Anglo-American formula of low-density development, comprising free-standing, single-family units, each with its own plot of land, but today its environmental sustainability has been challenged.

The rooftop sundecks, pool, running track and gymnasium of Le Corbusier's Unité d'Habitation (opposite) in Marseilles, 1951, represented an enthusiasm for hygiene, health and physical fitness.

buildings, it became imperative to reduce that figure, ultimately to a level of zero demand on conventional energy sources. The slow production of environmentally friendly buildings in response to these concerns has featured private houses, among some of the more interesting experiments, because they are so often used by architects as prototypes for wider application, and because architectural competitions designed to foster innovative thinking often adopt the domestic residence due to its innate public appeal.

The popular image of the environmentally friendly building usually takes one of two forms: either the high-tech structure clad in photovoltaic cells to generate energy, and equipped with advanced electronic gadgetry designed to regulate air flow, temperature, humidity and solar glare; or the supposedly backward-looking building made of rammed earth. In both cases, the perceived solution intensifies use of material resources, and an emphasis on materiality itself. Perhaps the more valuable area of environmental thinking for industrialized society, as it spreads across the entire globe, is the development of lightweight, prefabricated construction systems, which are economic and efficient in their use of recycled or reusable materials – as recommended by the Egan Report of 1998, for the future of the construction industry in the UK. More radical are the possibilities offered by biotechnology of artificially replicating natural substances for use in construction, as outlined by Neil Spiller and noted earlier.

The other important area of change is the re-evaluation of the now traditional Anglo-American formula of the low-density development of free-standing, single-family units, each with its own plot of land, which provided the highly successful recipe for the classic twentieth-century suburb. As the influential British writer on the environment, Colin Ward, has argued, this model has much to recommend it as 'the child-rearing sector of the city … a comprehensible setting', where, in the 1950s, 'the produce of the ordinary domestic garden … more than equalled in value the produce of the land lost to commercial food production', and to which, in the 1990s, many wild and rare species have fled from the countryside, in search of a safe haven.[23] But much of the suburban environment in its current, degraded form has become indefensible in terms of environmental sustainability, characterized by greedy land consumption, disorganized sprawl threatening green belts, and heavy dependence on motorized transport exacerbated by the intensification of a residential monoculture served by 'out-of-town' retail parks. This has stimulated a search for new models of densification in development and land use which could create greater efficiency in the use of resources, improved social cohesion through the integration of shopping, education, work and social provision with residential development, and a drastic reduction of dependence on the car. Notably, the discredited high-rise model has attracted some renewed interest as an appropriate domestic form for educated, relatively well-to-do, primarily urban communities. The urban 'loft-living' phenomenon has created a market for recycled, multi-occupancy, mixed-use industrial buildings, often comprising commercial units at ground level and rentable work space alongside the domestic accommodation. In the suburbs themselves, new models, building on earlier traditions, for terraced, semi-detached and even underground houses have been mooted,[24] with the aim of intensifying land use and consolidating shared infrastructure.

In 1995, just at the point of the internet revolution, the French philosopher Paul Virilio warned that cybertechnology posed a threat to the 'spatial relations fundamental to intimacy and democracy' and that, in a world where the notion of distance is replaced by that of a transmitting power, 'all the conceptual bases of architectonics are literally collapsing'.[25] Silverstone, Hirsch and Morley have also discussed the potential threats posed by domestic technologies and media to the maintenance of the 'moral

23 Ward, Colin. Sustainable Settlements, from Resurgence magazine, January/February 2000, No 198.
24 See for example Pierre d'Avoine's Invisible House, London, which he describes as an imaginative elaboration of the cellar or basement tradition in London houses.
25 Virilio, Paul. Open Sky (London: Verso, 1997).

economy' of the household, as an 'economic, social and cultural unit' which 'engages in a process of value creation in its daily practices'.[26] They argue that each household's achievement of what Anthony Giddens has defined as '"ontological security" – a sense of confidence or trust in the world as it appears to be' is complicated by the way that the increase of technology and media in the home allows the outside, public world to penetrate and influence the bounded, private, domestic environment, and the relationships between household members. It seems clear that technology has the potential both to unify households, but also to contribute to disengagement and lack of cohesion within the household by encouraging individuality and independence in its members. However, as the twenty-first century opens before us, there is considerable consensus that electronic communications are seemingly reintegrating societies, and strengthening personal relationships in a way that was not foreseen – facilitating, rather than destroying, embodied, face-to-face human contacts. This suggests a reading of the 'wired' dwelling as a dynamic, connected, communicating base unit of social organization, as opposed to the commonly envisaged image of the introverted, isolated, individualized 'home-as-prison'. It is arguable that this reinjection of vitality into the house-organism, which had been drained

of life by the development of the office society, has opened the way for a revitalization of the 'conceptual bases of architectonics' in domestic architecture, particularly as they relate to the experience of embodiment, because it reinstates a more holistic association between the home and the body.

One identifiable aspect of this development has been the exploration of local and regional expression in domestic architecture, a theme which emerges in many of the houses featured in this book. While there is a great deal of truth in Christopher Tilley's argument that the capitalist world system has 'resulted in the systematic erosion of locality as meaningful', because 'everywhere [is] homogenous in its particular exchange value for any particular project',[27] it is also true that intensified occupation of the home, facilitated by global communications and the growth of the information economy, allows the development of the home as local base, anchored in the day-to-day life of a local community, and so strengthening the meaningful character of locality. These factors suggest a departure from 'universal' ideals of architecture, be they classical, modernist, or post-modernist, and an embrace of local conditions. This reflects the findings of other anthropologists and researchers in the field of globalization, which reveal a strong, and perhaps

unexpected, link between the development of the global economy and growing expression of regional and local cultural identities: a globality defined by the theorist Saskia Sassens as not so much an over-arching condition, but rather a 'multitude of localities' involved in global projects.[28]

While there is much to be positive about in the process of social and cultural change at the beginning of the twenty-first century, it is undeniably the case that the sheer speed of change during the course of the last century, and particularly in its final decades, has created a world of intense pressure, uncertainty and doubts about the future for most individuals. For those in a position to commission a house, the retreat to an isolated spot in an untouched rural landscape, remote from the ever-advancing tentacles of urbanization, remains a strong temptation. For the architect, the commission to design an escape from the pressures and endless self-questioning of contemporary life, in which to be reassured of nature's timeless cycles of slow growth, decay and rebirth, may be both the most demanding and the most inspiring of his or her career.

The appeal of the pastoral ideal, and its evocation in the realm of domestic design, has been traced back at least to the nineteenth century by Joyce Henri Robinson: 'The quest for an uncomplicated moment of felicity in the midst of a highly complicated

26 Silverstone, Roger; Hirsch, Eric and Morley, David. Information and Communication Technologies and the Moral Economy of the Household, from Consuming Technologies, op cit.
27 Tilley, Christopher. A Phenomenology of Landscape: Places Paths and Monuments (Berg, 1994).
28 Sassens, Saskia. First BJS Millennial lecture, London School of Economics, Jan 25th 2000.
29 Robinson, Joyce Henri. 'Hi Honey, I'm Home': Weary (Neurasthenic) Businessmen and the formulation of a Serenely Modern Aesthetic, from Not At Home, op cit.

society is the concomitant to life lived in the city, and since ancient times (as Horace reveals) the onward and increasingly fast-paced march of civilization has been habitually accompanied by the laments of weary sojourners longing for a realm of pastoral calm.'[29] Robinson reveals that from the end of the nineteenth century, when nervous exhaustion amongst exhausted 'brain-workers' was identified as a prevalent medical disorder, numerous treatises emphasized the importance of a calm, serene, psychologically and emotionally restorative, domestic environment offering an oasis of restfulness in, or away from, the city. It is from this time that we can date ideas about forging connections between home and landscape – whether by introducing artists' representations of the pastoral landscape into the home, or, as in the modernist tradition, framing views of the landscape outside the house to be enjoyed from within. Also noticeable from this time is a developing interest in the psychology of the planning and decoration of the domestic interior, and subsequently, corresponding to the historical emphasis in Western thought on the individual and self-realization, the concept of the home as an extension of the self.

In the 1990s, contemporary social and cultural developments rendered the concept of the serene, simple domestic interior once again very appealing, as described earlier –

and in stark contrast to either the pop aesthetic of the 1960s and 70s, or the post-modernist artifice in form and colour, and its pseudo-symbolic content, of the 1980s. But the defining feature that distinguishes the manifestation of that ideal in recent domestic design from that of the modernist period, is the added emphasis on sensuality. Whereas the modernist architects certainly acknowledged the importance of the body and physicality in their work (one only has to think of Le Corbusier's design for the Unité d'Habitation in Marseilles, with its rooftop sundecks, pool, gymnasium and running track, and its views of the mountains and the sea), it represented more of an enthusiasm for hygiene, health and physical fitness, almost as moral values, than an interest in a genuinely hedonistic experience of domestic living. For many clients today, whose values have been shaped by the moral and sexual revolution of the 1960s, as well as a consumer explosion encouraging the legitimation and unabashed, deserved gratification of personal desire, it is the wish to build this kind of experience into everyday domestic life that often leads them to an architect in the first place.

The result is an architecture which aims towards a manifest expression of the client's sense of self-identity and social relations, whether as individual, couple or family, or all of these things, and as experienced at

both the bodily, sensual and psychological, emotional levels. Indeed, the process of dialogue involved in developing a design programme capable of achieving this ideal may often cast the architect in a perceived or actual role of psychologist, therapist, confidante – and even lover – to the client. Certainly, the development of a dialogue around a domestic design brief will always have an intense and personal aspect, which explains the reluctance among some architects to engage with domestic commissions at all.

For many architects, the contemporary ideal of the house as an idyllic home created in the image of the self represents the most difficult challenge. It has been highly developed in the popular press and media of the 90s, for example in the proliferation of TV programmes about home design, which have been blamed for encouraging unrealistic aspirations and expectations in an expanding lower end of the market. It implies a notion of design strongly coloured by resistance to functionalism, in which the possibility of developing objective, rational and abstract solutions to organizational, spatial and formal problems of house design is drastically complicated by the need to explore and realize the ever-variable and fluctuating sensual and psychological dimensions of 'home' at the start of the twenty-first century.

Glenn Murcutt's Marika Alderton House in Northern Territory, Australia, 1994, was designed to be a 'healthy building', constructed out of industrialized plywood sheeting and with a roof of corrugated metal.

For years, the environmental agenda in Western architecture was widely viewed as the preserve of a particular type of practice linked ideologically to the European and American counter-culture movements of the 1960s and 1970s, or to the intervention work of Westerners acting as enablers for community building projects in the 'developing' world. The concept of environmentally sound architecture was packaged in organic forms, earthy materials and labour-intensive construction which represented, to many practitioners, a simultaneous denial of industrial progress, intellectual content, urban culture and the economic logic of capitalism. It was fundamentally anti-modernist, over-emphasizing the 'natural', or 'primitive', emotional and sensate identity of human beings, without acknowledging the significance of learnt culture, urban sophistication, the necessity for economic survival, and the value of technological advances.

This situation has changed dramatically since the public acknowledgement of the severity of the ecological decline, underpinned by fears about the global threat posed by the industrialization of vast new tracts of the earth's surface, and by the inexorable growth of the global population. According to 'deep-green' theorist Mayer Hillman, of London's Policy Studies Institute, emissions must be cut by ninety per cent over the next ten to fifteen years if environmental catastrophe is to be prevented. Such predictions have promoted the institutionalization of a level of environmental awareness across most sectors of society, and certainly within the construction industry, responsible for a vast proportion of the world's energy consumption. The American economic analyst Amory Lovins has identified a newly emergent stage of economic development which he calls 'natural capitalism', and which recognizes the environment as 'containing and sustaining the whole economy'. He believes that the international business community is the only sector of society with the necessary economic and technological know-how – and the political leverage – to achieve a transformation of mankind's relationship with the planet, and that this process, which is already in place, will be accelerated by natural competition among companies to reduce 'unsaleable production', or waste, and move away from the production of goods to the delivery of services. Lovins points to the political trend towards taxation of waste rather than work, and competition between national governments to catch up on the environmental issue, as a natural corollary of economic evolution towards sustainable practices based on sound capitalist business principles.

According to Lovins, 'natural capitalism' represents the second big intellectual shift after the fall of communism in the last century, heralding a new economic order where

The steel and canvas 'tent house' by Gabriel Poole (left), at Eumundi, Australia, 1996, which embodied the principles of connection between house and natural environment, was the immediate predecessor of the Poole House at Lake Weyba.

The Baeta House, São Paulo, 1993 (right), was the first among the 'tree houses' designed by Marcos Acayaba to explore the use of a plan generated by triangular geometry, so as to reduce its impact on the site.

Like his Mexican Whale House, Javier Senosiain's earlier house built for himself, the Organic House, Mexico City, 1987, is generated by organic curves which give the impression of being constructed out of earth, in fact it is made of sprayed polyurethane foam (far right and below).

GDP no longer constitutes the gauge of economic success, and the contradictions between home and work life can be removed. Within this context, 'environmentalism' in architecture has taken on new, more sophisticated and subtle forms which represent an easy accommodation of values formerly regarded as conflicting. It would be rare now to discover any intellectually engaged, urban architect producing high-profile work that did not incorporate a level of environmental awareness.

The impact of the environmental agenda on the production of new domestic architecture can be identified at two levels. On the one hand, there are the architects working on individual projects within a general framework of environmental values which may be more or less cosmetic in character; and on the other, are those architects who have become engaged in research towards the development of new sustainable building systems which might have a widespread application. For the latter, each individual house takes on the role of a potential prototype.

In the past, the design of building systems has been regarded as fundamentally associated with the industrialization of the building process, and therefore anti-environmental in character. However, the re-evaluation of the industrial process as a potential route towards improved environmental sustainability, through the

development of new manmade and even artificially produced natural materials, and cycles of reuse (or 'loops of material flows' as Lovins puts it) has changed the received wisdom. Of the projects featured in this section, three use timber or steel structures specifically intended to be prefabricated. The Poole House makes use of PVC sheeting and polycarbonate, as well as the more 'natural', though also manufactured, canvas as infill materials, while both the Acayaba and Marika Alderton Houses make use of industrialized plywood sheeting, and, in the case of the latter, corrugated metal for the roof. It is now accepted that a lightweight, factory-manufactured, well-insulated prefabricated system which sits lightly on the ground, is easily erected and dismounted and potentially recycled in other buildings, as well as easily adaptable for future use, may very often be a more environmentally sustainable solution than a heavy construction with thermal mass which is intensive on materials and difficult to alter or remove in the future.

Of particular interest, in the light of this debate, is the work of Javier Senosiain, whose Mexican Whale House and earlier Organic House, which to all outward appearances seem to conform precisely to an outdated image of environmentally friendly architecture. The buildings encourage the assumption that their ground-hugging, swelling form, generated by organic curves, must be constructed out of

earth. On the contrary, these are lightweight structures made of polyurethane foam sprayed over a balloon form inflated with a fan. Once the balloon has been deflated, the exterior and interior of the hardened foam is spread with cement mortar mixed with metal fibres, creating a habitable enclosure with thermal properties such that neither mechanical heating nor cooling of the house is necessary.

This is a case which reveals a play-off between the use of industrially manufactured materials, and the achievement of long-term energy efficiency at the level of one domestic unit, and potentially many, depending on how the system is developed in future. The other

slowly developing investment of this sort is the use of photovoltaic cells as an integral part of the architectural structure, to harness solar power in the goal of drastically cutting levels of energy consumption. The Charlotte House, featured in this chapter, is an example of a traditionally constructed timber-frame structure, and cellulose-based recyclable insulation materials, which incorporates a series of solar panels into a distinctive barrel-vaulted, metal-clad roof. But in most countries of the world, this technology remains prohibitively expensive, and relatively inefficient, to encourage the development of a sophisticated architectural approach to its incorporation within pre-existing concepts of architectural form and materiality. Significantly, perhaps, architect Wes Jones (see Concept Houses), proposes that the technology might rather become a part of the streetscape than a standard element of the domestic house form.

It seems clear that the gauge for environmental performance in the architecture of the future will not, then, be a return to natural materials and construction methods per se; but, rather, the reduction of material density, the use of thermally efficient and environmentally responsive new materials and mechanisms activated by high-tech sensor devices, the inbuilt potential for recycling, and a minimization of physical disturbance and contamination of the ground itself.

Charlotte House
Stuttgart, Germany
1993
Behnisch & Partner

Opposite, clockwise from top left: the barrel-
vaulted roof of the Charlotte House represents
an eye-catching variation on the conventional
typology of the suburban context, while also
providing a large surface-area for the
installation of photovoltaic cells; the glazed south
elevation looks out onto the street, emphasizing
the relationship between public and private life,
and maximizing the advantages of solar gain
during the cooler seasons; the sides of the
house reveal a variegated surface texture to
the building, emphasizing the materiality of the
architectural conception.

The drawings of the house show that the
timber-clad north elevation (bottom) is more
enclosed, with smaller windows to inhibit cooling,
while the south elevation (top) is largely glazed,
with sliding slatted screens and louvres. The
cross section (middle) reveals the extent of the
internal volume contained within the roof space,
designed with the potential to be reorganized as
an autonomous flat in the future.

The well-established German practice of Behnisch and
Partner is primarily associated with large-scale, public
buildings with an explicit social programme – amongst
which the Munich Olympic Park of 1972, and the more
recent Plenary Hall of the German Bundestag in Bonn,
1992, are particularly notable. Both schemes have a
high public profile, not just because of their national
significance and civic symbolism, but also because of their
implementation of an architecture which is unusually open
to the environment. The Olympic Park is particularly
remarkable, conceived as a transparent, floating 'roof
over the landscape', on land that had fallen into disuse.
The undulating acres of open-sided, tensile canopy
structures, designed in consultation with Frei Otto,
provide shelter from the elements without obstructing
the view of the sky, or of the landscape all around. The
scheme for the Bonn Parliament met with an initially
hostile reception because of the extensive use of glass
to create a high level of transparency to the plenary hall,
symbolically exposing to view the activities within, but
also creating a strong connection between the interior
of the building and its external environs.

The 'solar-powered' Charlotte House, then, seems
a natural extension of this relationship between architecture and the environment in the practice's work.
However, the architects have questioned whether the
house, designed for Günter Behnisch's daughter Charlotte
and her sons in the wooded suburbs of Stuttgart, is really
worthy of that description. They have also revealed that
they have relatively little interest in designing small-
scale residential buildings of this sort, because of the
restrictions which make it difficult to produce anything
new or experimental. Notwithstanding their protestations,

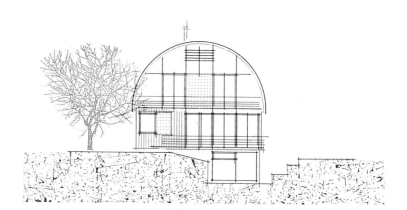

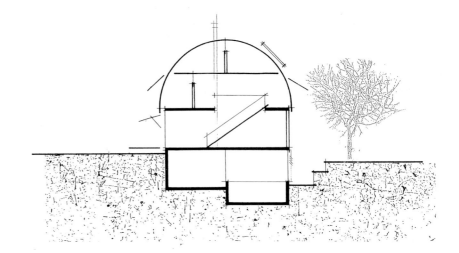

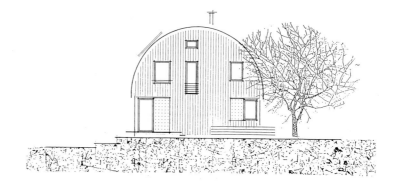

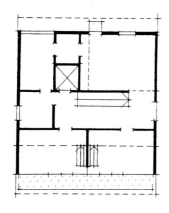

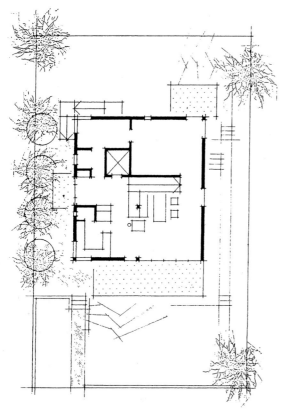

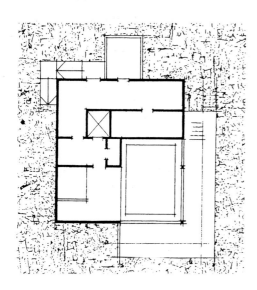

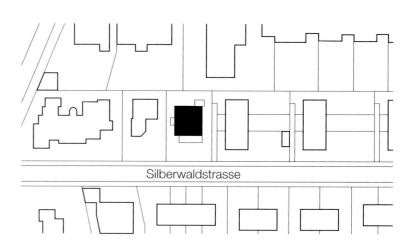

Silberwaldstrasse

this house still stands out as a relatively rare example of a refined contemporary design which makes use of roof-mounted solar collectors to heat the water supply, and seeks to meet the 'principles of biological building' in a general sense by using natural materials and minimizing the impact of construction on the site as far as possible.

Ken Shuttleworth's Crescent House in the UK (pp58–65) is a typical example of a house where provision is made for the future implementation of solar collectors 'when it becomes economically viable', and it is a fact that the installation of photovoltaic cells, certainly in domestic buildings, still remains rare in most parts of the world. As a result, the questions surrounding the ways in which they might be integrated into an architectural approach have been largely unexplored to date. Certainly more progress has been made in Germany where the technology has far greater currency. Even so, it is most common to find that solar panels, when installed, do not meet the full energy requirements of a house, and that energy for heating usually has to be supplied by additional means. This is the case at the Charlotte House, where the seven solar collectors – covering 18.6 square metres of surface area – a solar water heater of 500 litres capacity and a heat exchanger for the swimming pool comprise a solar collection plant on the roof. This heats the hot water supply and swimming pool in summer but, at other times of year, must be supplemented by a gas-fuelled boiler.

Despite these limitations, it seems appropriate that the most obvious architectural feature of the house, which distinguishes it from its suburban neighbours, is the roof itself, designed as a large barrel vault, or 'drum' roof – although not specifically in order to accommodate

The house plans (opposite) reveal a form of spatial organization which satisfies the archetypal image of the house: a 'cellar'-type basement (bottom), containing a swimming-pool and sauna, and 'attic'-like upper storey (top), containing the bedrooms, with a largely open-plan living space at entrance level (middle), giving onto the garden. The site plan reveals the context of suburban houses and gardens.

The main living space (top left) is light and airy, opening onto a terrace overlooking the street. The kitchen area is visible in the background with the dining area to the fore. The kitchen zone (top right) looks out onto the entrance passage, which provides a more private zone of arrival and greeting at the side of the house. This provides a counterpoint to the sense of connection with the houses across the street which is enjoyed from the living space (bottom).

the solar plant. This unusual shape, which maximizes the usable internal volume, was only accepted by the neighbours because it brought a reduction in the overall volume of the building from the original proposal. The preliminary design was three storeys in height, instead of two, with a saddle-back roof, responding to the client's wish that an upper storey could potentially be separated off and rented out when her sons leave home in the near future. Other requirements included a lift and special fixtures in all rooms, since the client has difficulty in walking, as well as a small swimming pool and a sauna for her physical training and fitness. These have been located in the basement, or cellar area, which becomes a clearly defined area of domestic activity apart from the primary living zone. The pool opens out onto an excavated courtyard within the garden terrain.

The main living areas are on the ground floor, entered via a side entrance to the house, with an open staircase rising from the open dining area to the upper level. The bedrooms and two bathrooms are located under the protective curve of the roof, as if in an enlarged attic, and each of the son's rooms has its own ladder providing access up to separated gallery areas within the height of the roof space, as well as access to a terrace at the front of the house. This floor still has the potential to be reorganized as an autonomous flat, and provided with separate access via an external staircase, when the sons are no longer based at home.

The predominant materials used in the construction of the house are timber, glass, and, for the roof cladding, metal. Considerable care was taken to use wood that had not been treated with chemical products – paints and lacquers are made from natural resins and cellulose-

The two bedrooms (top) on the south elevation
each have an upper gallery level (opposite),
which allows a special enjoyment of the roof
space, and which is reached by separate ladder
stairs. The main staircase from the ground floor
to the bedroom level (bottom) is an understated
structure which appears to be part of the
furniture of the living space and dining area.

based recyclable materials are used for insulation instead
of mineral fibre. The treatment of the south facade, facing
the street, as a largely glazed elevation equipped with
sliding slatted external screens and ventilating louvres,
helps to maximize the warming effect of the sun at cooler
times of year and daylight levels, while guarding against
over-heating of the interior in summer. The timber-clad
north facade is more enclosed with smaller windows to
prevent cooling, and has almost the appearance of an
industrial agricultural building.

The architects describe the house as being 'free from
the conformism based on building regulations' and, at the
same time, within those liberating parameters, nurturing
the sense of security and self-confidence of the client's
family. Perhaps this is because, although in terms of its
external appearance it asserts its difference from
conventional houses, its spatial and volumetric character
satisfies the archetypal image of the house which the
French philosopher Gaston Bachelard subjected to
illuminating psychological analysis:

'A house constitutes a body of images that give
mankind proofs or illusions of stability ... To bring order
into these images, I believe that we should consider two
principal connecting themes: 1, A house is imagined as
a vertical being ... 2, A house is imagined as a concentrated being ... Verticality is ensured by the polarity of
cellar and attic, the marks of which are so deep that, in
a way, they open up two very different perspectives for
a phenomenology of the imagination.'

Marika Alderton House
Yirrkala, Northern Territory, Australia
1994
Glenn Murcutt

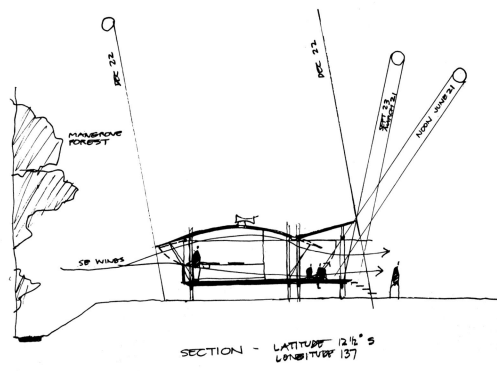

SECTION – LATITUDE 12½° S
LONGITUDE 137

DEC 22
DEC 22
SEPT 23 / MARCH 21
NOON JUNE 21

MANGROVE FOREST

SE WINDS

Murcutt's preliminary sketches of the Marika Alderton House reveal how the scheme is generated by a response to environmental conditions. The section (top) explores formal possibilities in relation to the angle of the sun's rays and ventilating air flow through the interior. The diagrammatic sketches (below) show the outline of the house as built, in relation to air flow (top left) and the organization of the roof structure to generate shade around the house.

The house takes on an animated appearance when the panels in the timber-built walls are opened (opposite), increasing air flow through the house, and transforming the whole perimeter of the house into an active threshold between the house and the surrounding landscape.

When Mies van der Rohe's Farnsworth House, designed for Edith Farnsworth, was illustrated in the magazine Architectural Forum in 1951, Glenn Murcutt's father, a house-builder in New Guinea and Clontarf and a subscriber to the magazine, interrogated his thirteen-year-old son on the design. Later on in Murcutt's own career as an architect, renowned for his private houses, he was himself to be described as 'a timber and tin Miesian' by the British architect Alison Smithson. However, his sense of empathy with the aims and means of the modernist tradition is fundamentally mediated through a deep awareness of the way that landscape, climate and culture shape architecture and ways of life. Perhaps the most fundamental way in which this sensibility and response to natural context manifests itself in Murcutt's work is through the consistent development of an environmental design programme which generates both the functional dynamics and the poetics of his architecture.

Coincidentally, the Marika Alderton house was also designed for a woman: Marmburra Marika, a well-known Aboriginal artist, along with her partner Mark Alderton, and children. Unlike Edith Farnsworth, however, Marika maintains regular contact with the architect of her house, even though they live 2,500 kilometres apart. Murcutt admits 'the house is not perfect – it is not a prototype, it is a start', but 'it does achieve many of the important cultural, spatial, climatic and technological requirements ... last year [1999] another house was constructed in the same community using the same principles.'

At one point during the realization of the building, Marika suggested it might be a 'bridging house' between

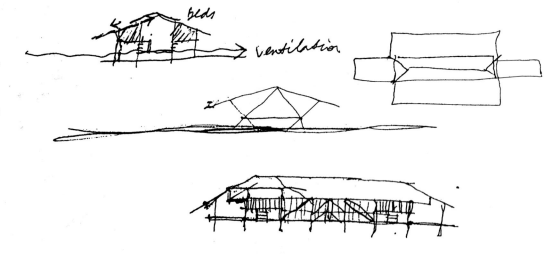

beds
ventilation

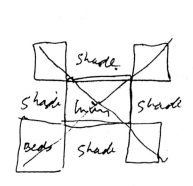

shade
shade | main | shade
Beds | shade

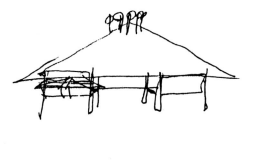

When the wall panels are opened, the side
elevations reveal the transparency of the house
and emphasize the lightweight nature of the
structure (opposite and right). It is raised off
the ground on stilts to protect against animals,
insects and rising water levels, and sheltered
from the sun above by the expansive roof
volume. Along the ridge are situated a series of
'windworkers' which help to suck air through
the house, assisting the process of natural
ventilation.

The detail of the side elevation (middle)
highlights the way the whole edge of the house
is elaborated with openings and ledges. From a
distance (middle left) the roof expanse is the
most solid visual feature of the house but, at the
same time, it seems to merge into the sky. The
elevation and ground plan (bottom) reveal the
distinct but interactive relationship between the
core and the peripheral zone of the structure
and living spaces.

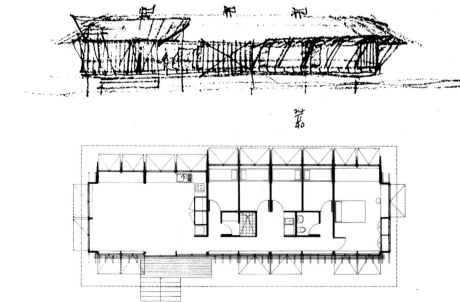

the cultures of the Aboriginal community and the
dominant white settler community. It represents a stage
in the natural evolution of Murcutt's work over a period
of thirty years, which manifested a similarity with
Aboriginal structures even before he began documenting
them in the 1980s. Marika had stayed in a building
designed by Murcutt four years before the project was
initiated, and asked him at that time whether he would
agree to design a house for her in the future, should
she ever be able to afford it. In the event, the budget
would only stretch to the house itself, and the additional
studio/sales building which the client had hoped for
had to be dropped from the original brief. The architect
and engineer had already agreed to provide their
services as honorary consultants, recognizing the
considerable significance of the project as an opportunity
to develop and test a culturally and environmentally
appropriate prefabricated system that could provide an
alternative in the future to the unsuitable concrete block
bungalows typically built for the Aboriginal people by
the Australian authorities.

Marika's brief hinged on the notion of a 'healthy
building', which was very much in tune with Murcutt's
architectural approach. However the Yirrkala house was
the first project he had designed in the monsoonal
Northern Territory, where summers are hot and humid,
bringing north-west winds accompanied by immense
storms and cyclones reaching wind speeds of sixty
metres per second. In winter, temperatures can drop to
twenty degrees Centigrade at night, which feels very cold
to the local people. Murcutt's response was to propose a
well-ventilated house, lightweight so that heat could not
be stored, completely shielded from the penetration of

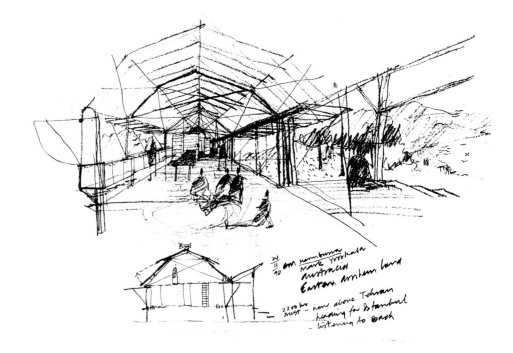

The interior of the house is light, airy and sparsely furnished. All furniture and fittings are integrated into the timber structure of the house, leaving an open living space with views out to the landscape on all sides. The use of slatted timber panels for doors ensures a consistent level of through-ventilation even when they are closed.

The timber structure of the house (opposite) was prefabricated by a team of carpenters near Sydney, transported across Australia to the site by lorry and barge, and erected in two months by two craftsmen with previous experience in boat construction.

the sun, and raised one metre off the ground to allow air flow underneath, but also to protect it from dogs, insects, reptiles and fluctuating water levels: monsoon downpours can deliver 200 millimetres of rain in an hour, and a cyclone on a high tide can bring a tidal surge where the sea covers the site up to a depth of half a metre.

The process of developing the brief took place in close contact with the client. Murcutt spent considerable time staying with the family, giving him a deeper insight into the cultural practices and values of the Aboriginal community in this part of Australia, and the environmental conditions that shape them. One of the most important factors in the design was the need for the inhabitants of the house to have constant visual contact with the surrounding landscape: the horizon, weather patterns, fish, turtles, rays and movement of saltwater crocodiles, as well as to see who is coming and going. The living space, combining cooking, eating and sitting activities, was orientated towards Marika's father's totem banyan tree and towards the mouth of the freshwater creek. The sleeping spaces are located at the other end of the house, looking symbolically westward towards the setting sun and the day's end (the children's rooms are located to the east of the parents', facing the rising sun, or the beginning of the day). It is an open, free-plan space – very much in the modernist tradition – capable of accommodating one or twenty people, for clan relatives might stay in the house at any time. But the communal nature of everyday life meant that privacy was also an important issue, resulting in the location of the bathroom, wc and laundry at the core of the house, where they also double as havens from the cyclone, being constructed of reinforced plywood.

The view of the interior from above shows how the lofty roof structure creates a large, open volume of space for air circulation at the top of the house, above the level of the room partitions. Hot air is drawn into the roof space and out at the ridge by the windworkers, which create suction by the Venturi effect. The sketched section reveals the structural principles informing the relationship between the walls, roof and floor, as a unified 'breathing' organism.

The overall form of the house is a long, relatively narrow hall, raised on stilts, and covered with a steeply pitched, corrugated metal roof with a deep overhang to keep off the overhead sun (the site is only 11 degrees south of the equator). Venturi (ie, suction) principle 'windworkers' on the ridge assist ventilation and ensure an equalization of internal and external pressure in cyclonic conditions. The walls of the house are made of opening panels of waterproof plywood and framed slatted tallow wood timber which ensure a well-ventilated structure. The floor is made of timber planks with gaps between them to allow foot-borne sand to fall through onto the ground below. The wall panels can be opened wide if desired, but even when closed during the daytime the slats allow family members to see out while maintaining their privacy within.

Because of the lack of local building skills and the remoteness of the site, the house was completely prefabricated by a team of carpenters near Sydney, transported across Australia by lorry and barge, and erected on the site in two months by two craftsmen with experience in boat construction. As a prefabricated system it has considerable potential for future development and use, even though it was never intended to be a true prototype.

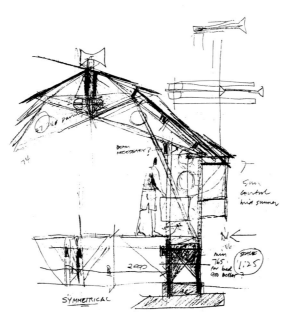

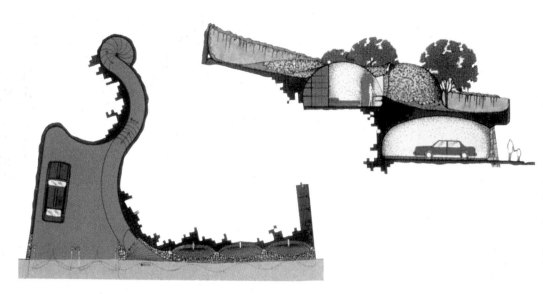

Mexican Whale House
Mexico City, Mexico
1994
Javier Senosiain

The lower-level plan of the Mexican Whale House (top left) shows the subterranean car-parking area opening directly off the street, and connected to the rest of the house by a tunnel and spiral staircase. The living spaces are set above street level by one storey on a sloping terrain (top right).

The plan of the main living accommodation (middle) is informed by the architect's belief that curved spaces are the natural habitat of humans; it also evokes the form of a whale, with the head lying towards the back of the site, containing the more private activities of the house, and the tail towards the front, containing the more communal and social functions. The roof plan (bottom) indicates the swelling contours of the dome and the positions of the top-lights in the upper surface of the building

Mexico City is situated in a bowl in the landscape which effectively traps contaminated air, and it has a reputation for being one of the most polluted cities on earth. From the surrounding plateau, the city's location is marked by a red cloud of dust and fumes, intensified by the action of the sun. Most of the major cities of the industrializing nations of the world face comparable problems of air pollution, as the volume of motor traffic escalates, and industry develops, and inadequate regulations are in place to control the impact on the environment.

In such cities, everyday life can become almost unendurable, and the central issue in designing for urban domestic life becomes that of how to alleviate, or minimize, the effects of the polluted environment – both on a day-to-day basis for the client concerned, and as a long-term strategy for widespread application.

Javier Senosiain's response is based in traditional wisdom, but embodies a radical aesthetic within the contemporary norms of urban design. Indeed, there are many cities in Europe where planning restrictions would make it impossible to realize a scheme comparable to his so-called Mexican Whale House, or the earlier Organic House which he designed for his own family. The Whale House is so named because of its resemblance to a whale emerging from the sea. The curvaceous, swelling outline represents a complete rejection of the conventional typology of the box in house design, while the submergence of the house in the earth represents a decisive response to pressing environmental concerns.

Senosiain's clients were a Latin American climber – the first to reach the summit of Mount Everest – and his wife, a well-known Mexican journalist. He identifies the key influences shaping their attitude towards the house

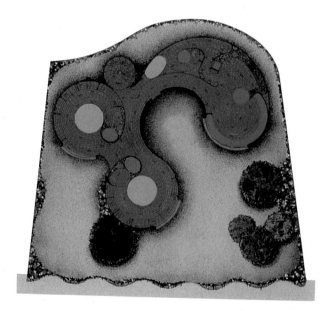

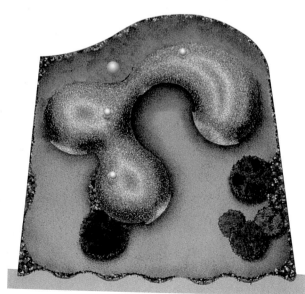

The street elevation (top left and bottom)
comprises a solid masonry retaining wall,
with a highly decorated, overhanging parapet,
reminiscent of Gaudí. The garage doors, treated
like a coarse mesh, have an organic form, while
the coloured tile mosaic embedded in the parapet
introduces an area of vibrant polychromy into the
streetscape.

The swelling form of the house itself can just
be seen above the parapet level (top right). The
whale-like form (middle right) spreads across
the natural contours of the site, with three
main window openings located at key points
commanding outward views (middle left).

as the work of Antoni Gaudí, Feng Shui and the desire
for close contact with nature. The relationship with Gaudí
is obvious, in terms of the curved forms and use of
coloured tile mosaic. But more significant factors than
aesthetic genealogy in the development of the design
would seem to be Senosiain's own belief that curved
spaces are the natural habitat of humans, and the
related understanding that architecture should accord
with the rules of nature, rather than exist in a dialectical
tension between nature and culture.

In a discussion of the Organic House, also known
to the clients, Senosiain refers to the importance of
bioclimatic control for the psychological and physical
wellbeing of the inhabitants. He says, 'it is important to
ensure that the earth and the sun work together to
maintain a stable temperature inside the house'. The
handling of the site topography, and the role of plants
and trees, are crucial in controlling the force of the sun,
and protecting the house from dust and dirt. The Whale
House is not covered with earth and vegetation like the
Organic House, nor is it strictly speaking buried in the
ground, but in other ways the architectural-
environmental conception is very similar.

The site is located in the suburbs of Mexico City, on
the edge of the surrounding plateau, in an area of lush
vegetation. These factors provided natural advantages:
the actual plot is elevated some three metres above
street level, leading to an interesting massing effect,
where the visible part of the house on the upper level
appears to be merely the tip of an iceberg, emerging
through verdant lawns. The entrance from the street is
marked by double gates in a hefty, stone retaining wall
crowned by an exotic undulating parapet clad in

Top-lights in the upper surface of the building,
embedded with broken coloured tile, (opposite)
allow light to filter into the internal spaces from
above. The internal spaces have a cave-like
quality (above), even though the house is not
actually excavated from the ground, but is made
from sprayed polyurethane over an inflatable
temporary armature. Once this has been
deflated and removed, the internal surfaces
are plastered with cement mortar and stucco.

patterned coloured tiles. The house itself is accessed
via a tunnel leading from the subterranean parking
area, immediately within the gates, to a spiral staircase
which takes the visitor up to the one-storey living
accommodation at the elevated ground level.

The organization of the habitable space is primarily
determined by the orientation of the rooms and views of
the outside which effectively link the internal and external
spaces. It falls into two distinct areas, the head and tail of
the whale: the former, towards the back of the site,
containing the more private functions of the house; and
the latter, looking towards the road, with the more public,
or social, functions. The two sections are linked, but also
separated, by a curving corridor which doubles as a
library. This layout generates a sculptural volume which
is sheltered by planting on all sides, but also forms a
protective embrace around an area of the garden.

The interior of the house has a cave-like quality, even
though the living spaces are not actually excavated from
the ground. The apparently natural form was created by
means of inflating a pneumatic structure on a concrete
base, and spraying it with polyurethane foam, allowing an
extremely plastic treatment of the building mass. Once
the shell had hardened, the internal armature was
deflated, and the internal and external surfaces of the
shell plastered with cement mortar mixed with metal
fibres. This was then covered with broken tile on the
outside, and stucco on the inside. The result is an
enclosed, protected environment, providing an antidote
to the harsh climatic conditions outside – and the clients
have indicated how much they look forward to their
return to the house at the end of a day working in the
city. Window openings in the sides of the building are

limited to three, large, irregularly shaped apertures
located at key points commanding outward views, while
other sources of filtered daylight are provided by a
number of top-lights, like a whale's blowhole, in the
upper surface of the building.

The key aesthetic issue in the design of the house
is the emphasis on the decorated external surface. The
typical grey of the whale is transformed by embedded,
polychromatic mosaic, which reflects and refracts the
sunlight into the carapace of a magical creature.
Although the heavy masonry retaining wall at street
level was intended as an evocation of a prehispanic, pre-
colonial past, the use of ceramic tile for both exterior
and interior surfaces, was a deliberate reference to
Mexican cultural identity expressed through a tradition
of craftsmanship first established by Spanish artisans
during the second half of the sixteenth century.

But the emphasis on the building surface, particularly
the use of polychromy, also represents a rejection of
modernist dogma concerning the primary importance of
structure and the need for its clear expression, unmasked
by decorative treatment. Here, the structure is rendered
invisible and unimportant, compared to the emotive,
sculptural effect of its form, which the architect
attributes in part to the influence of Henry Moore. The
surface is understood as the primary element of the
architecture, providing a rich variety of stimuli to the
senses and the imagination. In this sense, the house can
be understood as fulfilling needs of the human body and
spirit, as opposed to a primarily intellectual impulse, in
very much the same way as nature itself. Thus the
boundaries become blurred, as architecture and the
natural environment fuse into one entity.

The distinct roof profile of the three-pavilion Poole House is orientated towards the north. The north-facing verandah (top left) is a typical feature of the traditional Queensland house. Viewed from the south-east (top right and opposite), the large metal drums used to store water can be seen in the spaces between the pavilions. The elevations (below, bottom to top) show: north-west, north, south-east and south facades.

ENVIRONMENTAL AWARENESS

44

Poole House
Lake Weyba, Queensland, Australia
1997 Gabriel Poole

Gabriel Poole and his wife Elizabeth had occupied 'about 15 houses' before they moved into the new house at Lake Weyba, personally living out – as architect and client rolled into one – their interest in exploring alternative visions of dwelling. The immediate precedent to the Lake Weyba house was a steel and canvas 'tent house' in the mountains behind Eumundi, which embodied the principles of connection between house and natural environment driving the Pooles' research. This house is described by Poole as 'an experience to be remembered for a lifetime', but the reworking of the ideas at Lake Weyba was intended to produce 'a more practical version ... retaining the quality of light, the freedom of spirit and the ventilation controls which made the tent so memorable'.

The site was located in a 'fine example' of native Wallum, or coastal scrub land, in Queensland, but one which unfortunately was being gradually eroded by residential development. The native species were being displaced by new foreign species, and the outlook onto the bush was slowly disappearing. Elizabeth Poole pointed out that as 'the only view that mankind could not destroy in the area was the sky', the house should be designed so that the sky could be seen from any part of it. This led to the development of the distinctive steeply sloped north-facing monopitch roof to each of the three linked pavilions which make up the house.

The roof structure represents an advancement on that used in the Eumundi tent house, comprising an outer PVC fly and inner canvas ceiling. This concept had itself been taken from the old railway settlers' tents, where the layered composition ensured a 'cushion of cool air' between the two surfaces. In the Eumundi House, it had

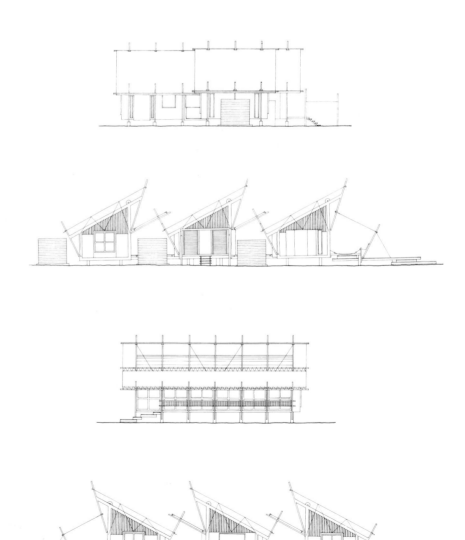

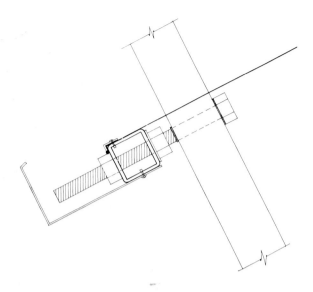

also generated a 'wonderful quality of light' filtering into the space from overhead, which the Pooles were eager to recreate in the Poole House. The PVC outer fly was retained, but the inner canvas layer was substituted by a twin wall polycarbonate sheet, creating a more solid, better insulated structure without detracting from its luminosity.

Each roof ridge projects beyond the north-facing, timber-framed window lights, preventing any leakage of solar glare, while a series of stretched canvas awnings beneath shades the timber decks connecting the three pavilions. In winter, however, the high windows can be shuttered with steel roller-shutters which heat up in the sun to the north, contributing to a natural warming of the house. Throughout the house, the windows are interpreted as dynamic, environmentally responsive, elements serving a variety of functions other than simply providing a view out and flow of light inwards. Some are designed as vertical slots with pivoting fins, located at the corners of rooms, to promote a cross-flow of air. Others are conceived as vertical sliding frames in the external walls of the house, glazed with clear vinyl in order to preserve their lightweight character, and operable by ropes and pulleys to vary the permeability of the building envelope as required. On the north-facing verandah, a typical feature of the traditional Queensland house, large two-metre-square windows are counter-weighted so that they can easily slide back and forth along the length of the verandah, dissolving the boundaries between external and internal space when desired. Some windows are conceived simply as large frames of insect screening with roll-up PVC walls behind, zipped into place down both sides.

The lightweight canopied roof structures and open-air walkway connections between the three pavilions help to ensure good cross-ventilation and protection from the glare of the sun, creating a comfortable habitat in the Australian bush (opposite and above). The detail of the roof tensioning system (opposite top) shows how each panel of PVC fabric awning is framed by sections of steel bolted to the eaves structure with winding nuts to stretch the frame. The plan reveals the relationship between the three connected pavilions, with the largest containing the main living spaces, the 'bath house' in the middle, and the sleeping quarters at the far end, well away from the architect's 'home office'. On the west side is a sheltered sitting-out area (centre), while the north facade opens onto the verandah (bottom right).

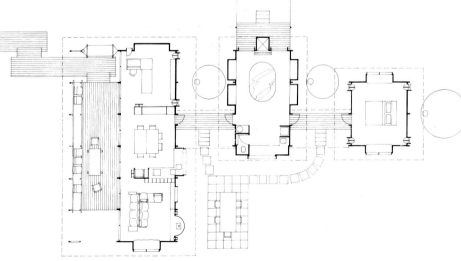

The overall structure of the house, into which these elements are incorporated, represents a continuation of Poole's research over the years into the development of innovative building systems. In an earlier resort development, The Hastings, he had personally taken on the role of builder in order to demonstrate to the developers the feasibility of an experimental prototype prefabricated building system, locked into place by cyclone rods. From 1983 to 1988 he constructed a series of quadruped houses using a construction system of slender branching poles which allowed the footings on a site to be minimized. This concept evokes the traditional Aborigine saying, 'to touch this earth lightly', as a basis for environmentally responsible construction in the future.

The Eumundi House made use of a lightweight, prefabricated steel portal frame system, with bracing infill panels and vinyl and canvas cladding to both walls and roofs. The same system is used in the Poole house to create the three linked pavilions between which the living and working activities of the house are divided. However, the walls were designed as more solid structures, developing the alcove system used in earlier houses, and clad externally in galvanized iron 'with the knowledge that [it] would lose its shine and gradually grow back to the colour of the bush surrounding the house'. The whole structure is raised above the ground on lightweight platforms just high enough for the house to 'float gently' over the native grasses of the site, without destroying the natural vegetation.

The planning of the house was originally developed around what was to have been a lap pool the full length of the building, as a 'heat beater'. In the event, the pool

The design creates a sense of interwoven internal and external space throughout the house. The initial scheme was developed around what was to have been a lap pool the full length of the building; in the event, this was replaced by a large plunge bath (above) housed in the central of three pavilions. The north-facing verandah (right and top middle), sheltered by awnings, creates a continuous extension of the main internal living space.

The north facade illuminated by night. The large awnings provide an extension of the interior space contained within this, the largest, pavilion. The 2-metre-square windows slide back and forth along the whole length of the verandah and allow views into the main living space, kitchen and dining accommodation.

was replaced by a large plunge bath, measuring 2 metres by 3 metres, housed in the central pavilion of the three, and so forming the focus of the domestic arrangements. The other two 'modules' house, on the one hand, the main living space, kitchen and dining accommodation, plus an office, and, on the other, just the bedroom – the separation of bedroom and office having emerged as an important requirement of the design. Indeed, the segregation of living, working, bathing and sleeping functions in separate pavilions of diminishing size, connected by a covered, timber-deck walkway forming the spine of the house, represents one effective solution to the problem of accommodating work and domestic life on the same site – albeit one which would be not only less congenial in different climatic conditions, but also of dubious environmental sustainability.

Poole regards the Lake Weyba house as 'the most significant development' of his ideas to date, but is uncertain how it will inform his future work. For the time being, it is enough that the house makes 'living in the heat ... more bearable', and 'adds daily to the joy' of living for him and his wife.

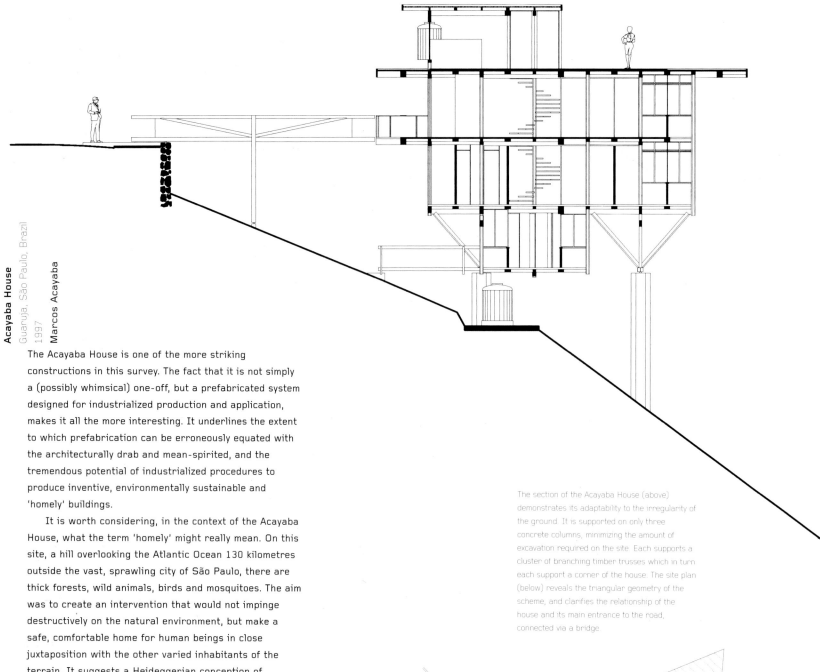

Acayaba House
Guaruja, São Paulo, Brazil
1997   Marcos Acayaba

The Acayaba House is one of the more striking
constructions in this survey. The fact that it is not simply
a (possibly whimsical) one-off, but a prefabricated system
designed for industrialized production and application,
makes it all the more interesting. It underlines the extent
to which prefabrication can be erroneously equated with
the architecturally drab and mean-spirited, and the
tremendous potential of industrialized procedures to
produce inventive, environmentally sustainable and
'homely' buildings.

It is worth considering, in the context of the Acayaba
House, what the term 'homely' might really mean. On this
site, a hill overlooking the Atlantic Ocean 130 kilometres
outside the vast, sprawling city of São Paulo, there are
thick forests, wild animals, birds and mosquitoes. The aim
was to create an intervention that would not impinge
destructively on the natural environment, but make a
safe, comfortable home for human beings in close
juxtaposition with the other varied inhabitants of the
terrain. It suggests a Heideggerian conception of
'dwelling' as a contemplative, almost mystical, experience
of being, between earth and sky – far from the
connotations of cosiness and small-minded comfort which
are usually attached to the term 'homely' in the English
language.

Acayaba's response to this scenario was to propose
a structure elevated into the space among the trees. He
knew the site very well, having owned it for ten years,
and visited a nearby beach with his family throughout
that period. During the time, he built nine other houses
for clients in the vicinity and elsewhere, using
industrialized timber systems in four of them, one of
which was for Helio Olga de Souza, the engineer who

The section of the Acayaba House (above)
demonstrates its adaptability to the irregularity of
the ground. It is supported on only three
concrete columns, minimizing the amount of
excavation required on the site. Each supports a
cluster of branching timber trusses which in turn
each support a corner of the house. The site plan
(below) reveals the triangular geometry of the
scheme, and clarifies the relationship of the
house and its main entrance to the road,
connected via a bridge.

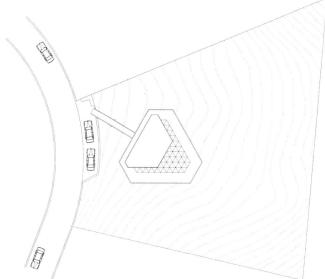

The elevated timber structure of the house seems to be suspended between earth and sky among the trees. The roof terrace provides a vantage point from which to view the sea and the surrounding landscape, and listen to the waves, river, waterfall and birds.

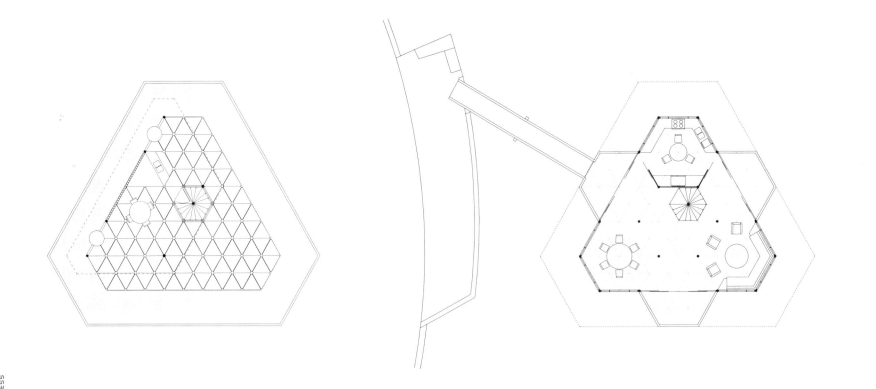

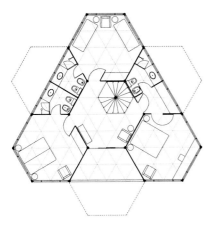

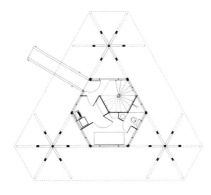

collaborated on the structural design and fabricated all the timber elements in his factory. The elevation of these houses on pilotis represented a practical solution to the problems of earth movement on the site, an irregular ground plane, and other hazards of being too close to the ground, such as the need for excluding animals and insects. At the same time it provided vantage points from which to view the sea and the surrounding landscape through the tree-tops, and listen to the 'constant music played by the sea waves, the river and its waterfall, and the birds', as the architect describes it. The vertical construction also minimized the extent of the surface area which would have to be claimed from nature. But the synthesis of these factors was realized in the development of a form of structural expression which has considerable architectural 'effect'. In the words of a commentator, 'details convert the work of engineering into poetry.' But in fact, it is the slightly ungainly quality of the houses – like large birds alighted precariously in the forest and illuminated with beauty through their poise and balance – that makes them appealing.

The Helio Olga House, located in the city of São Paulo, was awarded the National Architecture Prize of the Brazilian Institute of Architects in 1991; the Acayaba House received the Grand Prix at the III Bienal Internacional de Arquitetura de São Paulo in 1997 – affirmation of national recognition for Acayaba's technical and architectural achievement. The later house represents a development of the first, and a fresh prototype for future development, in that the supporting structure was reduced to only three columns, further minimizing the impact at ground level, but also exaggerating the poetics of equilibrium. The columns are

constructed out of concrete, each supporting a cluster of branching timber trusses, which in turn support one corner of the house each. The triangular geometry of the plan had been explored in an earlier building, the Baeta House, as a workable solution to limiting the number of trees which would otherwise have to be felled, but it also generates a natural logic to the layout, with the staircase suspended from steel cables at the centre, and the living functions focused in each of the corners projecting into the landscape, on the principle of the bay window.

The floors and roof are assembled out of triangular, precast concrete panels, and the walls and parapets of industrialized plywood panels held in a frame of vertical timber columns. These are held in tension by steel cables running across the diagonals. The walls are solid all the way round at the lower level, but glazed in the upper half, forming a continuous strip of fenestration on each of the three levels that can be opened and closed as required by means of sliding panels of un-framed, edge-polished glass, allowing for natural cross-ventilation against the humidity. On the exterior, sliding framed screens provide protection against mosquitoes. All these separate elements, structural and otherwise, pre-cut and numbered at the factory, had to be as light and manoeuvrable as possible to allow for easy and quick assembly on the site. This was indeed achieved by four workers, who completed the building in only four months.

The living accommodation is organized with an open-plan kitchen and living room on the main level, directly connected to the road by a wooden footbridge, which is the main point of access. Below it is the more intimate space where the bedrooms for the architect, his wife, two grown-up daughters and any visitors are located.

The staircase (right and opposite, below) reveals the extreme lightness of the structure, which in the context of the 'tree-house' is reminiscent of a rope ladder. Views through the internal space (below right) show how the trees, and glimpses of the sea beyond, are omnipresent. On the roof terrace (opposite, top) the triangular, precast concrete floor plates are exposed, while in the enclosed living areas they are hidden beneath warm-textured timber flooring (below and opposite below).

Beneath that, there is a service area which hangs down between the clusters of trusses, and a further bedroom has also been created there. At the top of the house is a terrace which is open on all sides.

Acayaba's 'tree-houses' represent a new departure from the attitudes to construction and the environment which built cities of concrete blocks like São Paulo. While the Acayaba House is primarily intended as a summer house, indeed a refuge from the city, and not for full-time use, both the Olga House and the Valentim House of 1996, in Blumenau, are full-time city residences which demonstrate the potential for the system to be applied in the urban context. For Acayaba himself, they represent a natural development of a distinctively Brazilian tradition enshrined within the architecture of Oscar Niemeyer, acknowledging 'the lightness of his buildings and the way he always characterizes them through the structure; his boldness, a permanent challenge to gravity', as his greatest inspiration.

The glazed, concave elevation of the Crescent
House (opposite) faces towards the south-east,
with long views across the garden towards the
downs. The orientation maximizes daylight in the
main living space of the house and generates a
level of natural solar warming.

The section shows the double-layered
structure of the house, with a double-height
circulation space running through the middle.
The sun's rays are shown penetrating the top of
this space through a glazed clerestorey, and
passing through into the back of the living room.
The lower part of the section contains the more
private sleeping quarters of the house, which
are top-lit. The plans (below) clarify the layout at
ground level (top) and gallery level (bottom), and
reveal the contrast between the solidity of the
facade to the north-west, as the 'back' of the
house, and the transparency of the garden
facade. The gallery level of the central circulation
space contains a library.

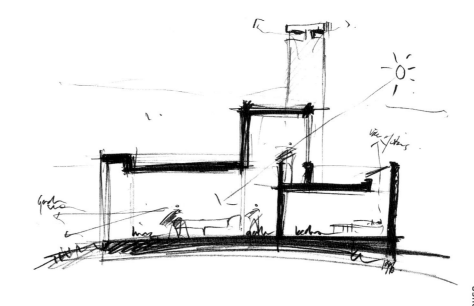

Crescent House
Wiltshire, UK
1997
Ken Shuttleworth, Foster and Partners
59 ENVIRONMENTAL
AWARENESS

The growing awareness in Western society, during
the 1990s, of a global environmental crisis has had a
significant impact on attitudes towards the land. In
the UK, where land has always been in short supply
and at risk of encroachment from urban or suburban
development, the vast increase in the number of
travellers adopting a nomadic lifestyle in the countryside,
coupled with the devastation of the farming economy
through a number of causes in the latter half of the
nineties, have served as catalysts in a process of re-
evaluation of society's attitudes and relationship to the
land, in which ecological values have come to the fore.

As many farmers contemplate, with deep anxiety, the
question of whether or not it will be possible to make a
living from working on the land in the future, and others
embrace the new trends towards organic cultivation
stimulated by a metropolitan market, a variety of other
groups have started to make more vocal claims to their
rights to the land – including ramblers, new age
travellers, 'landscape artists', conservationists and
ecologists – as a source of holistic spiritual and bodily
nourishment which must be respected, even at the cost
of food production.

The Crescent House, designed by Ken Shuttleworth
of Foster and Partners for himself and his family, is
a useful case study revealing the influence of these
cultural forces on architectural approaches to building in
the countryside, in which it is essentially the nature of
the relationship between the house and the land, and a
recognition of the spiritual power of the land, which
provides the core of a gentle ecological agenda. It is
particularly interesting in this respect because of its
genesis within the office of Foster and Partners, one

which has established an international reputation through the aestheticized technological sophistication of its buildings, rather than the subtlety of its approach to the relationship between buildings and their contexts, whether natural or urban. While environmental performance has always been central to the design agenda of Foster's office, it has formed the basis of an explicit functionalist architectural aesthetic which is emphatically different from the language of symbolically charged, sculptural form used in the design of the Crescent House in the Wiltshire landscape.

It is no coincidence, perhaps, that the house should be located in a region noted for its prehistoric stone circles, ancient burial mounds, and, a more recent phenomenon: its mysterious crop circles. In the mid-eighties, the nearby monument of Stonehenge became the site of one of the most politically charged and violent confrontations in modern British history over the use of the site for a regular free festival at the summer solstice by 'alternative' groups who proclaimed the sacred nature of the land. The architect describes Wiltshire in highly romantic terms as a 'unique county of unspoiled, wild landscapes [with] a most fascinating archaeological heritage ... and features which evoke immense visual and spiritual power'.

In their brief to themselves, the Shuttleworths declare, 'we are suspicious of modern boxes dumped on unsuspecting landscapes', and outline an architectural approach conceived in terms of a response to nature: 'its simple form reacts strongly with the location ... the critical ingredients are: a variety of spaces related to their function; a response to the changing quality of natural light; sensory contact with the elements of nature

The garden facade (above left) is protectively enclosed within the curving walls, with the entrance to the house located between the two crescent-shaped volumes. The architect has described the crescent solution as being like 'a medieval castle wall with the cells contained within its thickness' (above right and middle). It also provides a shield to protect the house from some unsightly features in the landscape, while the garden facade (bottom) is designed to pull the garden into the house and take advantage of the views.

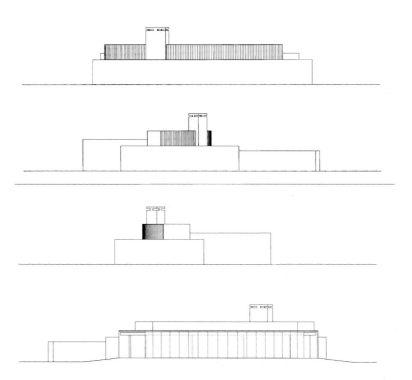

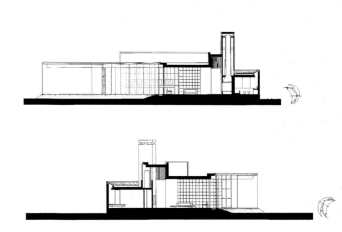

The elevations (above) show the extra height of the building on the north-west (top), highlighting the visibility of the clerestorey design, compared to the south-east elevation (bottom). The side elevations (middle) emphasize the composition of the house as a series of interrelated, mainly horizontal volumes, punctuated by the prominent vertical chimney feature. The sections (top right), viewed from the east (top) and west (bottom) underline the large scale of the main living space compared to the bedroom block.

The transparency of the garden facade (overleaf) becomes particularly apparent when the interior is illuminated at night, revealing the whole volume of the main living space.

and the changing seasons and a model for family living which is ecologically sensitive.' The evolution of the double crescent-shaped design seems to be an overt, symbolic reference to the forms of the stone circles of the region, but at the same time it works at a practical level in relation to the environmental considerations of building on this particular site.

While the scheme was clearly inspired by romantic notions of the landscape, the design approach also embraces the reality of the countryside in the industrialized countries of the twenty-first century. Shuttleworth makes no bones of the fact that the site was a 'fringe' location, with beautiful countryside on one side, but a road, rubbish tip, sewage works and recycling plant on the other, 'distinctly unpleasant' side. It was essentially these characteristics of the site which led to the crescent form: 'one side needed to be like a shield to protect the house [and the other] to pull the garden right into the house'. The house sits in the worst corner of the site, with its back to it, with long views in the other direction across the garden towards the downs.

Shuttleworth also describes the crescent solution as being like 'a medieval castle wall with the cells contained within the thickness of the wall'. It provides similar protection from the wind and weather to the north-west, as well as privacy, while the concave crescent of clear glass to the south-east warms the internal spaces, maximizes daylight and provides a strong sense of contact with nature. The idea of the medieval 'cell' is explored in the design of top-lighting to the bedrooms, bathrooms and dressing rooms, but no windows, to achieve a 'contemplative', intimate, character to the spaces, communing only with the changing sky above.

Shuttleworth observes, 'I always remember sleeping under canvas as a boy with my head out the tent so I could see the stars at night'.

The more private sleeping quarters in this zone of the house are separated from the main living-zone, or 'garden room' by a double-height circulation space with an upper gallery containing a library lit by clerestorey glazing. Compared to the introverted, private quality of the bedrooms, the garden room is open, transparent and communal: 'we wanted to feel that we were living in the garden', Shuttleworth explains. Not only has it allowed the family to become more cohesive as a unit, but it is also used occasionally by the local community as a second church hall for Sunday School meetings. The entrance to the house is inconspicuously located in the join between the two crescents, opening into the lower gallery space and allowing use of the main living area without impinging on the privacy of the bedroom zone.

The emphasis on the connection between the house and nature is reiterated in the colour scheme – white throughout, reflecting the use of whitewash in the local vernacular, and enhancing the play of natural light, offset by a changing seasonal cycle of colours for linen and other loose items. Towels, cushions, tablecloths, vases and so on, are faithfully changed at the end of each season, from red in winter, to yellow in spring, blue in summer and green in autumn.

But these aspects of the scheme are underpinned by more pragmatic ecological concerns. The energy consumption of the house is the same as a standard three-bedroom semi-detached house, satisfied by two small boilers, and there is also the potential to install solar panels and rainwater storage when they become

The interior is painted white throughout, to enhance the play of natural light (bottom right), offset by a changing seasonal cycle of colours for linen and other loose items for example, yellow in spring (top left). The hearth (centre) focuses attention inwards around the core of the house, countering the emphasis on outward connection with the external landscape through the glazed garden facade (centre right)

The central circulation space (opposite) runs between the rear wall of the main living space and the bedroom 'cells', but is bathed in light from the clerestorey high above.

economically viable. This economy of energy usage has been achieved through the use of a concrete structure with masonry infill, which provides a very high thermal capacity, acting as a heat store and reducing the rate of temperature change in the building. 100 millimetres of additional CFC-free insulation is wrapped around the external walls, and 200 millimetres is laid on the roof. The planting of new trees adjacent to the house also reduces the chilling effects of the wind, while providing shade from solar glare in summer.

In all, 1,000 new trees were planted across the site, while the demolition of various outbuildings and the concentration of the new development into a compact form in one corner of the site ensured that the maximum amount of land could be returned to nature. The use of concrete for the structure was prompted by the presence of a nearby concrete plant, which allowed for minimal transportation of materials and the maximum use of local resources. These considerations demonstrate a level of ecological awareness and responsibility towards the land underlying the less tangible, more 'spiritual' sense of connection which runs through the project as an inspiring force. As Shuttleworth puts it, 'the quality of light and an uplifting feeling is important. The building should make you feel good about the world.'

The Corson/Heinser Live-Work house, San Francisco, 1992 (opposite), designed by Richard Stacy, contributes to the recolonization of a former industrial area of the city, and to the breakdown of rigid spatial zoning between domestic life and work.

Le Corbusier's sketched section of the Certosa d'Ema monastery near Florence (below), which he visited in 1907, and which profoundly influenced the subsequent evolution of his ideas about housing design.

It is a striking characteristic of the houses featured in this book that, in almost every case, they subscribe to a notion of free space commonly regarded as having its origins in the Modern Movement. Divisions and differentiations are removed wherever possible, or minimized in their physical form – reduced to light moveable screens of various sorts. In fact, such a conception of internal house space goes back to much earlier models of vernacular construction throughout the world, when the only real internal segregation was between humans and their animals. Le Corbusier himself, and other pioneers of the Modern Movement, were strongly influenced by the model of the great religious houses of the Middle Ages, characterized by the relationship between individual cells and large, open communal spaces for eating, praying,

contemplation and work. Viewed from a longer historical perspective, the specialization and formalization of activities within the Western urban house – which led to the breakdown of internal space into a proliferation of smaller units – can be seen as representing a relatively short-lived period. All the same, it is this model to which the commercial providers of speculative housing everywhere adhere.

Most contemporary architects have been interested in exploring the possibilities of the alternative model, perceived as representing a looser, more flexible type of household structure, with the potential for evolution into new forms. Part of their interest stems from the fact that new construction techniques and materials have made it easier than ever before to span large, open spaces, free of structural supports. But it is also rooted in an intellectual liberalism which has, in the past, opened architects to the accusations of arrogance and social engineering – ie, attempting to force change in living patterns which most people do not want.

Surprisingly, it has been shown that most tenants of modernist council housing, designed with open-plan interiors, like the internal layouts of their flats. There can be no doubt that Western society, at the start of the twenty-first century, revolves around considerably more relaxed, non-hierarchical notions of family and household life than it did for most of the last century, and that a more

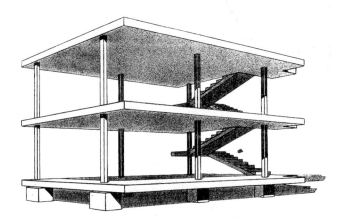

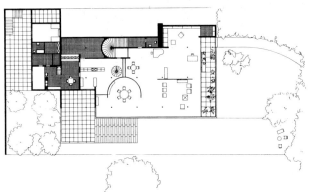

flexible approach to the design of domestic space is an appropriate response to this area of social change.

Alongside the reconfiguration of the ideology and practice of family life – embodied in the decline of marriage, the increasing acceptance of serial partnerships and the begetting of children from successive unions – one can identify two key factors shaping the evolution of living patterns at the end of the twentieth century. Technology is the first, and cultural relativism the second.

At the same time, it can be argued that Western society is also witnessing a level of fragmentation of the household unit – not in terms of a breakdown, but more in terms of increasing autonomy for each member. The rapid development of technology during the 1990s represents an important dimension of this process. As the architect Wes Jones has suggested, the Internet represents the potential for 'children [to] become self-sufficient citizens of the virtual world.'

The dramatic advances in computer technology and communications represent the single most fundamental point of difference in the everyday life of individuals in Western society today, compared to that of society fifty years ago, although its effect on the spatial and temporal organization of domestic space is only just starting to be seen. The philosopher Paul Virilio predicted in 1992 that technology would condemn people

to inertia, and a loss of the capacity to experience themselves as 'a centre of energy'. He also suggested that 'the old public services are in danger of being replaced by domestic enslavement [and] insularity'. But, by allowing people to work from home, developing new patterns of association within the house, as well as new forms of engagement with the outside world through effective interactive communications, technology has the potential to transform the psychological perception of the home into a dynamic organism within the wider social structure, and perpetuates the use of the home by a variety of different people with different interests. This promises a development of the house as a more variable structure, encompassing a greater range of functions, public and private, than it has done, certainly in its more recent past.

Furthermore, advances in the development of computerized technological systems capable of running everyday functions and services, open up vast possibilities for people who have been 'condemned to inertia' in the past by impaired physical mobility. The interior of the house becomes reconfigured as an interactive, kinetic landscape of moving and still parts (for example: lifts, stairs, doors, lighting and the whole range of domestic gadgetry), operating in collaboration with the human body, and invigorating the senses, in its capacity as a true 'machine for living in'.

The Dom-ino system skeleton and sketch
(opposite), designed by Le Corbusier in
1914–15, used the emerging technology of
reinforced concrete to create a new freedom
of spatial organization on each floor, with
a suspended facade.

Mies van der Rohe's Tugendhat House
(opposite below), of 1928–30 embodied an
ideal of flexible, open interior space, using
a system of partitions.

The Corson/Heinser photography studio
(right) is located on the floor above the main
living accommodation, illustrating the principles
of 'live-work' space.

The mechanized lift 'room' in OMA's House
near Bordeaux, 1998 (below right), offers
new possibilities of movement which transform
the interior of the house into an invigorating,
kinetic landscape.

Communications technology has also
played a role in the growth of cultural
relativism, a second significant factor in the
evolution of new patterns of living. Building
on the foundations laid by the great flows of
people and goods around the world during the
last century, it has opened a global forum for
the articulation of transnational cultural
identities – albeit much more heavily used by
certain groups than by others. It can hardly be
disputed that the imposed cultural hegemony
of Western social values, religion, philosophy,
politics and economics has been challenged
with at least partial success, however bleak
one's view of the situation may be. That
hegemony can no longer be assumed, even if
one accepts that, as the historian Dipesh
Chakrabarty suggests, 'just as the
phenomenon or orientalism does not disappear
simply because some of us have now attained
a critical awareness of it, similarly a certain
version of "Europe", reified and celebrated
in the phenomenal world of everyday
relationships of power as the scene of the
birth of the modern, continues to dominate
the discourse of history.'

Much of the most interesting new domestic
architecture has been fundamentally shaped
by an awareness of 'how the other lives', or
by the dialectical relationship established
between two sets of cultural values, differing
conceptions of the normative in patterns of
daily life. It is not surprising then to find that
many of the most provocative domestic
design projects are no longer located in the
West, the traditional home of 'avant-garde'
architecture, but in the former 'margins' of
the globe, generated by a dynamic and
passionate awareness of cultural identity
and difference. This suggests that, in the
future, Western architectural history,
particularly the various forms of domestic
typology, will be increasingly shaped and re-
invigorated by the richly textured architectural
manifestations of other cultural practices
emerging across the world.

Lannoo House
Sint Martens Latem, Belgium
1992
Robbrecht & Daem

The Lannoo House can best be understood as a continuation of the tradition established by the Renaissance country villa, reinterpreted within the context of contemporary patterns of life predicated on ease of communication and travel. The result is a model of domestic living which revisits old ideas to project new possibilities for the future.

The Renaissance country villa was essentially designed around the principle of pleasure. It provided an occasional retreat from the city for the sensuous enjoyment of nature, completely dissociated from the burdens of working on the land experienced by genuine country dwellers. Its raison d'être was the pursuit of leisure and sociability, designed to facilitate the entertainment of guests at often lavish parties. To a large extent, the brief for the Lannoo House was driven by the same ideals. The client was a couple with three children and busy professional lives. They decided that they wanted a house in the countryside which would be a place of rest and pleasure, providing an escape from the pressures of work – but in which they would live permanently – interjected by long business trips. One of the fundamental characteristics of the house they envisaged was that it would function, in its entirety, as a place for large-scale entertainments for friends and family.

In the development of the brief, this then brought to the fore the house as public, permeable place, rather than traditional private, introverted family home. The architects designed a scheme comprising a succession of rooms opening into each other with sliding doors, allowing the whole of the ground floor to be opened up. All the rooms look onto the garden, through a completely transparent facade which opens via sliding glazed windows onto a long, canopied terrace. The internal flexibility of the layout, in

The house forms a variant on the typology of the
traditional simple, long white box of the Flanders
farmhouse. The architectural expression is
understated, but animated by the drifting drapes
on the garden facade (opposite). The entrance
facade (above) seems to be less the public face
of the house than the garden front

The house is designed as a succession of
rooms opening into each other and onto the
garden through a transparent, glazed facade.
The view through the kitchen reveals the tiled
screen with a narrow opening leading to the
patio and garden beyond.

which all the lateral partitions can be removed, also allows
for future variation when the children leave home and the
disposition of functions and activities can be reconsidered.

The building has been described in terms of the
typology of the traditional Flanders farmhouse, insofar as
it is a simple, long white box. It is located, however, in the
vicinity of a village which became known for its inter-war
artistic community. This establishes a local precedent,
then, for the architects' intellectual refinement of the
traditional typology, in a house which can be immediately
distinguished as somewhat out of the ordinary.

In a way, it is surprising that this should be the case,
because the construction and specification is understated,
even baldly conventional. Yet certain aspects of the detail
mark it out for attention – most obviously the external
drapes hanging from the edge of the perforated metal
canopy over the terrace, which, drifting and blowing in
the wind, constitute an almost surreal, animated inversion
of the normal relationship between exterior and interior.
The moving fabric relieves the austerity and rigidity of
the glass, metal and grey-rendered garden facade, which
seems to make a virtue of standardization.

A further distinguishing aspect of the scheme is the
distortion of the regular orthogonal geometry at the two
ends of the house and the self-conscious use of screening
devices. One corner of the house is dragged forward
towards the garden, pulling the facade out of line to
enhance views of the garden from the living room within.
A large horizontal window in the top of this section of the
facade allows more daylight to enter the grand double-
height space. The end elevation is drawn in a gentle arc,
projecting beyond the edge of the garden facade, to form
a perpendicular screen containing the end of the terrace.

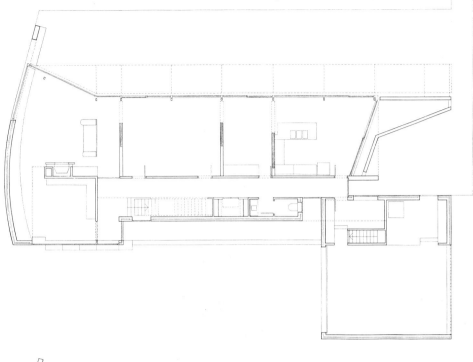

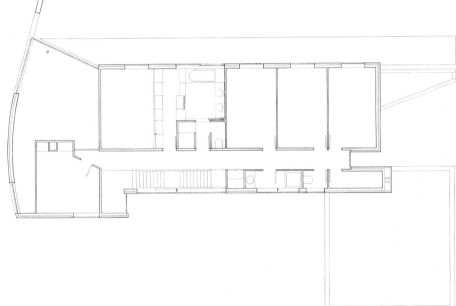

The ground floor plan (top) reveals the parallel, linear character of the circulation, repeated on the upper level (bottom). This creates a vista through the house from one end to the other along the garden facade (opposite right). The end elevation of the main living room is drawn in a gentle arc projecting beyond the glazed corner of the house (opposite top). The exaggerated chimney-breast forms a screen between living room and study (opposite left, top). The staircase is a simple straight structure running inside the entrance facade (opposite left, bottom).

However, a large opening is cut into the plane of the screen, revealing the junction of the glazed lower walls of the living room as a variant on the conventional bay window.

At the other end of the house, the side elevation is sharply cut back to create a sheltered patio within the rectilinear plan. The screen appears again as an angled wall directly in front of the glazed kitchen elevation, forming a strange, narrow, enclosed space between the kitchen windows and the patio, opening through a thin, dramatized, gap onto the edge of the garden.

The garden facade seems so much to be the public face of the house, that the location of the main entrance almost appears to be at the rear, concealed in the return of the facade to the study and living-room block. The approach elevation of the house is solid and impermeable, making a secret of its internal, particularly its festive, aspects. It emphasizes the more sombre side of the northern European environmental and cultural context, and, through the prominence of the garage and its entrance, dependence on the car and, more generally, ease of movement and travel as the basis for contemporary lifestyles.

Contemporary attitudes such as these have consolidated the ground during the twentieth century for the evolution of new patterns of domestic life in rural settings, geographically detached from urban centres where new generations of country-dwellers make their livings. In this culture of leisure, the transformation of the indigenous farmhouse, bound to the countryside through the labour of its inhabitants, into a more abstract, often exotic, species with roots in the ideal of the Renaissance villa, becomes an intriguing area of investigation for the architects of twenty-first century houses.

Villa Anbar
Dammam, Saudi Arabia
1993
Peter Barber

The Villa Anbar is particularly interesting because it embodies a deliberate critique of the social conditions in which it has been produced. Through a discreet but explicit manipulation of architectural form and space, it sets out to instigate changes in the normal, and normative, patterns of social usage. It is worth considering whether it is ever really possible for an architect to achieve this within the context of his or her own culture. In this case, the architect was a stranger to Gulf society, resulting in a scheme which represents the operation of an objectifying Western gaze, to the extent that the client herself was hardly aware of the 'subtext' of the design. On the other hand, the scheme could never have come into being had the client not acquired a cultural identity that was both of, and apart from, that of the Gulf, embodying the contradictions and tensions that arise at the interface between conditions of local and global culture.

As a widow with grown-up children and grandchildren, who is also a romantic novelist and, for half the year, a resident of London, the client's view of Gulf culture was mediated by cosmopolitan influences. She commissioned the house for a site in the run-down suburb of Tobaishi, in Dammam – a city built from the oil wealth of the 1920s – which also, therefore, exhibits a subtle fusion of Western and local influences. Tobaishi itself was built up in the 1930s and 1940s with detached, concrete-frame houses embellished with the occasional Art Deco motif.

The Villa Anbar takes its architectural references from different historical sources, but they are also essentially Western: Le Corbusier, obviously, Oscar Niemeyer, Álvaro Siza. It is a modernist canon, redefined by Barber as 'souped-up minimalism'. But within the Gulf context it has been modified by certain significant changes: a high

The aerial perspective of the house (above) shows how the modernist concept of the free-standing villa, with large windows opening onto the landscape, has been transformed into a clearly bounded family compound, with small windows looking into a private courtyard. The view over the courtyard (below) reveals something of the surrounding suburban context and the clear separation from the street. The single entrance into the courtyard from the street allows visitors of both sexes to mingle in the same space. The tilting form of the block containing plant on the roof (opposite: top and bottom right), sets up a provocative dialogue with the upright minaret beyond; and a small window to the driver's room (opposite bottom left) looks over the private courtyard. The entrance gate (opposite bottom centre) obstructs views into the compound.

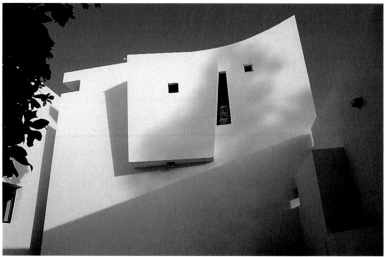

The view from the entrance gate into the Villa Anbar (opposite) is strictly constrained by the presence of the lateral wall screening the courtyard and swimming pool, while the small windows in the facade of the house provide points from which the inhabitants may survey the approach of visitors without themselves being seen. The lintel overhead carries water into the swimming pool.

The sections through the house (right) reveal the layering of enclosures. From bottom to top: the outermost courtyard wall; the front elevation of the house onto the front courtyard; the inside wall of the central courtyard; the outside, facing wall of the central courtyard.

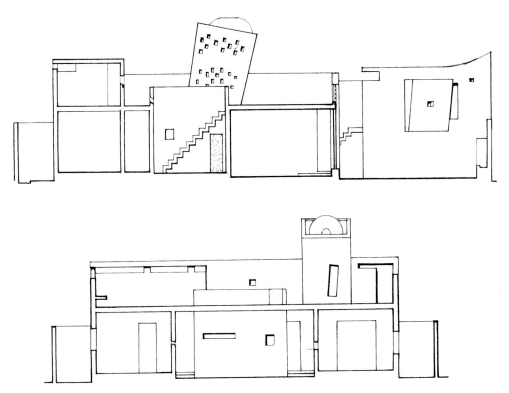

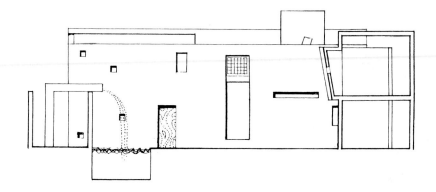

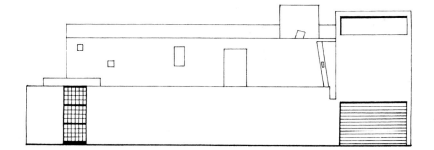

boundary wall, transforming the free-standing villa into an integral element of a family complex; small windows, to protect against the relentless sunlight and temperatures of 45 degrees in the shade; a sheltered internal courtyard; and clearly defined servants' quarters.

Barber acknowledges that, influenced by his readings of Fatima Mernissi and Beatriz Colomina on gender and the regulation of space, he embarked on the project with the explicit intention of challenging the operation of Saudi society through a rigid system of hierarchies and segregation. The client's brief itself was straightforward, merely specifying the accommodation required for herself, her children and grandchildren during the cooler periods of the year, and a certain number of staff. The normally rigid issue of segregation between male and female occupants of the dwelling was treated with relative informality, partly because the client's status as a widow meant there would be fewer male visitors than there would otherwise be. For example, the house has a single street entrance into the front courtyard, so that visitors of both sexes cross and mingle within the same space.

Inside the house, however, the traditional segregation between male and female living space is observed in the provision of separate living rooms. The male space is larger, with a full-length window looking onto the front courtyard and the family swimming pool. In this way it provides a focal point from which the activities of the family can be surveyed and regulated. By contrast, the women's living room is set to the side, with a much smaller window allowing limited views of the communal space. However, Barber has also provided a small window in the partitioning wall between the rooms, in a subtle gesture of subversion. The client's family immediately objected to this

Many small openings in the walls (above) create an effect similar to that of the traditional mashrabiya screen, allowing good ventilation and views out, but privacy within.

The planning of the house is generated by a nine-square grid (right) centered on the internal courtyard **8**. The ground-floor plan (right) accommodates the main living spaces at the front, looking onto the pool courtyard: the women's living room **1**, men's living room **2**, and dining room **3**. The entrance is located to the side, with the bedrooms **7**, shower **4** and WC **5** at the back, and a separate garage **9** is directly accessible from the street. The maid's room **10** is on the roof (far right), with the laundry **11** and plant **12**, while the driver's room is located over the garage **13**.

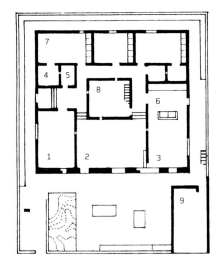

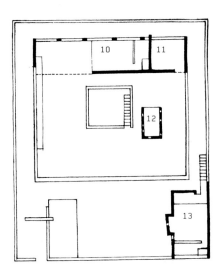

The swimming pool is well screened from the entrance gate, allowing privacy for the family in the courtyard space (top). Water splashes down into the pool from the lintel over the entrance passage, acting as a small viaduct (middle). The full-height window – the largest in the house – in the men's living room allows the courtyard to be surveyed from the interior (bottom).

opening, but, ironically, the shutter installed to screen the view was located on the women's side, giving control over its use to the female members of the family.

Other subtle challenges to the social hierarchy are implemented through the location of the servants' rooms. The maid's room is situated on the roof, away from the family quarters, but occupying a place within the roof garden – the part of the house that was established by the modernist tradition as the zone of greatest freedom. Here, people were invited to enjoy their bodies in the sun and interact unconstrained by the social codes embodied in the organization of the house beneath. Within the Gulf context, the subtle implications of putting the maid's room here might not be perceived, but the way in which the window of the room opens a line of vision into the central courtyard, as the heart of the house, would have considerable implications. Likewise, the driver's accommodation projects out of a lateral wall into the family courtyard. It establishes a visible presence, and commands a line of vision over the space from a small window.

Barber stresses that these design tactics are 'gentle questions, not heavy gestures', and that 'they do not interfere with the easy use of the building'. If this is indeed the case, one might question whether they achieve any real purpose, or if they are little more than a conceit. On the other hand, it is legitimate to question whether an architect should ever attempt to force change in a status quo he does not really understand. Barber makes it clear that his intention is not to force change but to introduce a level of ambiguity which might provoke equally legitimate questions about social practices and social change, and that this is an approach he aims to implement in his work in any cultural context, not just that of the Gulf.

The choice of materials for the Corson/Heinser Live-Work house fits in with the raw, industrial character of the neighbourhood. The main volume is mostly glazed towards the street, while the adjacent ancillary block is clad in sheet-metal panels. The plot is very narrow, and the building is divided vertically into three separate zones.

Corson/Heinser Live-Work
San Francisco, California, USA
1992, rear addition 1996
Richard Stacy,
Tanner Leddy Maytum Stacy

Richard Stacy has identified his clients, a photographer and a graphic designer, as 'pioneers in [a] new post-industrial community'. The dwelling he has designed for them in the formerly industrial South of Market area of San Francisco can be seen as archetypal of what is probably the most significant development informing the future of Western cities: the conversion of industrial space to so-called 'live-work' accommodation for self-employed people, so breaking down in one fell swoop traditional concepts of office work, the segregation of domestic and work life, and the rigid spatial zoning of those two realms which has been the dominant factor in the life and use of Western cities in the twentieth century.

The loft phenomenon, as it is often described, can be traced back to the 1950s and 60s in New York, when artists began to take over redundant warehouse and industrial structures in SoHo as studio space, taking advantage of the high levels of natural light and the uncluttered open spaces which they offered. By the 1980s, the phenomenon had spread to California, where it was taken up by companies and individuals working in the emerging media and high-tech industries, for whom flexible layout, team-working, and easy installation of telecommunications services was important – as well as the excitement to be had from an awareness of working at the edge, conceptually and geographically, of the traditional city and its economy. The term 'pioneer', then, is appropriate to describe the self-perception of those involved in the process of recolonizing increasingly deserted and derelict, 'uncivilized' urban areas with new types of creative economic activity that opened the door to greater independence for the individuals in formulating ways of working and living.

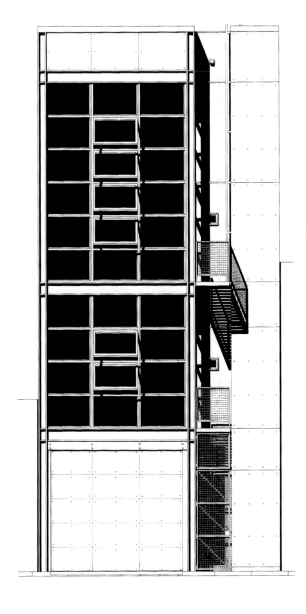

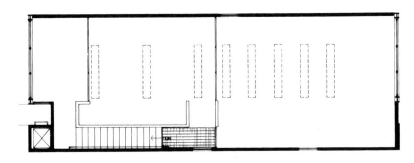

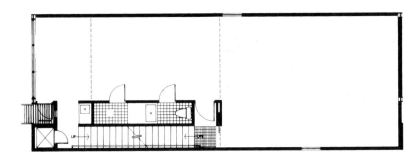

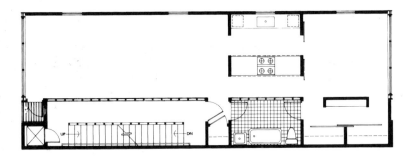

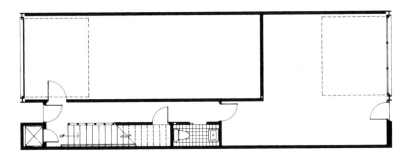

The Corson/Heinser Live-Work house provides a valuable case study for a consideration of the interrelationship between the new live-work practices developing around the home and the revitalization of inner city centres, in terms of both their social and physical fabric. The new building fills a very small plot, measuring 20ft by 75ft, situated next door to Heinser's former photography studio on an alleyway. The couple had been looking for an existing warehouse to convert into combined accommodation for their separate businesses and domestic life, but were unable to find a suitable building. Heinser approached the architect to ask him to study whether or not their requirements could be fitted onto the small plot available, and within the constraints of a very modest budget, while also achieving the sense of generous, open, well-lit space which they sought in a warehouse building.

Stacy's initial response to the problem was hardly modified during the realization of the project. He proposed a tall, thin building which would be divided vertically into three separate zones, with the garage and graphic design studio on the ground floor, the shared living spaces on the first, and the photography studio – where ample natural light was needed – on the top floor, together with a meeting room and mezzanine level office and darkroom. This results in a set of long, narrow, high spaces, daylit mainly from the two end elevations, except for the domestic level which also enjoys side light from one direction. The small utility spaces (not including the kitchen) were segregated and grouped together, along with the staircase, in a secondary sliver of building running alongside the primary block, so freeing up the main block to be handled in as open-plan a manner as possible.

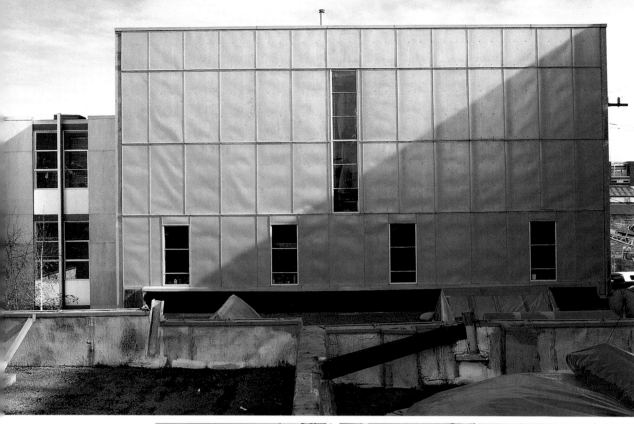

The house successfully accommodates new
live-work practices, as shown in the plans
(opposite, bottom to top): a garage and graphic
design studio are located on the ground floor;
the main living spaces on the first floor; a
photography studio, wardrobe and meeting-room
on the second floor, with an office at mezzanine
level. The fenestration of the side elevation (left)
reflects the internal organization, with a single
vertical strip window to the photography studio
and mezzanine office. Otherwise, daylight enters
the building through the glazed end elevations
(opposite and centre), held in a steel frame
(bottom). The graphic design studio opens onto
a paved area at the rear (below).

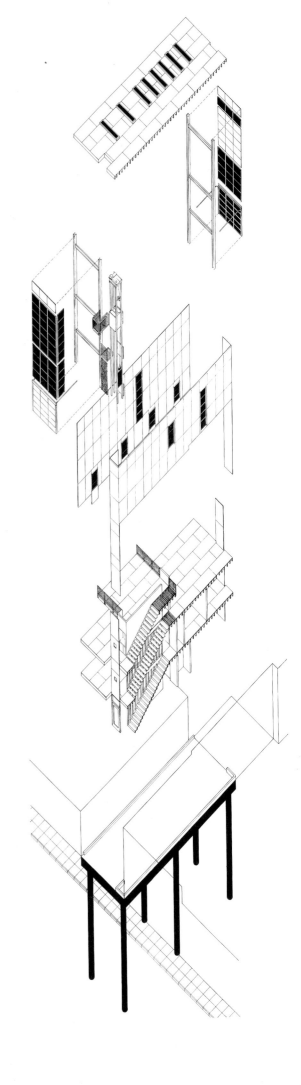

The internal spaces are long, narrow and high, fitted out in functional materials. The main living space incorporates a dining area at the far end, with an open kitchen towards the rear, forming a buffer zone to the bedroom at the back (opposite, top left). The exploded aerial perspective (opposite) reveals the organization of the house, with circulation spaces accommodated in the narrow ancillary block. The photography studio (top right) is open to the roof, in contrast with the more tightly enclosed, densely occupied office spaces (above)

This functional zoning of the building manifests a clear implementation of the concept of hierarchy between 'servant' and 'served' spaces, which is central to modernist ideology, and it is expressed in the outward form and cladding of the house. The 'ancillary' zone is separated from the main volume by a recessed, glazed slot running from top to bottom of the building, which contains the landing, or circulation areas, with a small balcony projecting over the street at the upper-floor level. While the street facade of the main volume is almost entirely glazed, with full-height studio windows at first- and second-floor levels, the smaller volume is entirely clad in sheet metal panels. These reflect the client's wish for the building to be constructed out of functional, maintenance-free materials, but they also fit in with the raw, industrial character of the neighbourhood, and flag up the hybrid identity of the 'live-work' typology. Cement-board panels are used in the up-and-over garage door which forms the solid ground floor frontage, while the steel frame of the structure, supported on 13 metre-deep piles, is exposed on the front facade. Structure and services are also exposed in the interior workspaces, the floors laid with timber panels, and the staircase constructed out of mesh metal. The simplicity and rawness of the approach is one which the client hopes will prevent the building looking 'dated' in ten years' time. The architect regards the design simply as the result of 'applying the basic attitudes of "modernism" to a 1990s building program and budget'. Above all, the clients no longer have to commute to work, or pay rent on three separate spaces, which represents a significant step forward in the rationalization of living and working patterns in the city of the future.

The house 'shapes itself' to the topography of the site: from the entrance at the north end (left) to the 'prow' at the south end overlooking the water (right and above), it slips down a steep gradient to the river's edge. The plan forms a straight spine elaborated by irregular, sharp-angled geometries, exaggerated by the sharply pitched roof form.

The elevation drawings (opposite) clarify the change of levels through the house. The north elevation (bottom) shows the entrance, with the house dropping down behind it. The south elevation (middle) reveals the full height glazed facade which addresses the river from under the protective overhang of the large pitched roof. The east elevation (top) shows how the ridge of the roof maintains one level from one end of the site to the other, while the volume of the building beneath it becomes progressively larger.

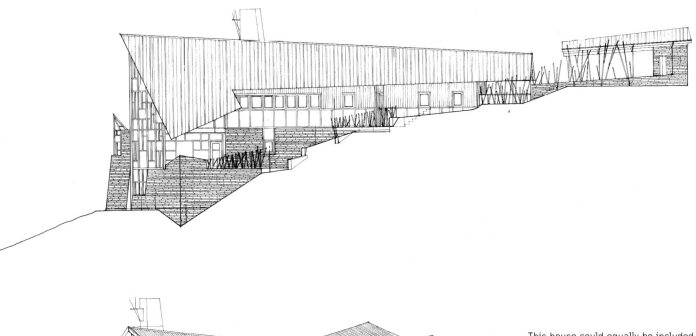

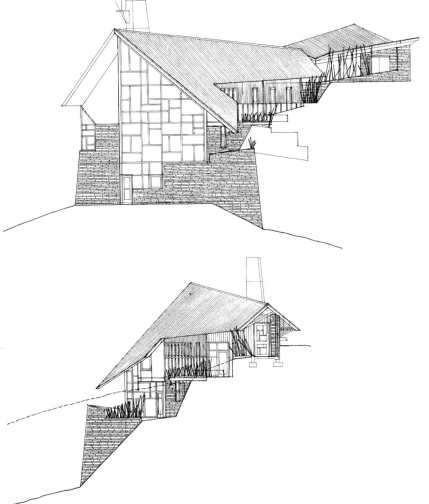

House at Shiloh Falls
Tennessee, USA
1996

Mockbee/Coker

89 CHANGING PATTERNS
OF LIVING

This house could equally be included as an example of the contemporary rural retreat. However, it provides an interesting case study in the way that its form might be developed to accommodate variations on conventional functions of domestic living in the industrial era. One of the key purposes of the house, otherwise intended only for weekend occupation, was to accommodate and provide a showcase for the clients' collections of contemporary photography and Pre-Columbian artefacts. This, as well as the steeply sloping topography of the site down towards the river, is the key to the concept of the house developed by the architect in discussion with the client – two brothers, both doctors living in Memphis – who had previously been intending to build a house from stock house plans published in the magazine Better Homes and Gardens.

In this sense, the house represents very clearly the notion of home developed as an expression of the self-identity of the client through the display of artefacts in his or her possession. While this has been a significant factor in the design of the grand houses of Europe throughout history (one only has to think of the classic long gallery of the Elizabethan country house in Britain, where family portraits provided evidence of social status, wealth, and taste) its contemporary realization is a manifestation of a rather different impulse. The sort of artefacts assembled into contemporary collections tend to be less connected with communicating family status and genealogy, than the personal tastes, desires and experiences of the individual, and how those link the individual to a particular social group of 'like-minded' people within an essentially consumer-based culture. The case of the Shiloh Falls house is interesting, because it demonstrates the ultimate manifestation of the house as a specially designed wrapping

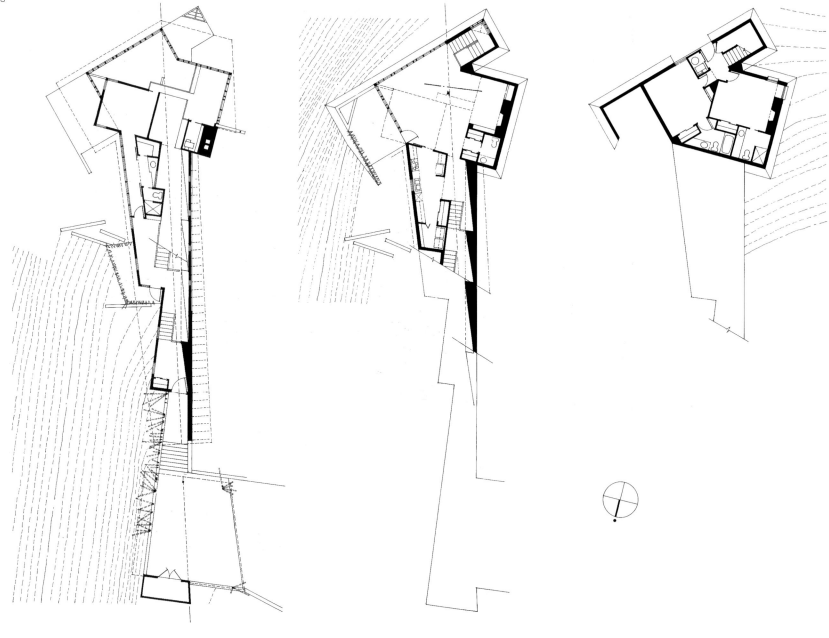

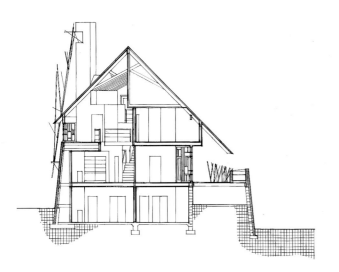

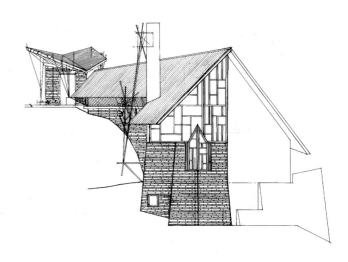

The section through the living and dining space on the first-floor level (above left) reveals the bedrooms below, and the master bedroom and study above. To the side is the open deck and terrace. The section through the gallery and kitchen (above middle) is taken further back, behind the large chimney flue, and shows the staircase moving up through the gallery space towards the entrance. The south-west elevation (above right) is orientated towards the river.

Views of the entrance (opposite), within a covered but open-sided garage area, reveal the jagged, decorative forms of the timber structure responding to the site. The plans show, from left to right: the entrance-level, or second-floor, plan, a narrow, terraced strip with small high windows, leaving room on the walls to hang artworks, the main dining and living spaces opening onto an external deck and terrace on the lower level or first floor; beneath the main living spaces in the ground-floor plan are two more bedrooms.

The house (right) is conceived as a challenge to 'the limitations of a regionalist rubric', drawing on industrial agricultural references as well as the more traditional domestic brick and timber.

for contents of this nature – its primary raison d'être, rather than the more routinized practices of everyday living.

This identity is well expressed in the demonstrative outward architectural form and style of the house, which was acknowledged by the clients to have taken on the character of a 'family art project'. As painters and sculptors themselves, the architects were predisposed to be sympathetic to such a project. The plan is organized along a linear axis extending down the slope towards the water, forming a straight spine elaborated by irregular, sharp-angled geometries. These are exaggerated by the sharply pitched roof form and the jagged, decorative forms of the structure to the open-sided garage at the main entrance, the chimney piece and terrace railings, all of which create an animated composition, responding perhaps to the drama of the topography. It can also be understood as part of the architects' intention to challenge what they describe as 'the limitations of a regionalist rubric'. Although the basic form, construction and materials of the building were consciously considered in terms of expressing a relationship with local vernacular – including industrial agricultural references as well as more traditional brick and timber of the domestic – the design emphatically asserts the architects' and clients' rights to invention and freedom of expression.

The internal layout is predicated around the construction of a narrow, 60-ft-long gallery which forms an extended entrance sequence into the heart of the house. It is a relatively cool space, with small, high windows, leaving room on the walls to hang artworks under gallery lighting conditions. By contrast, the main living space to which it leads, stepping down five levels, suddenly opens up to the river through the double-height glazed wall which encloses

the south end of the house. A staircase directly off this space leads down to two bedrooms, while the master bedroom and study are located over the living space, with a view down into it, on the entrance level. The overall form of the interior has been characterized by the client as an 'unfolding' of overlapping spaces, as they slip down the steep gradient towards the light-filled 'prow' of the house at the river's edge. The architects describe it as a process of the house 'shaping itself' to the topography, and the clients have said that living in the house has led them to a greater appreciation of the surrounding landscape

The construction of the building was unusual, in that the architects deliberately allowed the contractor to make an input into the realization of the design, drawing on his own experience and capabilities, and so extending the significance of the house as 'art project' to all involved. The contractor's influence determined the patterning of the brickwork and the framing conditions, while the steel supports were spontaneously designed during installation by the sub-contracting steelworkers. The element of improvization was built into the construction process by the production of minimal working drawings by the architects, leaving the resolution of many details open-ended.

The redefinition of a house in terms of its artistic contents, and there are many examples to be found of contemporary houses designed around art galleries, opens up interesting avenues of thought about the evolution of living patterns into the twenty-first century. The architects speak of the effect on their clients of 'living in a place surrounded by extraordinary artworks', suggesting a notion of domesticity far removed from most people's experience, but one which could be used to formulate a blueprint for every new home.

The main living space incorporates a double-height volume (top left) running alongside the glazed facade towards the river, maximizing daylight. The master bedroom and study located on the level above (top right), underneath the roof, look into the void. The gallery (left) is a 60-ft-long space descending through the house from the entrance via an open staircase. The suspended study (opposite) enjoys magnificent views across the water through the glazed gable-end of the south elevation. It is connected to the master bedroom via a bridge across the void below.

The main facade of the house as viewed across the entrance courtyard, with its distinctive 'spiral ramp' (opposite). The contrasting qualities of the three living zones are revealed, highlighting the transparency of the main living space on the middle level, with its views out over the city of Bordeaux beyond.

The cross section through the courtyard (below top) and long section through the main house (below bottom) show the tripartite structure clearly, with the 'elevator room' as the key vertical connecting element, the 'machine at the heart of the house'.

The site plan shows how the main wing of the house is excavated into the side of the hill at the lower level, creating a cave-like zone for family activities entered directly off the entrance courtyard.

Rem Koolhaas describes the schema as one of three houses laid on top of each other, each defining a linked but essentially separate world. The transparent middle section contains the main living spaces, while the more intimate family rooms are placed below it, and the bedrooms are located within the cantilevered box on top.

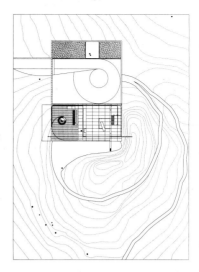

House near Bordeaux
Bordeaux, France
1998

Rem Koolhaas, Office for Metropolitan Architecture

95 CHANGING PATTERNS
OF LIVING

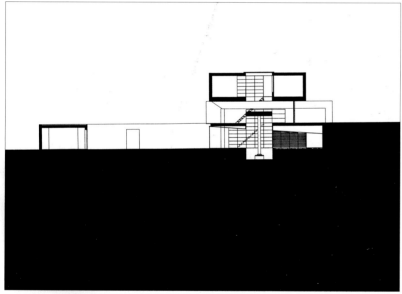

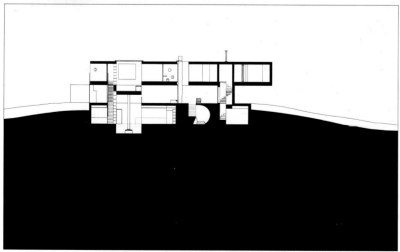

Anthropological research into houses built by traditional, small-scale societies tends to emphasize the significance of their role as part of a 'domestication of the world', by which the indigenous cosmologies are represented in microcosm through house form and symbolism. This provides a basis for an understanding of house design beyond style and technologies which has particular resonance in the case of this project (notwithstanding the disparity in cultural context) designed in response to the physical and psychological needs of a man confined to a wheelchair, after a car accident, and his family. 'Contrary to what you would expect', the client told the architect, 'I do not want a simple house. I want a complex house, because the house will define my world'. The precise, but open-ended brief, suggested a design for a dwelling which could encompass a whole topography of physical and synaesthetic experience that could compensate for the newly imposed restrictions on the client's life, and allow for an inhabitation of the house in the imagination as well as by the body.

The choice of a site, on a hill overlooking Bordeaux, established from the outset the possibility of strong visual links between the house and the world beyond, which can be enjoyed to the full from the transparent first-floor accommodation. In this sense, it immediately establishes a strong contrast with the client's former house, a 'palais bourgeois' in Bordeaux itself, which had begun to seem like a prison to him in his altered circumstances. In the new house, the walls of the main living space are completely glazed, minimizing the separation between interior and exterior, and it opens onto a generous west-facing terrace commanding views across the city in the distance. This level seems to form

The unusual and daring structure of the house (left) seems to affirm its character as a container for new patterns of living. The cantilevered box on the top level has a thrusting quality intended to express an idea of 'launch', while the visual impact of its sheer physical weight and solidity is dramatized by the transparency of the main living space on the middle level (opposite).

a void between the lower and upper storeys, which are dedicated to the more private aspects of family life – informal eating and sleeping.

The second floor level takes the form of an elevated, enclosed box, apparently held aloft only by a cylindrical steel drum anchored into the terrace and containing a spiral staircase. The children's bedrooms at the west end are reached independently via the spiral stair from the terrace, and the husband's and wife's rooms open out onto another narrow terrace facing towards the east: incidentally, not unlike the symbolic arrangement in the Marika Alderton House (see pp32–9).

The lowest level of the house, which is entered via a drive-in, walled courtyard, is excavated into the side of the hill, giving the spaces devoted to family life (kitchen/dining area and family room) a particularly protected and intimate quality: 'a series of caverns carved out from the hill for the most intimate life of the family'. On the opposite side of the courtyard is a free-standing, one-storey wing containing the caretaker's house and guest house. The circular, almost spiral pattern of the driveway as it arrives in the courtyard relates to the figure of the spiral staircase on the terrace, serving to emphasize the concept of upward movement through the house. It is also picked up in the large circular openings in the courtyard wall and the wall of the children's bedrooms on the upper storey, creating a series of cross-references which are suggestive of some symbolic, cosmographic content.

OMA's Rem Koolhaas describes the schema for the main house as one of three houses laid on top of each other, each defining a linked but essentially separate world. The key element which sustains vertical communication

between these separate layers of living, in addition to the staircase access, is an open elevator rising from the kitchen, through the heart of the living space and up to the parents' bedrooms, alongside a three-storey high wall of shelves containing books, files, artworks, wine and other items. In Koolhaas' words, 'the movement of the elevator continuously changes the architecture of the house. A machine is its heart': an intriguing, perhaps indirect reference to Le Corbusier's aphorism, 'the house is a machine for living in'.

In the Corbusian vision of the modern house, considered from a highly functionalist perspective, circulation was the most important element, efficiently serving the different spaces designated for the routine activities of domestic life. But in OMA's reinterpretation of this notion to meet the special circumstances of the client, the circulation of the house becomes its raison d'être, a dynamic ritual route through a constructed landscape, which infuses meaning and significance into day-to-day existence. The concept of the house as a machine – embodying a lofty rationalist ideal well-established within the French philosophical tradition since the Enlightenment – becomes subverted by the explicit evocation of emotion and feeling in the reference to the 'heart' of the house, and the identification of that heart with a machine in the tradition of certain fairy tales. There is also the suggestion of identification between the lift as a machine, and the mechanization of movement embodied in the wheelchair habitually used by the client. Thus the two come together as one entity constituting a principle of 'transformation', in an almost magical sense, at the heart of the house, promising a continuous process of change and discovery into the future.

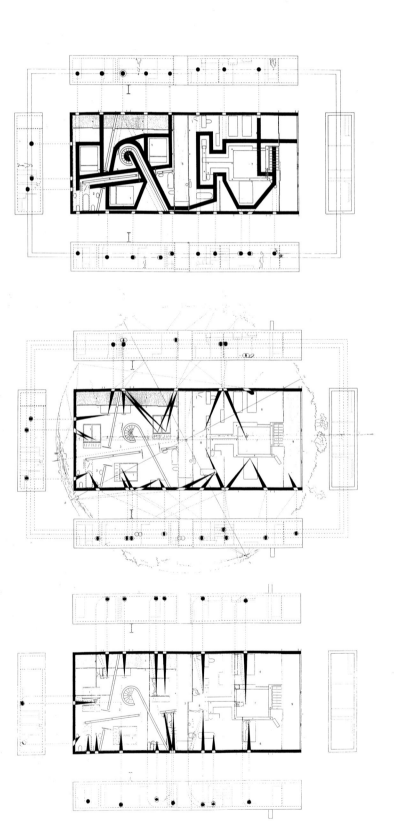

The three plans of the bedroom floor show the varying angles of light entering the spaces through the porthole windows, according to the degree of aperture. The large circular opening to the children's bedrooms (opposite left) looks out west towards the city.

The parents' bathroom (top) on the top level is treated as a long strip of functions. The 'elevator room' (middle) represents the mechanization of movement embodied in the wheelchair habitually used by the client, thus the two come together as one entity constituting a principle of 'transformation'. The kitchen and dining area (bottom) are part of the lowest level of the house, described as 'a series of caverns carved out from the hill for the most intimate life of the family.'

101 House near Bordeaux Rem Koolhaas, Office for Metropolitan Architecture

It seems reasonable to suggest that this deliberate subversion of modernist rationality in the conceptual programme and realization of the house, through various symbolic and magical references, also lies behind the provocative structural resolution of the building, which, viewed from a classical architectural perspective, lays itself open to accusations of mannerism or formalism. Designed in collaboration with structural engineer Cecil Balmond, it encompasses only two structural supports within the footprint of the house, and gives the disturbing impression that the upper storey is insufficiently supported in comparison to its weight. It 'floats' somewhat uncomfortably over the void at the middle level, while the apparently delicate system of balances is dramatized by the presence of an external steel beam running across the top of the box, anchored to the lower ground level by a steel cable; and by a contrastingly hefty projecting leg, extending to one side of the house from under the parents' bedroom.

Balmond describes the project as 'not about a cantilever, but a series of interdependent offsets ... equilibrium stretched to its absolute limit'. He also suggests the intention was to create 'a feeling of launch'. However, the deliberate dramatization of a suggestive irrationality to the structure suggests a consciously formulated desire to set a recognizable distance between this house and the perceived functionalism of the modernist tradition to which, in many other ways, it owes much.

Check House 2
Cluney Park, Singapore
1999 **KNTA Architects**

Check House 2 is located on a densely planted hillside site near the Botanical Gardens in Singapore, and represents a transforming transposition of modernist architectural ideals to the ambiguous urban conditions and distinctive cultural context of a Far Eastern location.

The house was designed for a successful Singaporean who considers himself, to some extent, a patron of the arts and architecture. Some years before, he had commissioned the architects to design a smaller house for his family. The new house in District 10, an upper-class area of many colonial bungalows traditionally inhabited by a largely expatriate population, was designed to accommodate the client's parents as part of an extended family.

This pattern of living is still unusual in the West, despite increasing concern over the care of the elderly in a progressively ageing population. Check House 2 is interesting because it brings an essentially Western form of expression – albeit modified by references to South-East Asian vernacular architecture – with a fundamentally non-Western understanding of family structure, underpinned by strong cultural values. As such, it offers a potential model for the Western world, that might open the way to solving some of the social problems of the future.

The client's brief included not only a separate, private parents' wing, with a sense of connection to the main house, but also a private family living area, and a more public living room for entertaining. Further amenities were to include a gymnasium, cinema, wine cellar and a large swimming pool. The kitchen also had an outdoor area for Chinese cooking.

The architect's response was initiated by the site, which had a four-metre high retaining wall on two sides, resulting from previous excavation and levelling of the land.

The client's growing family and need for more space prompted the commission of Check House 2. The original Check House (left), also by KNTA and located in Cluney Park, was completed in 1994.

The entrance (east) and courtyard (west) elevations (below) play on modernist imagery, in terms of horizontal fenestration, portholes and pilotis. The sections show the organization of the elevated entrance and internal entrance sequence to the main stair.

The double-skin roof is a distinctive feature of the house viewed from a distance (opposite): it represents a fruitful reinterpretation of the classic Corbusian roof garden within the context of regional tradition and climatic conditions.

The plan of the house forms an irregular U-shape around a central swimming pool, suggesting a more relaxed, informal attitude towards the modernist agenda.

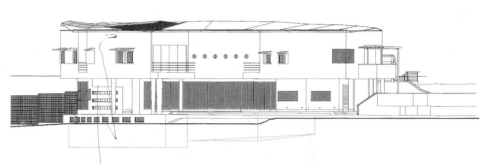

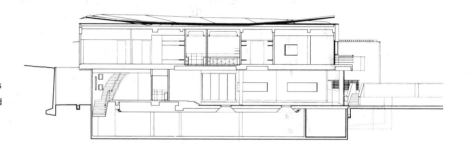

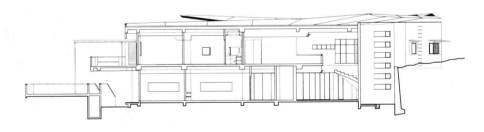

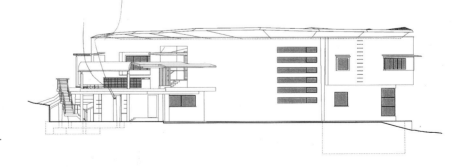

Despite the modernist references the overall approach is intended to avoid 'any kind of strict minimalism'. All the main living spaces look out over the central courtyard and pool. The main entrance is unassertive, recessed at the top of the sharply ramped drive (opposite below).

The site plan shows the ramped link to the 100-metre-long driveway connecting the house to the road. The floor plans show, from top to bottom: the basement level, with cinema, wine cellar and gymnasium; the ground-floor level, containing the main living space, dining room and access to the courtyard and swimming pool. A grand staircase ascends to the entrance level, leading to the grandparents' rooms, family hall and bedrooms.

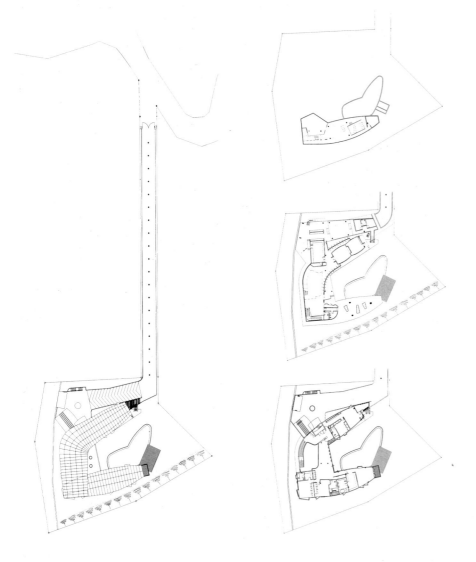

This gave it a sunken, secluded feeling, exaggerated by a 100-metre long driveway connecting it to the main road. To counter this, the main entrance to the house was raised to first-floor level, reached by a sharp ramp in the drive. The entrance hall opens into a family 'living hall' on this upper level, forming a gallery looking down the main staircase and into the living room, and outwards over the courtyard and pool. The main family bedroom accommodation is located at the far end of the living hall, extending over, and sheltering, the open pool deck beneath. The parents' accommodation – a bedroom and living room also at the upper level – is located in the opposite wing, opening directly off the entrance hall, and allowing easy independent movement in and out without impinging on the rest of the family space.

A dining room and study are situated on the ground floor of this wing, in close proximity to the internal and external kitchens and service accommodation: the curved walls of the dining room in both this and the earlier house were generated by the round form of the traditional Chinese dining table, seating twelve to sixteen people, with a central rotating and elevating lazy Susan. The basement level is given over to the cinema, wine cellar and gymnasium, plus a spacious gallery accommodating displays of the client's collected artworks. This focuses attention once again on the points raised for speculation in the House at Shiloh Falls, although in this case it is tempting to propose a reading of the space as a reformulation of the artificial leisure environment of the shopping mall, rather than a form of communion with artworks in the context of the natural landscape. As such, it represents an investigation of new patterns of domesticity as an extension of consumer practices which were formerly part of the public realm and regulatory system, but are

An elegant formal staircase (opposite and far right) leads down from the entrance into the main family living room opening onto the courtyard through a glazed window (middle), creating a ceremony of arrival. The family living hall is on the upper level (bottom). The window also dematerializes the juncture of the walls at the right angle as one turns towards the master bedroom, and forms a contrast with the porthole windows in the upper part of the wall.

increasingly being brought into the more private and autonomous enclaves of the home.

These developments might be seen as part of a predictable evolutionary progress started by the domestic experiments of modernism – embracing an increased emphasis on health and fitness – and on the domestic dwelling as a magnet for complementary facilities and amenities that could be combined in larger, multi-activity units. Certainly, the architectural and spatial language of Check House 2 – the white-rendered, undecorated external elevations, the use of pilotis, extensive glazed areas to the ground level facade, wrap-around window openings and open free-flowing internal spaces – appears to be a conscious evocation of the modernist tradition, while the double-skin roof, with suspended metal roof to deflect heat from the top of the house and create a ventilating void, represents a fruitful reinterpretation of the classic Corbusian roof garden within the context of regional tradition and climatic conditions.

The architects confirm that their intention is to retain 'the modernist play' embodied in Check House 1, while avoiding 'any kind of strict minimalism'. The gentle curvaceous lines of the building and the irregular, vaguely U-shaped plan are suggestive of a more relaxed, informal approach which might be an effect of the tropical climate and lifestyle – in the same way that Corbusier's own work became more plastic when he started working in South America and India, away from the chilly climate and the cultural and religious strictures of Europe. That understanding also has relevance in relation to the conception of the house as an accommodating, flexible home for a fluctuating household unit which has little relation to the rigid Western notion of the nuclear family.

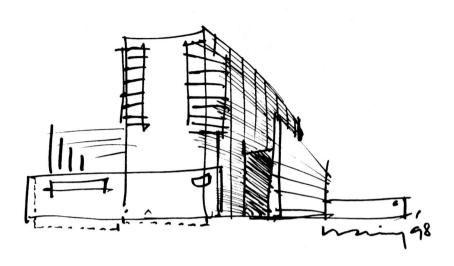

Craig House
Christchurch, New Zealand
1999
Thom Craig

'All iconic references confirming "house" are removed', writes Thom Craig of his family home in Fendalton, Christchurch: 'I became interested in the way of enjoying the house as "theatre".' Described as a 'black box' in the architectural press, the building sustained a debate in the city's newspapers for several months, by virtue of the way in which it challenges received notions of home, domesticity and home life.

Much of the contemporary architecture of the Antipodes has deliberately drawn on a mixed vernacular/colonial heritage, as part of a project to develop distinct forms of material culture which might express a fresh sense of national identity. Craig's house, by contrast, deliberately eschews the use of such referents and can be read as a subtle subversion of the social order which they represent and sustain. Traditional European and American notions of the house interior, and their structuring of acceptable patterns of inhabitation, are swept away through a conscious embrace of minimalism, flexibility and generic space. Craig observes that, 'There was never really a change to the programme except in maximizing our resolve to attempt to push the house beyond just a theoretical notion of flexibility into a physically achievable and livable home that challenges architectural norms and ideas about residential living.'

The radical nature of the programme was underscored, not only by the conventional suburban physical environment in which the house is built – consisting mainly of two-storey Californian-style bungalows – but also by Craig's wife's background in 'a more traditional domestic environment in which her family home and other residential experiences have been of a more English character.' This commentary highlights the continuing grip of essentially colonial ideals

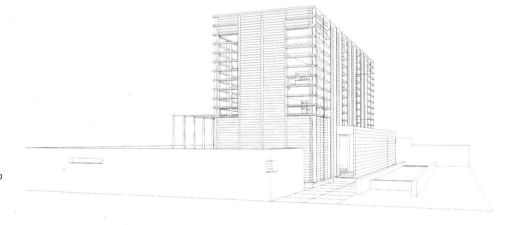

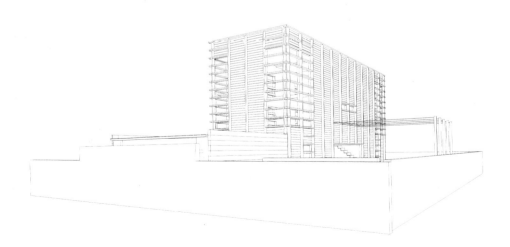

The multi-purpose living room on the ground floor extends into the courtyard space when the folding glazed doors are pulled back (opposite and bottom).

The structure seems to be designed as a magical lightbox, capturing, reflecting, refracting and projecting light out into the street. The four glazed corners of the building (right) light up like lanterns against the black stained weatherboarding.

The exploded aerial perspective shows the structural layering of the house, from the ground plane (bottom), to the structural frame, the internal skin, and external weather-proof cladding (top).

Overleaf: the electric blue lighting scheme (left) transforms the exterior of the house at night and contrasts with the 'white gallery' room spaces. These are also animated in unexpected ways by coloured neon tubes hidden in recesses – the yellow kitchen lighting (right) can be changed throughout the day.

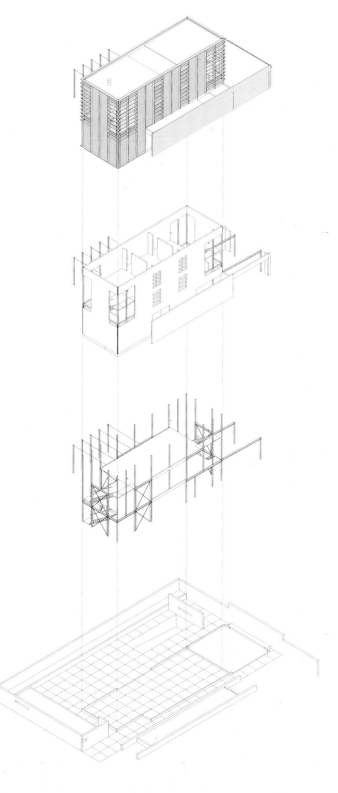

of family and social life rooted in the historical European class system, on the cultural value systems of the settlements of the former 'New World', created by pioneers cut free from their cultural roots. In contrast, Craig's work is supported by a conceptual framework of ideas about discovery and 'wonder', and the importance of intellectual freedom, evolving from his early political and emotional experiences in South Africa.

Craig points out that the very notion of the family has been increasingly challenged during the 1990s, so that 'architects now contend with a vast array of conditions, including single parenting, gay households, extended families, the house as office … ' In fact, his own family of two parents and two children (with the possibility of expansion in the future) represents a highly conventional household structure for the latter half of the twentieth century. But the internal layout of the house is divested of the normal domestic codification and institutionalization of that structure, opening the way for possible future changes in occupation patterns.

The house has two separate, but equally-used staircases, one at each end of the house (left). Both are framed by the glazed corners of the house, contributing to the 'theatrical' interior lighting. The unconventional vertical circulation arrangement is clarified in the section (below, top), which also shows the location of the bathrooms in the centre of each floor (opposite, far right) and the double-height, galleried space of the bedroom on the west side (opposite). The east and south elevations (below, middle and bottom) show the fenestration organization within the grid of the weatherboard cladding treatment.

The plans (opposite) reveal the simplicity and neutrality of the internal organization: an open living space on the ground floor (bottom, and above centre) and on each of the upper levels (top) a bedroom either side of the bathroom block.

The box-like structure and plan of the house, on three floors, is, on the face of it, very simple, with no divergence from the linear norms of conventional construction to suggest a radical break with the past. It comprises a multi-purpose living space at ground-floor level, and two equal-sized rooms on each of the upper levels, separated from each other by a core in the middle containing bathrooms and storage. The two outstanding features of the internal organization are the lack of segregated horizontal circulation spaces and the use of two separate, but equal staircases for vertical circulation, one located at each end of the house, instead of one main, communal staircase: a significant reconfiguration of the traditional house layout. Hence the rooms on one side are accessed directly off the west staircase and, on the other, off the east staircase, with inter-communication between the rooms on each floor provided via the bathroom facilities. On the west side, there is also vertical intercommunication between the rooms above and below, via a gallery at the upper level looking onto a double-height void.

The rooms themselves are conceived more in the manner of 'white gallery' spaces, providing a changeable backdrop for the activities of the occupants, than as conventional, identifiable, domestic living spaces. This neutrality, or generic quality, represents an ideal of 'free space' which is extended into the external areas around the house, consisting of a north-facing courtyard, or 'outdoor living room', and a south-facing stone garden which borders the street. It is in these areas that the concept of the 'house as theatre' becomes most pronounced, through the implementation of an electric blue lighting scheme on the south side which transforms the exterior of the house and the street at night. But theatrical lighting plays an

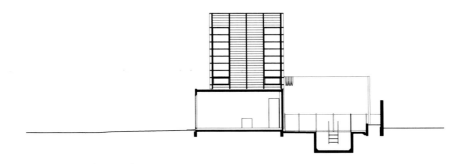

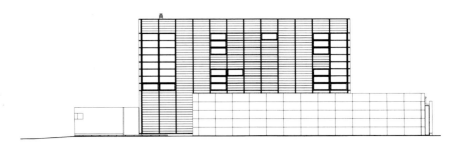

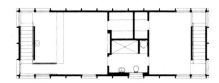

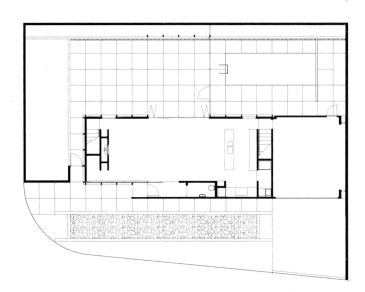

important role throughout the house, through the use of coloured neon tubes hidden in recesses. These can be operated to change the colours and illumination of the walls at different times of day and night, so generating a level of participation by the occupants in the materiality of the building itself.

Craig refers to the influence of artists such as James Turrell, Robert Irwin and Dan Flavin, and their work with light, in the development of ideas about art, light and space which underpin the design of the house. The structure seems to be designed as a sort of magical lightbox, capturing, reflecting, refracting and projecting light out again into the street. By night, the four glazed corners of the building, which frame the open stairwells within, light up like lanterns against the black stained cedar weather-boarding which forms the external membrane of the box. By day, they form transparent slots in the surface of the box, allowing light to flood into the edges of the house interior, and warm the upper levels through the natural process of solar gain.

The exterior of the house has a fine grain and quality of detail that speaks of concentrated workmanship, even though it seems to have been stripped bare of the traditional finishes and frills of domestic architecture. It is a far remove from the conventional suburban home, and as such it poses implicit questions about the norms of family life. But it is emphatically intended as a model to stimulate discussion around changing patterns of living that could generate new forms of collectivity in the future, and not as a signal for a destructive retreat into introverted individualism.

The townhouse by Tod Williams and Billie Tsien in
New York City is a demonstration of their belief
that 'we should build more in the city'.

III URBAN INTERACTION

From the Palladian villa to Le Corbusier's reinterpretation of the same in the first half of the twentieth century, and up to the present, the ideal model of the home as a detached house standing in its own domain has exerted a powerful influence over the European and, by extension, the American and colonial imagination. It is essentially a rural image, embodying a fundamental human sense of connection with the land that is enshrined in centuries of law-making reaching far back into history. But the dialectical and inseparable relationship between rural and urban life throughout this history, by which each profoundly shapes the other, means that it has also had an enormous influence on the development of cities.

The whole suburban movement of the late nineteenth century was predicated on the concept of the rural villa. As cities became transformed into industrial centres, they began absorbing enormous influxes of rural factory workers and manual labourers from the countryside – whose basic need for shelter was met by the rushed construction of the densely planned, back-to-back housing that would be condemned in the post-war slum clearance programmes of the twentieth century. The image of the city as a dark, stinking inferno of misery and disease quickly took root in the public imagination, and, as public rail and bus systems started

to develop, a whole new class of office workers took flight from the city centres to new homes around the perimeter from which they could commute to work each day. This process has continued to the present day, to the extent that many contemporary American city centres have been virtually abandoned by commerce, and left to decay through lack of basic operative urban infrastructure, due to the phenomenon known as 'white flight' to the suburbs and the ghettoization of minority groups subsisting on or below the poverty line in the inner city areas.

The classical suburbs of the West were largely pioneered in Britain, the first nation to become fully industrialized – using the capital acquired through the vast project of colonialism and empire started in the sixteenth century with the subsequent loss of much rural-pastoral landscape. As a result, Britain experienced an anguished yearning for its pre-industrial landscape, and the idyll of pastoral life in contact with nature, that was unequalled anywhere else. This sense of loss, combined with a growing fear of the moral decay and diseased atmosphere associated with the city, generated a perpetual pursuit of a rural ideal that found one of its main forms of expression in the development of the suburb, particularly in the hands of the picturesque and Arts and Crafts Movement. The early suburbs, with their characteristic village

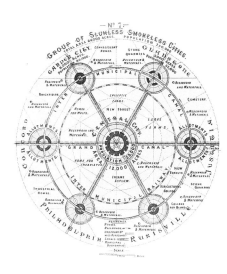

layout and detached or increasingly semi-detached housing units, provided the model for the development of the Garden City movement in the twentieth century. It had an extensive influence on European and American town-planning theory and practice.

Although there was considerable interest in the British garden cities abroad, it is fair to say that the ideal of low-rise, low-density urban development has never been so embedded in the European urban mentality as it has in Britain. High-rise, high-density dwelling in the form of multi-occupancy blocks has long been the norm in the great European capital cities. To this extent, Le Corbusier's radical concept of the Radiant City (1930), comprising huge slab blocks set amidst open parkland, was not such a radical departure from tradition. Today, as urban centres throughout the world grow at a pace that could never have been envisaged by previous generations, and the pressure of outward expansion renders land and resources increasingly precious, the high-rise, high-density model of urban dwelling is increasingly being recognized as the only possible way forward for future development.

While this situation may appear to spell doom for the eternally attractive ideal of the private house-villa as refuge and oasis in the city, it has also opened interesting new possibilities for its future. Some of the most significant new private houses of the 1990s

are those designed as small interstitial insertions in existing urban and suburban fabrics where larger-scale development would not be possible. This is a result of a shift of public opinion and government policy across the Western world towards the recycling of 'brownfield' or wasteland sites in existing city centres and their peripheries, and the imposition of severe constraints on further outward expansion.

This development both reflects, and has been encouraged by, social and economic changes in the post-industrial world, particularly in the realm of global digital communication, which have started to break down the old spatial and temporal boundaries between work, domestic life and leisure. For many people, the traditional commute from suburban home to city centre office has become redundant, as old-fashioned office jobs become more scarce, and the possibility of integrating work and home-life becomes a reality thanks to computer technology and the internet. At the same time, the steady move away from the city centres during the decades of the mid-twentieth century, when the popularity of the suburbs was at its height, has left them ripe for redevelopment and repopulation by those – particularly the young, childless and affluent – who relish the particular forms of sociability offered by contemporary urban culture.

These tendencies have offered new opportunities to architects, particularly because the sort of inner-city site typically available for new development is too small and awkward to attract the interest of commercial developers, allowing an increased involvement by private individual clients in the business of reinventing the city fabric. But running in parallel with the renewed interest in the possibilities of the inner city is the focus of concern on the existing suburbs, which now form an integral part of any major urban centre. The future of the suburbs, as dormitories for office workers and nurseries in which to raise children, has begun to look uncertain in many parts of the West, as office jobs disappear, the birth rate declines, and the old ideal of the self-sufficient nuclear family becomes less attractive to many city

Ebenezer Howard's ideal plan for a central city surrounded by 'garden cities' (opposite left) dates from 1898; Letchworth Garden City (opposite), designed by Parker and Unwin in 1903, embodied the garden city principles in its layout of 607 hectares of low-rise, low-density development and 1,214 acres of permanent greenbelt.

The re-planning of Paris in the 1880s (opposite below), overseen by Baron Haussmann, was based on the principle of carving wide boulevards through the densely built up areas of multi-occupancy residential blocks.

In 1930, Le Corbusier's proposed masterplan for the Radiant City (below), comprising huge slab blocks set amidst open parkland, was intended to solve the problems of congestion and pollution in historic city centres. He cited Haussmann's earlier initiative in drastically reshaping Paris, as a 'powerful dose of medicine'.

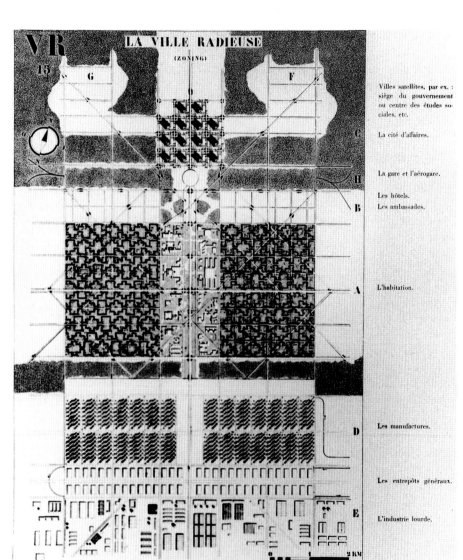

dwellers as well as less likely to match the reality of diversifying households. These issues have led many architects to embrace the opportunity of working on suburban projects with renewed interest, focusing particularly on diversification of the residential monoculture, the interaction between public and private space, more efficient patterns of land use, and a revitalization of the relationship between the suburbs and the city centre.

At the start of the twenty-first century it is widely recognized that the equal health and vitality of the suburbs and of the city centre is essential to the health of the whole as a unified, interactive organism. The American sociologist William Julius Wilson has identified a new era of 'city-suburban cooperation', based on the realization that 'in a global economy the health of the central city is the key factor in firms' choice of location', and that the suburbs cannot cope with their increasing 'sprawl-related problems'. Urban growth exploded throughout the world, particularly in the industrializing countries, in the last decade of the twentieth century, but the key factor in the continuing success of cities as a desirable form of human settlement will be whether they can continue to offer the jobs, trade, social contact and culture that represent the fundamental basis of urban life.

Nalin Tomar House
New Delhi, India
1992
Revathi Kamath

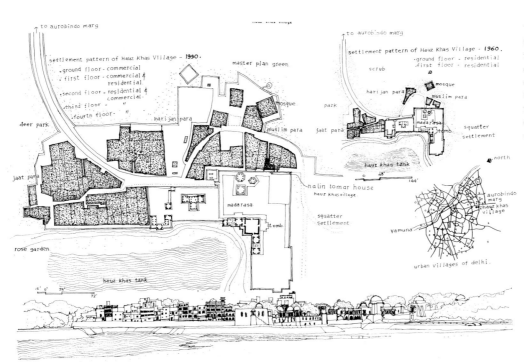

The site plan shows the location of the house in the historic Muslim quarter of Hauz Khas, in close proximity to the historic monuments dating from the thirteenth century. The rear elevation, facing towards the monuments, shows how the profile and detail of the house blend into the historic context, overtly borrowing elements such as chhajjas and donmes from its neighbour.

The opportunities for architects to build on a small scale in the historic quarters of most of the major developing cities of the world are scarce and tightly regulated. Land values are high, and planning policy is entrenched in a type of conservationism which is essentially aimed at serving the interests of tourism in whatever form that might be. As a result, it becomes impossibly expensive for ordinary working people to live in the central areas, leading to ever-increasing pressure on the urban peripheries and transport networks.

In the very rapidly developing cities of Asia, and elsewhere, these issues are of particular concern. Revathi Kamath's design for a new house for an art dealer in the historic Muslim quarter of Hauz Khas, New Delhi, addresses the complex problem of forging sound urban, architectural and environmental principles for the development of the historic city in the face of rampant commercialism and an unthinking importation of Western models of urban modernization and associated lifestyles.

At the heart of Hauz Khas lies a thirteenth-century theological college and reservoir. The monuments are surrounded by the village which grew up during the eighteenth century, and which is now itself 'engulfed by the modern city', as Kamath puts it. But the village itself has undergone a transformation into a chic quarter of restaurants, art galleries and boutiques selling expensive handcrafted, 'designer' garments and crafts, frequented by the fashionable set of Delhi and tourists keen to purchase high quality, 'exclusive' Indian goods. One of the most obvious effects of this process of urbanization has been a hike in land prices and the realization of a new high-density development which Kamath describes as 'not only crassly commercial but also hideously ugly and without syntax.'

The entrance elevation (below right) is an extremely narrow tower, fronting onto a narrow alley, and containing a staircase serving rooms on eleven different levels. By contrast, the back of the house (shown in elevation, below left, and viewed from the boundary to the monuments, top left and centre) has a sociable character, being a generous width, with open balconies at each level looking out over the monuments, and a terrace on the roof.

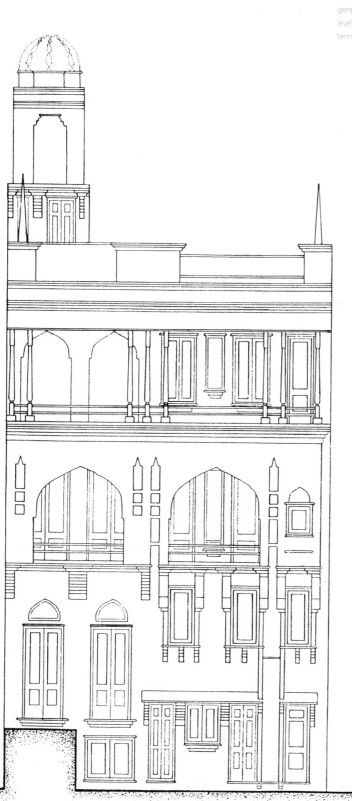

The side profile of the building (top right) shows how it steps down towards the monuments at the rear. Pointed arches (above and left) are used to root the architectural language in the vernacular and create a sense of space and airiness within the house, despite the constraints of the site.

In a sense, Nalin Tomar's commission to Kamath is glaringly representative of the process of urbanization and displacement of the poorer sections of the population by an affluent, educated, cosmopolitan elite. A wealthy, unmarried dealer and restorer of antique textiles and jewellery who ran a gallery in Hauz Khas, Tomar bought the L-shaped site for the house from an elderly vegetable seller who occupied an area of pavement outside his premises. Although it measured only 40 square metres, and was accessible only from a narrow alley terminating at the entrance to the property, it enjoyed an enviable position in close proximity to the historic monuments, with open views across them to the tank beyond – precisely the advantages which could make it, in the words of one Indian magazine, 'one of New Delhi's most amazing homes.'

However, Tomar embarked on the project with the express intention of 'setting a new precedent of building a contextually appropriate architecture in the area', as Kamath puts it. Kamath herself runs an architectural practice with her husband Vesant Kamath which produces work informed by an explicitly environmental agenda – including a new ecological house in the countryside for themselves, built of mud brick. They sum up their approach as the 'creative synthesis of attitudes and technologies into an aesthetic habitat and way of life', applicable not only to individual houses, but also to groups of homes and communities in urban, semi-urban and rural contexts.

In the case of Nalin Tomar's house, Kamath expresses regret that passive climate control, renewable energy, and sustainable waste management could not be on the agenda because, 'in dense urban situations ... they

The long section from front to back (below) reveals the relationship between the many different levels accessed off the central staircase, the backbone of the building. The cross section through the main body of the house (opposite below) demonstrates how the spaces open out behind the narrow entrance tower. The steel grille and beading designs for the dome, doors and windows (opposite) are part of the architectural vocabulary which Kamath has developed as an antidote to the lack of 'syntax' manifested by other new development in the neighbourhood

necessitate the conceptual, social and physical clustering of household units.' This was beyond the scope of Nalin Tomar's project. On the other hand, it represents part of a larger body of work by the architects which aims to integrate traditional architectural wisdom and practice into contemporary design, and vice versa. Both the client and the architect saw the project as an invaluable opportunity to explore how a harmonious aesthetic continuum could be established between the house, the monuments, the village, and the disparate elements introduced by the process of modernization: 'continuously establishing links and connections between seemingly contradictory realities through architecture.'

The recognition of the need to acknowledge the new conditions of 'daily living in contemporary time-space' without devaluing the traditional was of crucial importance to the project. The first impression of the new house is, indeed, confusing, since it is far from clear that it has only been recently built. It is constructed out of load-bearing brick walls, plastered with a local coarse sand and unpainted cement plaster, and the doors, windows and balcony elements are made out of recycled timber. The architectural language appears to be rooted in the vernacular, using pointed arches, a small dome, prominent corbelled cornices and wrought-iron metalwork designed around the motif of the tree of life. The intention was to produce a composition combining fairly simple, recognizable elements that could be copied and reinterpreted by others building around the monuments, especially traditional masons, even where no architects were involved.

The most striking aspect of the house from the outside is the narrow, towering entrance elevation onto

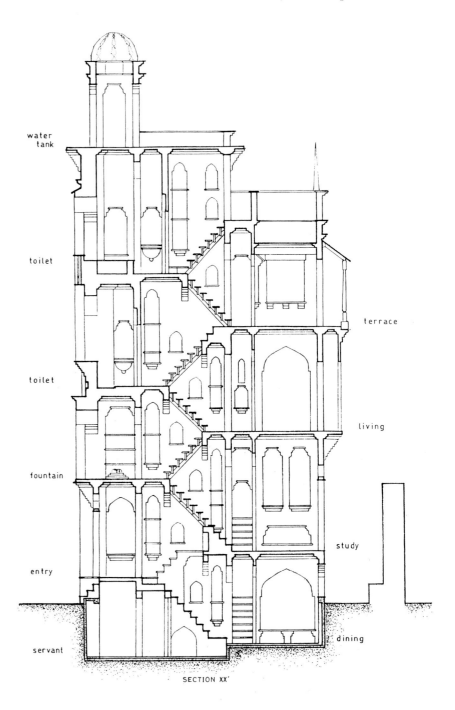

water
tank

toilet

toilet

fountain

entry

servant

terrace

living

study

dining

SECTION XX'

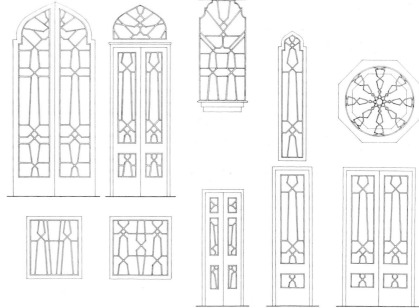

Nalin Tomar House
Revathi Kamath

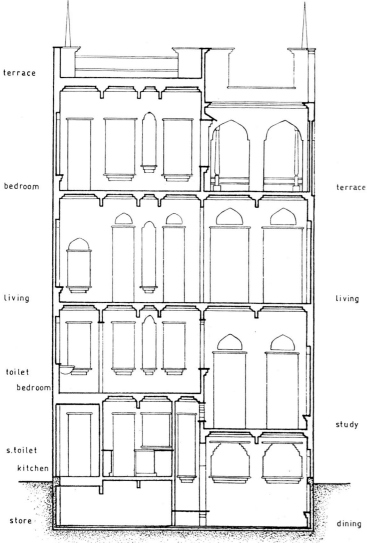

terrace

bedroom

terrace

living

living

toilet
bedroom

study

s.toilet
kitchen

store

dining

SECTION ZZ'

the alley, four storeys high, and only slightly wider than the doorway leading into the house. This narrow section forms the front arm of the L-shape, while the wing of the house at right-angles to it is twice the width, with generous open balconies at each level looking out over the monuments, and a terrace on the roof. The key to the planning is the stairwell immediately beyond the entrance hall which gives access to the rooms behind it on each of eleven different levels. The most public room is Tomar's study, on axis with the entrance, where he often receives clients. Otherwise the house has a quality of privacy and intimacy, deriving from the way in which the living spaces are folded into the awkward angles of the site.

The client has said that the house has 'made his life'. Kamath explains that he sees the house as 'an extension of himself and totally identifies with it'. The house is, then, the direct result of a close engagement with a personal agenda and the desires of a particular individual, but the architect has also deliberately worked through that process to reach a meaningful understanding of the dynamics of an urban society under the impact of dramatic cultural change.

Koechlin House
Basel, Switzerland
1994
Herzog & de Meuron

The Koechlin House was designed from the inside outwards. It is possible to see right through the house from the courtyard at its heart out to the street beyond (left). The architects considered glazing the entire exterior, breaking down the boundaries between public and private space; as it is, large sliding glass panels render much of the exterior transparent (opposite, top and bottom). The front elevation (opposite, top) is cut into the slope of the site, asserting a sense of connection with the earth; the rear elevations (bottom) look over a garden. The site plan (below) shows the relationship between the drive-in forecourt and the house at the upper level.

Concomitant with the redevelopment of former industrial zones as a major factor in the future of the cities of the post-industrial world, is the re-evaluation of the suburbs. Europe, and particularly Britain, led the way in the late nineteenth century and first half of the twentieth century in developing the model for the monocultural, residential zones of the periphery which were regarded as the locus of family life, and which provided a template for the new colonial cities of the empire and 'modernizing' cities everywhere – as, for example, in the oil-rich cities of the Gulf such as Dammam, the site of Peter Barber's Villa Anbar (pp76–81). But the changes in work patterns and family structure which have made such an impact on late twentieth-century city life have fundamentally undermined, in many ways, the identity of the suburbs. They are steadily ceasing to function predominantly as dormitory communities, abandoned by workers during office hours to housewives and mothers, and entrenched in their dependence on the private motor car, as internet entrepreneurs and others start earning their livelihoods through network connections in their homes. Suburban communities and their interests are becoming more variable and diverse, leading to fundamental questions about the accepted relationships between public and private space, and the channels of interaction between public and domestic activities.

The Koechlin House, in many respects, satisfies the traditional criteria of suburban living, as a permanent residence for a traditional family of mother, father and four young children. It is located in an area of Basel developed during the 1920s and 30s, with detached houses and gardens in varying styles, and it conforms to the established model. The major evolution of the design lies in the handling of the external envelope of the house, as the

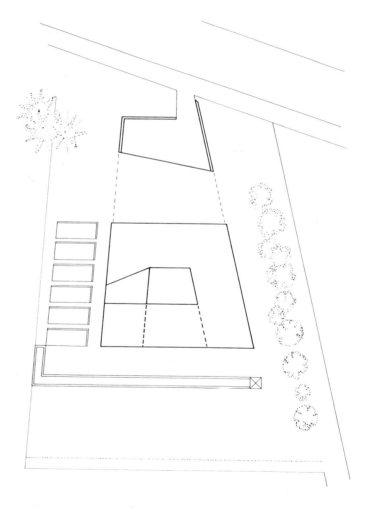

The house is organized around a courtyard as a
layered structure of vertically and horizontally
interpenetrating spaces (below). The lower
ground-floor plan (opposite top left) comprises
a seemingly subterranean zone, gently sloping
upwards to points of vertical access into the
main living areas of the house (opposite top
middle). This U-shaped plan around the
courtyard is turned through 90 degrees on
the upper bedroom level (opposite top right)
creating a bridge over the open end of the
courtyard (opposite bottom) and an open
view out to the side (right).

interface between public and private life, and distinguishes
the house as a conspicuous object of architectural attention
playing an important urban role.

Significantly, the architects have noted that, in contrast
to many of their other projects, they were unsure as to the
final appearance of the house, even after months of work
on it. The building's image was uncertain, quite unlike the
standardized, pattern-book approach implemented in the
original construction of the suburbs, where a familiar
domestic image based on the ideal of the detached villa was
all-important. The Koechlin House was designed from the
inside outwards, rather than as an enclosing envelope
around a plan, as a layered structure of vertically and
horizontally interpenetrating spaces. Indeed, the initial
intention was to eliminate altogether a clearly demarcated
external enclosure, possibly by glazing the entire exterior.

Such a breakdown of the boundaries between private
family life and the public domain of the street represents a
radical inversion of traditional suburban values. As it is,
large sliding glass panels render a good proportion of the
exterior transparent, and form a fully glazed skin around
the central internal courtyard so that, at many points from
the heart of the house, it is possible to see right through to
the street beyond and the neighbouring houses. This does
indeed represent a radical renegotiation of the relationship
between the suburban house and its neighbours – twitching
net curtains at windows become redundant in the new,
transparent, suburb of the future. Similarly, the
introversion of the nuclear family is blown open, as the
internal workings of the house and its intense familial
relationships are put on show.

In the end, it was decided that the transparency of the
exterior had to be accommodated within an overall concept

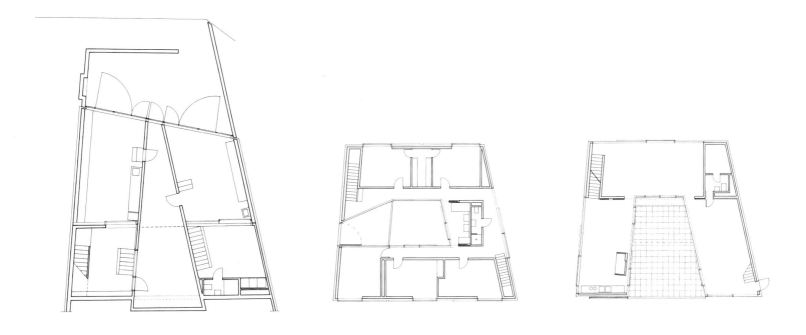

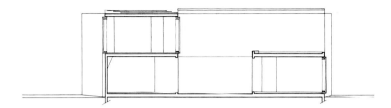

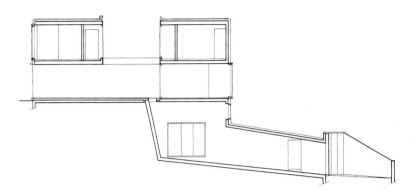

The subterranean sloping access to the
house interior is illuminated with a contrast of
artificial and natural light, the latter introduced
through a skylight and clerestorey window at the
innermost point, as shown in the long section
(bottom left) The cross section is taken through
the rear of the upper house (top).

of solidity and connection with the earth: an idealized, rural
image that continues to exert its power, as an assertion of
the physical and material, over the design of new houses in
an increasingly virtual world. The architects describe the
'almost black, completely smooth surface' as having 'a
sensual effect like a block of slate ... which also recalls
something organic and soft, such as animal skin.' Their
evocation makes the social yearning for the reality of
corporeal, synaesthetic experience explicit, and deliberately
challenges the validity of the thin, surface images
presented by so much of the historic suburban
environment.

The architects suggest that the fluidity of the facade
fenestration, compared to conventional models, allowed real
freedom in the organization of the ground plan. From the
street, the house appears to be three storeys high, with a
classic drive-in forecourt cut into the rising slope of the
site. Glazed doors open into a seemingly subterranean zone
beneath the main living accommodation, which gently slopes
upwards to points of vertical access into the house. The
level above is organized around the courtyard, opening
directly onto the garden under a bridge formed by the
organization of the upper storey, which spirals around the
central void, with its own upper-level outdoor space.

The design of the upper house through a complex
ordering of transparent and reflective planes of glass,
deliberately sets out to blur the boundaries between visual
understanding and the sense of its materiality. By
contrast,the lower zone is characterized by the most
tangible form and materiality, underlining its identification
with the earth. The structure of the house is rooted here,
rising skywards in 'a concrete image of the plan', which
manifestly represents a creeping transformation of the
culture and physical fabric of the suburbs.

New York City House
New York, USA
1996
Tod Williams, Billie Tsien

The newbuild townhouse is located in a highly populated, built-up area of uptown Manhattan (opposite) on the site of two demolished brownstones. The most striking feature of the house, compared to its neighbours, is the transparency of the garden facade (far left), and even on the street facade, where a large screen of hammered limestone is used to protect the privacy of the occupants (left).

The section (bottom) shows how traditional cellular rooms have been opened up into larger, more generic spaces, using steel beams to span the extended widths. The perspective (below) shows the view out to the walled, terraced garden from the living room. The garden is excavated to basement level, as shown in the section.

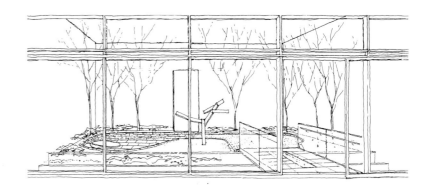

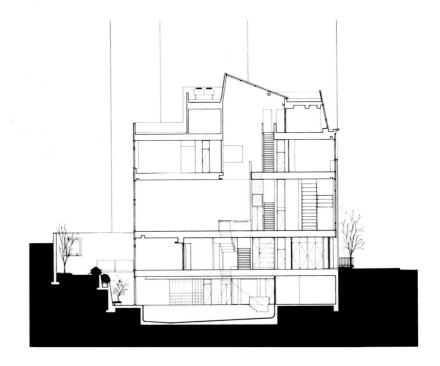

Until the implementation of Mayor Giuliani's politically highly controversial 'zero tolerance' crackdown on crime, there was only one way for family-minded professionals in Manhattan to go, and that was out. The historic heart of New York City was widely regarded as being simply too dangerous for anyone of any substance and social standing to live in, and indisputably inappropriate for raising children in. As architect Tod Williams points out, this spells doom for the future of the city: 'If the rich cannot live in the city, the middle class and poor cannot either. If the rich flee to the countryside the middle class and poor will soon follow. More of the constructed city need be torn down.'

In recent years, the flood of departures has been to some extent stemmed, partly due to reduced levels of crime, and partly to the flowering of the 'loft' phenomenon, reclaiming industrial buildings and warehouses in formerly non-residential, downtown zones of Manhattan, for domestic inhabitation. While this sort of accommodation is generally considered more suitable for double-income, childless couples working in the creative professions rather than for family life, Williams and Tsien's newly built townhouse in a more traditional residential district of Manhattan is designed to establish a new norm in response to those needs.

For the moment, however, it is very much the exception rather than the norm – to start with, the availability and cost of land in New York would put such a venture out of the reach of most people. The client for this project was, not unexpectedly, a developer husband-and-wife couple, the wife having formerly trained as an architect, who were 'very much aware of the advantages of owning a piece of land rather than simply a piece of a building'. But apart

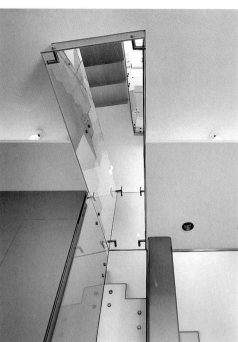

from that, they were committed not only to living in the city, but also to living in the uptown area of the city where their intense working lives were based: an interesting point in the light of discussions about the dissipating geographical effects of Internet use, and the cessation of the need for physical proximity in working life. They also had 'an adventurous and expanding art collection', in Williams' words, which needed to be properly housed. Their only regret was the lack of potential loft accommodation in this area.

Corresponding to the client's commitment to living in the city, is the architects' commitment to building in the city, despite the lack of opportunities. They make the observation that 'we should build more in the city and we hope this encourages others (owners and architects) to build more'. This is very much in line with the latest thinking on densification of the urban environment, and redevelopment of 'brownfield' sites, but continues to arouse antagonism among planners, developers and clients who regard the whole process of building in awkward existing urban situations as simply too complicated and time consuming. As it is, Williams and Tsien suggest that the new townhouse is one of very few built since 1968, when Paul Rudolph built a house for Halston (originally the Alexander Hirsch Residence), on East 63rd Street between Park and Lexington.

Somewhat perversely, the construction of the new house on this site involved the demolition of two nineteenth-century brownstones – the classic model of the New York townhouse. Its immediate neighbours are a five-storey brownstone on one side and an 18-storey apartment building on the other. Other buildings in the vicinity are mainly 15-storey residential blocks, a 30-storey tower and

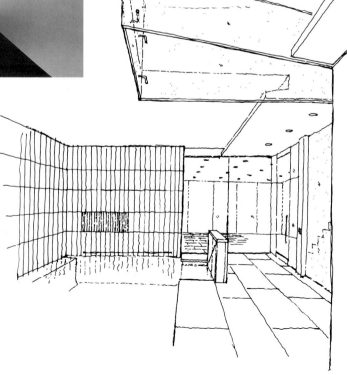

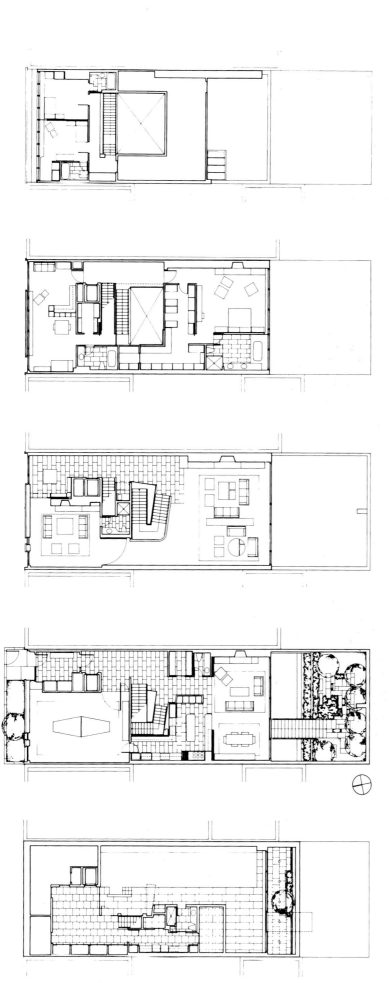

Vertical access through the house from the
basement to the fifth floor is encouraged by
a large skylight placed above the stairwell
(opposite). The basement (opposite centre and
see sketch below) contains a swimming pool
which is visible from the top of the house.

The plans (from top to bottom) show the
organization of the house with the staff rooms
on the third floor; the bedrooms on the second
floor, organized around the central light well;
the main living room and study on the first floor;
the family room and dining room on the ground
floor; and the swimming pool in the basement.

On each level, hanging space for artworks
are accommodated within the light well.

the odd brownstone: in short, a densely occupied, densely
built neighbourhood, but one of dramatic contrasts in scale.

In comparison to its neighbours, the most striking
aspect of the new house is its transparency, although
mainly on the southern, garden elevation, which suggests
a radical alteration of the conventions of urban design
mediating the relationship between the public sphere of
the city and the private sphere of domestic family life. It
can be read both as the ultimate expression of bourgeois
family values, understood as the foundation of public life
and citizenship within the capitalist system, and elevated
here on a pedestal to be displayed to the world at large. It
can be perceived as the precise inversion and subversion
of those values, by the very act of opening up the private
preserve to the public eye and so transgressing the
established boundary between the two realms.

In fact, the expression of transparency – through
large areas of glazing – is itself partly illusory, although
exaggerated by the photography of the house. A large
section of the street facade is composed of a hammered
limestone wall projecting forward from the house like
a moveable screen, specifically to generate a sense
of protection. It also establishes a parity of scale
and materiality with its neighbours, without resorting
to the mimicry of historical style. The fenestration is
worked around it in the recessed plane of the house,
and designed to bring a filtered quality of light into the
spaces within. The flow of light is maximized by the
design of the interior, another significant departure
from the traditional conventions of brownstone design:
the breakdown of cellular rooms into larger, more
connected and more generic spaces. Structurally this
is achieved by spanning the existing party walls with

The living room (left) is a vast cavernous space with views over the garden to the rear and buildings beyond. The garden is excavated deep into the ground within a high retaining wall and the upper terrace is linked to the street level of the interior by a bridge (below).

The skylight floods the stairwell with natural light from above, providing an ideal hanging space for art (opposite).

steel beams, and so obviating the need for internal structural elements.

The light and open character of the interior is exaggerated by a huge skylight placed over the central staircase, winding its way from the basement to the top floor, and opening directly down into the main living space facing over the sunken garden behind. This feature is also designed to encourage vertical circulation through the house, since the architects felt that 'the pleasure of moving through the house vertically would be essential to its success.' In the basement is a swimming pool which is visible from the top of the staircase, representing a somewhat disconcerting, but ethereal, inversion of one's expectations of solid ground at the foot of a house – particularly in such a large house.

On the top floor, the accommodation consists of staff rooms, revealing the existence of a household structure now untypical in the West except within the most affluent sectors of society, and the need for consideration of the relationship of cohabiting family and non-family members within the design of the house. In fact, the resolution of this relationship has been carried out along fairly traditional lines, albeit within the framework of a much more open, less closeted internal structure.

The architects believe that, if the opportunity to build in the city arises again, as they hope, their next house would be simpler as they have grown in confidence. Certainly, the challenge and impact of building on some scale on a historic city site, directly reworking long-established traditions of residential architecture, are considerable, and the architect cannot but feel a heavy responsibility for his or her actions in relation to the long-term future of the public urban realm.

M House
Tokyo, Japan
1997
Kazuyo Sejima and Ryue Nishizawa/SANAA

To the European or American, the urban landscape of Tokyo
may frequently seem chaotic or incoherent, a great sprawl
of concrete buildings, infrastructure and lights, but it is one
which has exhibited an unparalleled ability to accommodate
growth and change. After the destruction caused by the
1923 earthquake and the firebombing of World War II, it
was a necessity, but the concept of rebuilding is also
fundamental to the cultural understanding of continuity in
Japan, in stark contrast to Western ideas. The most revered
and ancient buildings are ritually rebuilt every twenty years
or so as a matter of course, to ensure their historical
continuity in an exemplary state of repair and newness.
Hence the principle of interaction in the built environment
is essentially dynamic in nature, embracing cycles of change
and obsolescence, unshackled by the forces of Western
'heritage' and conservation philosophy which seek to freeze
great swathes of the urban landscape in particular
historical periods.

As a result, Japan has provided a fertile seedbed
for innovative architecture in the post-war era, and in
the 1980s gave many of the West's more radical architects
the opportunity to translate their ideas into built architectural form, particularly in the major cities, such as Tokyo.
Kazuyo Sejima was one of the new generation of Japanese
architects to emerge during this period, working at
what was perceived in the West to be the cutting edge
of architecture.

The M House is built in an upper-class residential
district in central Tokyo. The urban historian Jinnai
Hidenobu has shown how, despite the city's continuous
reconstructions, its basic organization, in terms of the
relationships between different areas, still corresponds
to that established during its early formation in the Edo

period, and determined largely by topographical considerations. Hidenobu explains that 'living spaces for the warrior class were created in the high city, with its varied land formations [of valleys and plateaus], whereas the commoners made their homes on land reclaimed from the river delta and threaded with canals in the low city.' He also describes how, in each zone, 'classification rules for architecture according to land surface, structure and design were clearly established within each lot. Forms were elaborated to govern features visible from the street, such as the indications of status ... and structural elements were combined to create the special appearance of each neighbourhood.'

These comments provide an insight into the urban context of Tokyo which allows an appreciation of the radical nature of Sejima and Nishizawa's intervention. The architects explain that the increasing subdivision of plots in the neighbourhood of large residences in which the M House is situated is generating a process of densification. This in turn is leading to problems of privacy between neighbouring houses. Since the street frontage of the M House and its neighbours is south-facing, most of the houses have large windows on this side; but, because they look onto the public thoroughfare and therefore expose the interior of the houses to view, they are usually screened by high fences or permanently closed curtains. This has provoked the architects to radically rethink the way in which the architecture of the individual domestic dwelling should interact with the structure and visual design of the neighbourhood as a whole.

The starting point for their strategy is the excavation of the entire site, up to the boundaries, forming a large hole into which the house is dropped. Thus the normal

A simple open stair leads straight down from the front door and entrance into the main living room (opposite top and centre). The lower-level rooms: a music studio (opposite bottom) and study, and a dining room, are situated either side of the living space.

The more public rooms are on the lower ground floor (top right), and the garage and bedrooms are on the entrance level. No direct access to the bedrooms exists from the entrance level, except to the guest bedroom directly off the entrance hall. The family bedrooms are reached via an ascending staircase rising from the study area.

The front and garage doors are the only openings in the street facade (bottom). The vertical sections mark alternating areas of corrugated metal and metal mesh cladding.

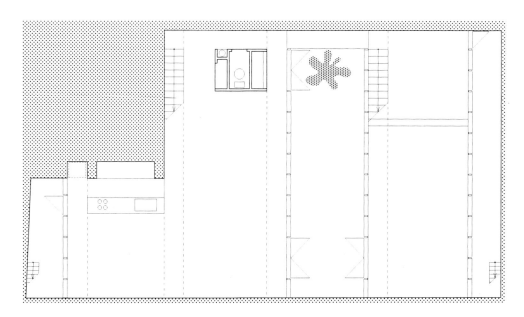

M House
Kazuyo Sejima and Ryue Nishizawa/SANAA

process of building upwards from ground level is inverted. The master bedroom, guest room and garage are situated at ground level, but the main living spaces are located below ground level, around a central open courtyard, or light well. The containing wall of the house site is formed by a one-storey, corrugated metal screen, without windows, apart from three sections made of metal mesh which allow the central and secondary light courts within to have a veiled visual presence on the street. This appears to eliminate any but the most neutral relationship, or level of interaction, between the house and its locale. At the same time, a quality of outside space is drawn into, and captured within, the interior of the house itself in the form of the sunken courtyard and tree at its centre, with views through the overhead louvres to the open sky above.

The client was a husband and wife, who at the outset gave the architects only a basic brief concerning their requirements and allowed them to develop the project in the way they felt to be appropriate. A key aspect of the programme was that the house should provide not only work spaces for both husband and wife, but also a large space suitable for entertaining visitors as a necessary dimension of the husband's work in the music and film industries. The living room is accessed directly from the entrance to the house, via a narrow, descending, open staircase, and opens up onto the central light court through double doors in a translucent screen which allows the penetration of indirect light. A study and studio are ranged on the opposite side of the light court, with a second staircase leading up to the bedroom, bathroom and children's room (for future use) at street level. On the far side of the living room is a smaller dining room and kitchen, with a guest room above at street level, entered directly off

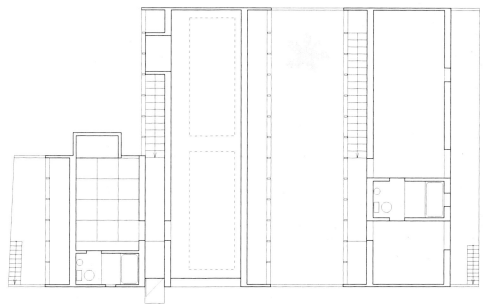

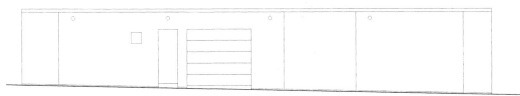

the entrance lobby. At the perimeter edges of the site are further, narrow light wells, introducing additional indirect light into the rooms, both below and at ground level.

In many ways, this house seems highly introverted compared to the norms of urban residential construction, but it does address important questions about the forms that residential development might take in the contemporary city. The trend towards densification of neighbourhoods in the planning policies of cities throughout the world means that issues of privacy and retreat will become increasingly acute, while the appropriation and consumption of the public space of the street by motorized vehicles has already made the ideal of permeability in the interface between the house and the street less desirable. One has only to look at examples of traditional, closely built, urban settlements in areas such as the Middle East to realize how alien the concept of the house open to the public street can be. As the architects observe, in the case of the M House, 'Sounds from above ground are heard through the punched walls as if from far away; this creates the impression of an appropriate distance from the surrounding environment.'

The Ozone House is based on the typology of the traditional Californian clapboard cottage, manipulated to reflect and express the reality of contemporary conditions (front elevation opposite). The front and back elevations (right) show a narrow, two-storey house with a garage and enclosed parking court at the back.

The cross sections (below) are taken through the centre of the house looking forward (top) and back (bottom). The roof is made of prefabricated wooden trusses, with a glazed clerestorey over the second study.

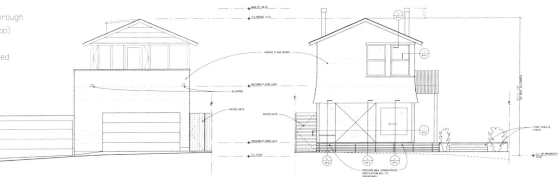

Ozone House
Venice, California, USA
1998
Koning Eizenberg
145 URBAN
INTERACTION

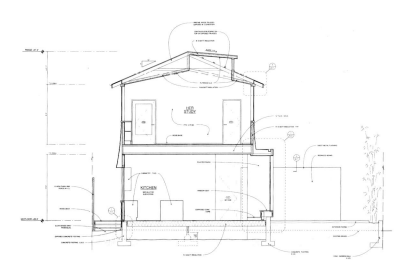

'In the 1980s ... the history of suburban development became an essential part of urban history', writes the cultural geographer Dolores Hayden – and no more so than in the great urban conglomeration of Los Angeles, California, regarded as the model for the archetypal 'Edge City', where the conditions and cultures of the edges become more significant in urban life than those of the centre.

The concept of Edge City became current towards the end of the 1980s, or the early 90s, amongst architectural theorists and planners who suggested that it represented the future for all big cities around the world. Los Angeles itself exercized a certain fascination as a prime example of a city designed for and around the motor car, where the concerns about preserving the pedestrian-scaled, historic centres of the great European cities and East Coast American cities had little meaning. The structure of Los Angeles was perceived as being very different from the traditional European city – a loose network of clearly defined neighbourhoods, some famous for celebrity like Beverly Hills and Hollywood, others notorious for social dysfunction and violence, connected by high-speed freeways, and enjoying the advantages of an extensive section of Pacific coastline. The very looseness of this structure seemed to generate a climate of freedom and experimentation with ideas that has manifested itself in the emergence of numerous architects producing work of considerable interest and vigour over the years – for example, Morphosis, Franklin D Israel, Eric Owen Moss, Frank Gehry and others.

Another characteristic, however, of more recent Los Angeles urban development which has attracted much attention and considerable criticism, is the increasing

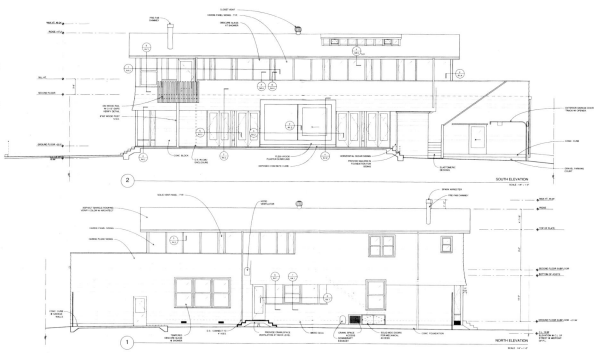

The south and north elevations (right) emphasize the length of the house, occupying almost the whole of its long, narrow plot. Glazed doors open on the south side from the living room onto a paved and landscaped area.

The aerial view highlights the diverse scale of buildings in the area. The Ozone House can be distinguished just right of the centre of the picture, by the high wall and garage entrance which forms the rear facade and its deck

emergence of 'gated' developments forming exclusive, high-security, 'anti-urban' enclaves within the urban fabric. Designed to be accessed by car at all times, they allow inhabitants to dissociate themselves entirely from the life of the public street, the all-important locus of the vitality of the traditional city. Since it has also become common for public buildings in the city centre to be designed for direct access from basement carparks, a drastic reduction of interaction with the external public spaces of the city has emerged as a very real possibility.

In this context, Koning Eizenberg's Ozone House at Venice, one of Los Angeles' better-known suburban beachfront neighbourhoods, is of considerable interest. Venice was part of what has been described as an 'historically democratic strip of coastline and beach', developed as a popular resort with canals, bridges and gondolas in the early 1900s, but it had fallen into decay after oil had been discovered there in 1927. In the late sixties it was famously described by Reyner Banham as a spectacle of urban desolation, replete with rusting oil machinery, but in more recent years some of Los Angeles' most prominent architects have contributed to its revival. The Ozone House is sometimes described as a beach house, suggesting only occasional holiday and weekend use outside a city; it is in fact a permanent home for its clients – a couple with grown-up children who had sold their long-standing family house. The site faces onto a pedestrian-only street set one block back from the beach front, but the street itself is what the architects describe as 'an eclectic mix of old California wood-clad cottages, apartment buildings and new, aggressively modern, large house or duplex developments.' In short, a classic example of the typical 'corniche'-style development exhibited by most

seafront cities, containing a mix of urban, suburban and even rural elements.

According to Koning Eizenberg, the clients specified in their original brief to the architect that, 'the house should feel beachy and not suburban' – let alone urban. They wanted a sense of privacy, yet at the same time not to feel isolated or appear un-neighbourly. Their desires seem to typify the outlook of the typical inhabitant of Edge City, who wishes to remain connected to the metropolitan centre, while at the same time indulging in a dream of apartness and closeness to nature. Ironically, for these people, the suburban areas usually represent the nadir of all their desires, but ultimately provide the perfect environment in which they can be lived out in a wholly acceptable form.

The architect's response was to take the typology of the traditional Californian clapboard cottage, and subtly manipulate it to reflect and express the reality of contemporary conditions. In this sense, their approach is very different from that enshrined in the architectural experiments carried out by neo-traditionalists in the 1980s, such as the wood-clad resort of Seaside, Florida, which aimed to achieve a perfect recreation of the morphology and building typology of traditional settlements, without acknowledging the implications of patterns of cultural and environmental change. The Ozone House acknowledges its contemporaneity even through its name, which to any informed global citizen of the twenty-first century is fraught with the implications of environmental anxiety. But apart from that, the massing of the building has been evolved in response to its existing neighbours – on one side, a high continuous facade with a few windows in it, on the other, a modest, modern, low-rise clapboard duplex. The

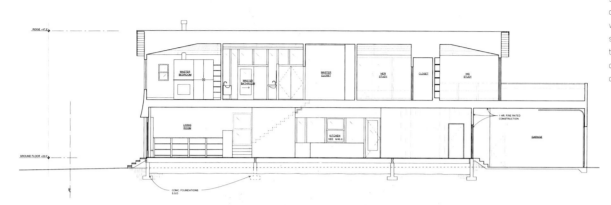

The section (left) and plans (below) clarify the
organization of the living area, kitchen, dark
room and guest bedroom on the ground floor
(middle and pictured opposite) and, on the
upper level (bottom), the master bedroom and
bathroom suite to the front of the house, with
'his' and 'her' studies to the back.

The living and dining room opens onto a
south-facing garden (opposite). The substantial
chimney-breast (opposite middle left) contrasts
with the glazed areas opening onto the external
spaces. A cool modern aesthetic was used
throughout, punctuated with areas of bright
colour – the architect intended the interior to be
calm and subtle rather than overly expressive.

Ozone House is a two-storey house with a long, thin
footprint, a parking courtyard and garage to the back, and
paved and landscaped garden space to one side and at the
front. The whole structure is elevated on a concrete-block
plinth, giving a slightly disconcerting sense of space
underneath the house, and the clapboard cladding of the
upper, overhanging storey is developed as a system of
external sliding shuttering on the ground floor, which allows
the facade to be opened up or closed as desired.

The primary space is the combined living, dining and
kitchen area which runs through the ground floor plan from
front to back. Segregated spaces at the back of the house
accommodate storage, a darkroom and a guest bedroom
and bathroom. The staircase to the upper floor wraps
around an enclosed pantry off the kitchen. The first floor
contains the master bedroom, bathroom and dressing room,
plus two studies, 'his' and 'hers', and a third bathroom. His
study opens onto an outdoor deck at the back of the house,
over the garage. The shallow pitched roof, constructed out
of prefabricated wooden trusses, is lifted like a flap over
'her' study and the internal bathroom, to create a glazed
clerestorey bringing in daylight from above, and revealing
views of the sky.

The architect intended the interior of the space to be
calm and subtle, rather than overly expressive. From the
outside, the house was to constitute 'a place to be
discovered, not confronted ... to recontextualize the obvious
and the familiar ... to be suggestive rather than explicit
about change and to play with the expectation of
the viewer.'

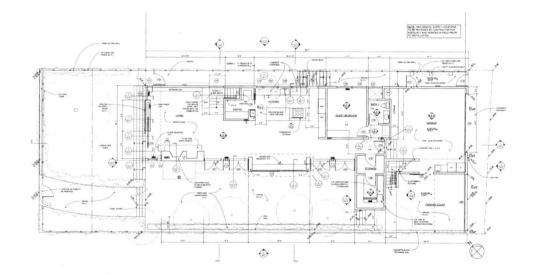

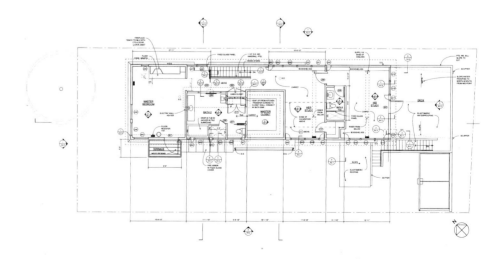

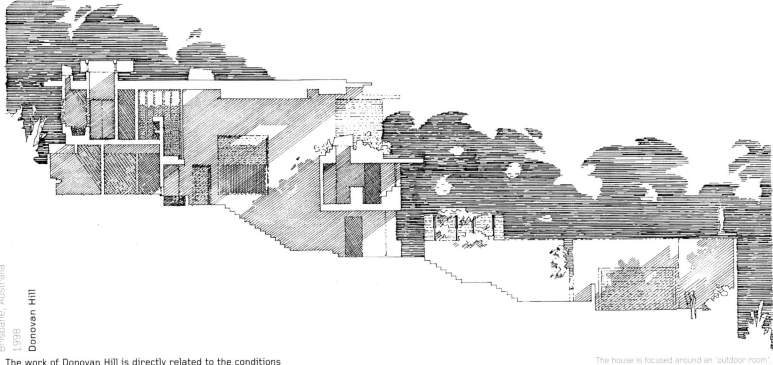

C House
Brisbane, Australia
1998
Donovan Hill

The work of Donovan Hill is directly related to the conditions of the expanding city which, in Australia as elsewhere, has prompted a debate about the problems of suburban growth. In Australia, where there has been no shortage of space for expansion, the concerns have been less focused on the issue of exhausting environmental resources than on the quality of 'place'. Most of Donovan Hill's work has been located in the area around Brisbane, which the architects describe as 'a rapidly expanding area of suburbs and resorts with a benign sub-tropical environment'. The practice has established a clearly articulated position of engagement with this ill-defined terrain of 'residual landscapes of underdeveloped sites', concentrating on the need to develop strategies of promoting the concept of public space in the suburban context.

This proposition might seem at odds with the monoculture of private domestic development which constitutes the typical suburban environment. Suburban life in its current form is sustained by a clear physical segregation of the zones of private domesticity and public life, the latter located at a distance within the inner city, and the relationship between the two mediated by private motor transport. Donovan Hill's work sets out to challenge the nature of the status-quo, and open new paths for the development of the suburban environment, by introducing a concept of public space into private domestic projects.

The C House is one of a series of suburban residences which develops this idea through the form of the 'outdoor room'. Indeed, the architects have noted that 'At both intimate and public scale the ordering, tectonic and memorable experiences associated with outdoor rooms have become a preoccupation.' In the C House, it is the main space on the site, creating a cavernous, double-height,

The house is focused around an 'outdoor room', introducing a concept of public space into the private, domestic domain (opposite, below left).

The section (above) shows how this central space forms the culmination of an extended ascent towards and into the house via a grand 'landscape stair'. Beginning at garden level, it passes underneath the front wing and into the heart of the building (see also plan below).

The entire structure of the house is formed out of concrete, giving the building a material homogeneity and weight which is thrown into contrast by the use of timber to create accretive forms on the inside and internal linings within (opposite top, below right and overleaf).

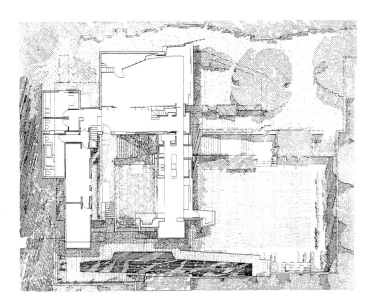

The view from the open kitchen into the central
'outdoor room' emphasizes the detached nature
of the kitchen, forming the front wing of the
house, which evokes traditional Arabic models
of domestic design

covered void at the heart of the house, onto which open
the surrounding internal spaces.

This layout is interesting, because it reverses the
normal morphology of suburban development, comprising an
endless repetition of compact boxes set in the middle of a
surrounding plot of land. In the case of the C House, the
edges of the house are pushed out towards the perimeter
of the site (while still maintaining a large garden at the
front), and an alternative outdoor space opened up within
the footprint of the building. This, in fact, replicates the
typical morphology of the traditional Islamic city, in which
one finds the houses pushed close together along narrow,
shadowy streets, but opened up within their boundary walls
by means of large central courtyards for family use and
entertainment; the same principle is vividly illustrated in the
design of the 'hôtels particuliers' of eighteenth-century
Paris, generating a rich urban fabric of interrelated,
variegated public spaces and tightly contained circulation
routes. It represents a much more efficient form of land
use, which eliminates the typical suburban problem of ill-
defined, leftover edge spaces lacking any obvious use.

The 'outdoor room' of the C House is rendered
particularly dramatic by the fact that the site is located
on a hillside. Hence the central space represents the
culmination of an extended ascent towards, and into, the
house, via a grand staircase beginning at garden level, and
passing underneath the front wing of the building into the
middle. This staircase, described by the architects as 'a
landscape stair', has a recognizably urban quality, going
back to the great city-building enterprises of the
Renaissance. This is acknowledged in the architects'
analogy between the outdoor room and a town square,
surrounded by clustered buildings.

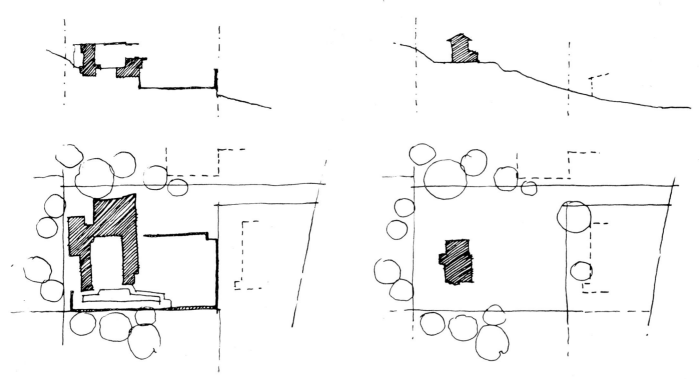

The architects have emphasized the significance of the construction technique in determining the formal resolution of the house. The structure is built of concrete, as a consequence of the client's involvement in civil engineering. Timothy Hill observes that, 'When working with concrete you can fashion both the landscape, the wall, the roof, the floor, the structure, the openings, the edge, the finish.' It opens up the possibility of creating an entire landscape moulded out of one material, because it can be used equally in internal and external situations, due to its weather-resistant qualities. This generates a material homogeneity and weight to the building, which emphasizes its physicality in a way that more lightweight materials might not do. This emphasis is deliberately exaggerated by the use of contrasting timber members and boarding to create accretive forms on the outside, and internal linings within.

The other important characteristic of concrete is its spanning potential, which was a crucial factor in the conception of the outdoor room as a space 'covered with a parasol'. The use of a concrete structure made possible the realization of this expansive, parasol-type covering, supported on hefty concrete columns at the corners and beams above. The frame is partially open to the sky, and partially lined with woven pine panels on the underside, softening the impact of the concrete, and establishing a literal sense of overlap between the artificially constructed, manmade nature of the house and the natural landscape of trees and plants surrounding it.

In view of the similarities between the typomorphology of the house and that of the traditional Islamic city, it is striking that the architects explicitly make use of the Arabic term 'Iwan' to describe the bower-like, lightweight timber-built structure attached to the front wing of the house at

The view o
(left) revr
support
corner
The house has
generated by the comu…
and timber, as shown in the imag.
(bottom), bathroom (opposite below) and a
room (below).

The concept sketches show the contrast
between the conventional model of the suburban
house as a compact, impermeable object (right),
and the realized model of the house as a
construction penetrated by the landscape,
representing public space.

the corner, where it provides a look-out point over the
garden ahead, and the pool to the side. The Iwan usually
takes the form of a terrace or colonnade, providing an
external, semi-protected living space vital to the functioning
of the Arabic home. The pervasive influence of an Islamic
model of dwelling in the C House can also be read in the
design of the kitchen as a detached structure, forming the
front wing of the house, opening directly onto the outdoor
room, but set well away from the more intimate areas of
the interior. This is a pronounced contrast to the traditional
European–American model of the kitchen as a fully
integrated element in the configuration of domestic living
space, representing the domain of the female head of the
household – wife, mother, housekeeper and cook rolled into
one person – from which she might hope to participate in,
and survey, the life of the family going on around her.

These cross-cultural references in the conception
of the C House generate an exciting counterpoint to the
conventions of European suburban typology and social
structures, which opens up new avenues of development
for the future. It is not altogether surprising that this type
of work on the redefinition of suburbs should be emerging,
with particular vigour, from Australia, due to the combination of vibrant cultural diversity and the unusual availability
of land which pertain there.

Film House
Paris, France
1998
Atelier Lab

Film-related ideas and images abound in the conception of the Film House. The garden facade (opposite left) exaggerates the image of the projection room, while the bedroom window looking across the top of the garage onto the street (opposite right) is more evocative of a camera's viewfinder. The garage (below and opposite right centre) is designed as a near-literal translation of the form and material of a car bonnet.

Paris is one of the most highly planned and historically complete cities in the world, renowned for its beauty, but also for the rigour with which its physical fabric has been controlled and ordered. It seems unthinkable that for several decades of the twentieth century, the threat of comprehensive demolition hung over the city, to make way for the implementation of Le Corbusier's Plan Voisin; but in fact, this ambitious proposal fitted quite naturally into an urban history punctuated by grand master-planning projects, most notably the so-called 'Haussmannization' of the city in the late nineteenth century which saw the creation of the grand boulevards and displacement of whole communities of the working class.

Radical alterations to the city inspired by the Corbusian agenda in the post-war era included the construction of the inner ring road, or Périphérique, forming a cordon sanitaire between the inner city and the suburbs beyond, the demolition of large areas of the historic centre to make way for the Pompidou Centre and Les Halles shopping complex, and the extensive recon-struction of one of the traditional artists' quarters: Montparnasse. It was the public reaction against these interventions that led to the implementation of measures taken to prevent further erosion of the historic urban fabric, although the tradition of large-scale, government-led building projects was continued in the series of prestigious new cultural buildings commissioned by President Mitterrand during the 1980s.

This history has created a particular interest in the issue of 'urban interaction' where new construction projects, especially privately commissioned, are concerned today, while there seems to be a greater tolerance of what is perceived as 'modern' design than in, say, a city such as

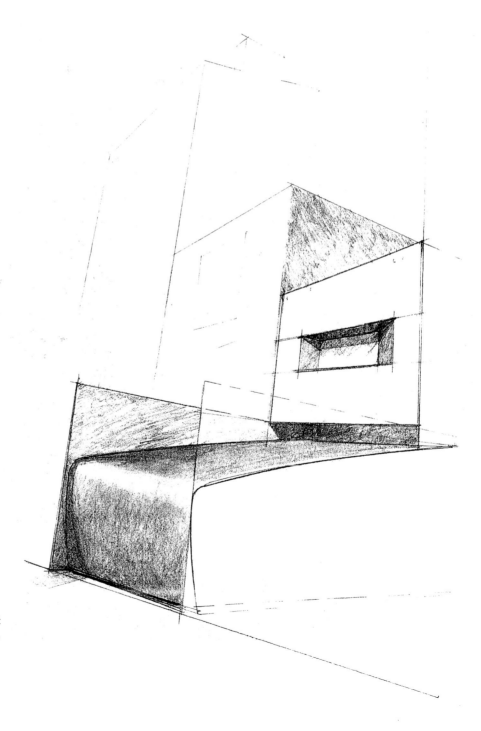

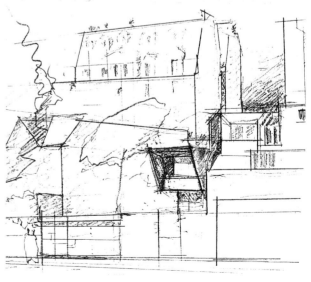

London. Atelier Lab's Film House, commissioned by a
'temporary bachelor' working in an area of the film
industry, is distinctively 'modern' in appearance – the
front of the building being dominated by a projecting,
moulded-steel garage construction designed to appear
and function similarly to a lift-up car bonnet. The rest of
the external construction is of polished concrete panels,
with windows designed to be reminiscent of the
viewfinder of a camera. These are explicit figurative
references to the iconic inventions that ushered in the
modern era, establishing a cultural distance from the
nineteenth-century urban landscape which is often
conceived as the quintessential, romantic Paris.

Notwithstanding these formal gestures, the house can
best be understood within the urban context in relation
to the special Parisian tradition of artists' studio housing.
It is this which has given the city its various enclaves of
small-scale residential development, comprising smallish
houses and attached gardens, and standing out in
contrast against the predominant, more distinctively
urban typology of the multi-storey apartment block. While
these enclaves often have a quaint, even picturesque
appearance and atmosphere, unlike the elegant urbanity
of the city's more familiar faces, it is worth remembering
that the model of the Parisian artist's studio also provided
an important source of inspiration to Le Corbusier in his
development of a radical new house-type for the future.

The Film House is located in the north of Paris, not far
from the established artists' quarter of Montmartre, and
close to the outer boundary of the inner city formed by the
Périphérique. This comparatively ragged edge, cut through
by the infrastructure of ring road, inner boulevard and
railway line, represents one of the more likely areas where

The preliminary plans explore the possibility of a ground-level swimming pool (middle), with main living spaces on the floor above (plan, top, and section, bottom), and steps down to the garden. The central lantern acts as the lynch pin, around which the internal layout is organized.

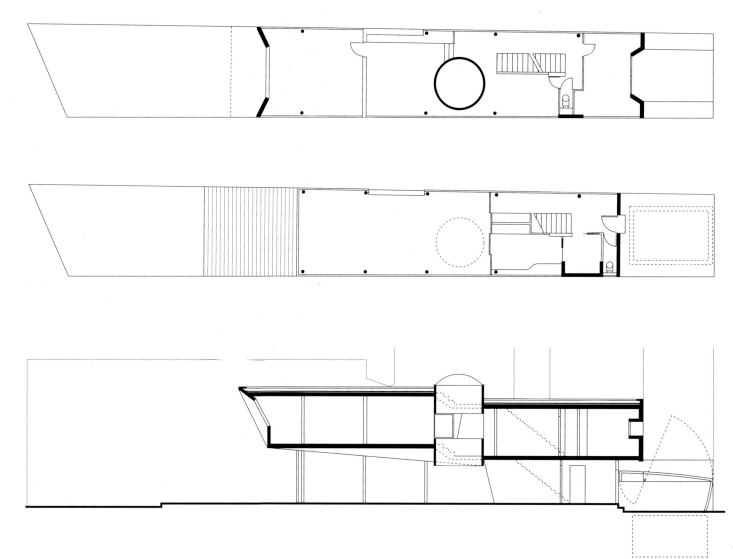

pockets of land and opportunities for new construction might be found (although Atelier Lab had built an earlier house directly overlooking Pére Lachaise cemetery, one of the city's better-known historic landmarks). The site of the Film House is long and narrow, bounded at each end by a side street onto which it has front and rear access, while both long sides are party walls.

The architects suggest that the site originally appealed to the client because it seemed to embody 'the ideas of depth of field and centering of image'. The language of film permeates the project – even its name – conjuring up an intimate connection between the house and the client's line of work, and also evoking the closely linked histories of the city of Paris and of cinema, the former frequently appearing as a subject of the latter. In this sense, it suggests an alternative basis for an approach to urban thinking, and in particular the issues of urban interaction, understood essentially from a filmic point of view, in terms of strong visual features, unlikely juxtapositions, and cuts and sequences through space.

The external scale of the house is diminutive, but its presence is emphasized and exaggerated by the eye-catching design of the garage and the monolithic quality of the facade treatment. The interior of the house constitutes an intimate, internal urban landscape, which belies the

constraints imposed by the limited surface area. It is described as 'a box of images, a camera obscura, where light can travel from end to end', and which 'presents the owner's life as if it was set in some sort of precious casket'. The metaphor of the camera obscura is embodied in the dramatic design of a large circular lantern light and void in the centre of the plan, bringing daylight into the heart of the house, which would otherwise be plunged into sombre gloom due to the lack of window openings in the long side walls. At ground-floor level, this opens into the main living room, which also has full-length windows opening onto the small rear garden. The kitchen, a small office, and staircase, are set towards the front of the house, accessed from the street through the garage, with a small clerestory light above the garage door to provide a level of daylight into these areas.

The staircase is set away from the party wall, to create a double circulation route between the front and back of the house. The first floor level comprises a bedroom at each end, enjoying the daylight and views out provided by the 'viewfinder' window openings. On the garden facade, the upper storey projects forward, overhanging the living-room windows, and exaggerating the imagery of the projection room – while also recalling Le Corbusier's characteristic use of the 'oriel principle' in his development of the new standardized house type. A bathroom and library are located in the central, 'internal' section, illuminated by the cool light entering from the top and sides of the glazed lantern void. This represents a striking feature in the very centre of the house, with a sliding metal mesh screen which allows the sides to be opened up for ventilation or communication between the two floors of the house.

The Borneo Sporenburg development is described as 'the most compact new housing district in The Netherlands', built on land reclaimed from Amsterdam's old harbour (below). The masterplan was developed by landscape practice West 8 (right). The houses face the street on one side and the canal on the other.

The double-height glazed facade of No 18 creates a lofty, light-filled box on the canal side (opposite), and a level of transparency intended to encourage a sense of interaction between the public and private realms.

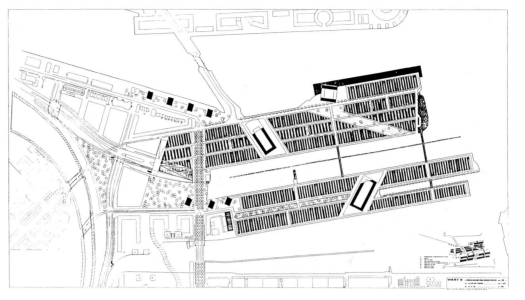

Borneo Sporenburg 18
Amsterdam, The Netherlands
1999
MVRDV   URBAN
         INTERACTION
165

The issue of urban development is particularly acute in The Netherlands, where extremely low density has created the phenomenon of the Randstadt: a continuous ring of urban development formed by the merging of one city into the next due to peripheral sprawl. The architect Rem Koolhaas has formulated the question, 'Is it a country surrounded by an airport? Or a city surrounding a meadow?', attributing the situation to the existence of no less than 47 separate municipalities, each 'feverishly planning its own periphery'.

The architects MVRDV, based in Rotterdam, are committed to developing research on 'FARMAX', or maximum floor:area ratio, explaining that, 'confronted by the growing acreage of "grey" suburban sprawl, FARMAX poses the question whether the situation can be reversed by extreme increases in local density. The introduction of programmes absorbing ultra-high density areas into the existing texture can enable the pastoral landscape to be preserved from total suburbanization.'

Borneo Sporenburg 18 is one of two new houses which they have designed in Amsterdam as part of a new residential development described as 'the most compact new housing district in The Netherlands', and built on reclaimed, recycled land, in accordance with the latest thinking on sustainable urban development. The second house, due for completion in 2000, is Borneo 12, a few doors away. The two projects have provided an opportunity to explore in detail the implications of 'ultra-high density' for day-to-day living in the contemporary city.

The masterplan for the Borneo Sporenburg development was developed by West 8, a radical landscape architecture practice based in The Netherlands.

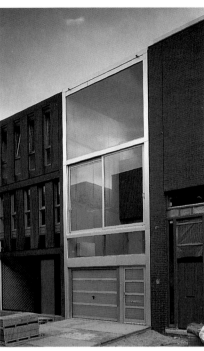

The aerial perspective of the the Borneo Sporenburg housing quarter also features buildings by Steven Holl, Fritz van Dongen and Koen van Velzen (below).

The plot is extremely narrow – just under 4 metres wide. On the canal side (far left), the glazed facade to the kitchen is recessed beneath the projecting structure of the bedroom level, with its oriel window. The street facade (left) is almost fully glazed, with a garage at ground level (see also elevations, opposite below).

The section (opposite) shows the organization of interlocking horizontal volumes reminiscent of the section used by Le Corbusier at the Unité d'Habitation in Marseilles.

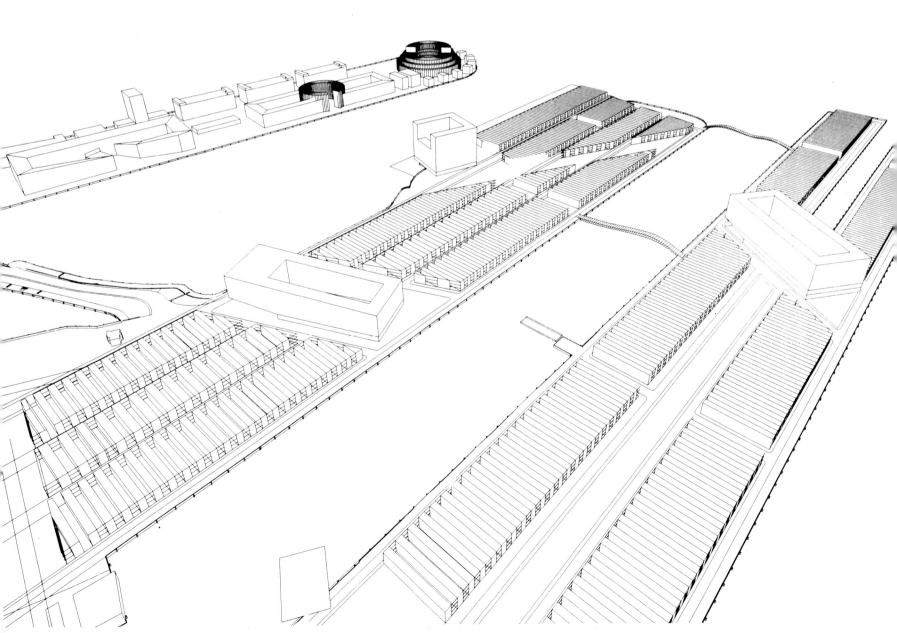

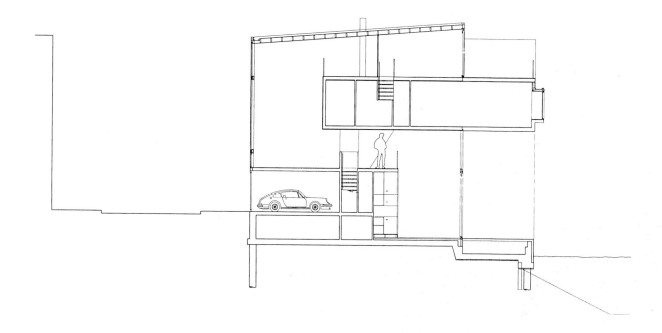

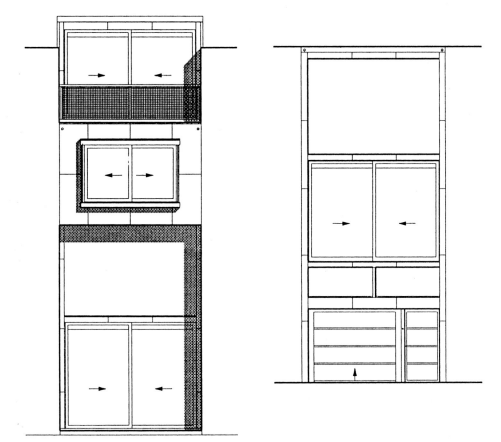

The layout comprises terraces of single-family houses, marshalled along fingers of land projecting out into the water, and separated from each other by narrow canals. Each plot measures a mere 5 metres in width, by 16 metres in depth, with a 9.5 metre height restriction, and all the houses look out over the water, with street access running down the middle of the site between two rows. Some of the plots, of which Borneo 18 is one, are designated garden plots, having a 4-metre deep garden at the back, running to the canal edge, but all the houses have an interesting double-fronted character due to the exposed, public nature of the facades on both sides, facing the street on the one hand and the canal on the other.

The situation is unusual compared to the construction of most new private houses in major cities, because the sites are not infill sites within an existing urban context, subject to the constraints of historical conditions, but an integral part of the development of a whole new city district. On the other hand, the architects' freedom is constrained by the conditions and restrictions imposed by the overall masterplan, and by the need for some level of formal dialogue, or interaction, with neighbouring houses designed by others. The public nature of both exposed facades means that the issue of the interrelationship between houses is particularly sensitive, and this constitutes a significant area of difference from the traditional nineteenth-century terrace, where the houses had a very clear 'back' which could be handled much more freely, and usually less coherently, than the street facade. It was on this side that various accretions would grow through time, reflecting the individuality of occupants and

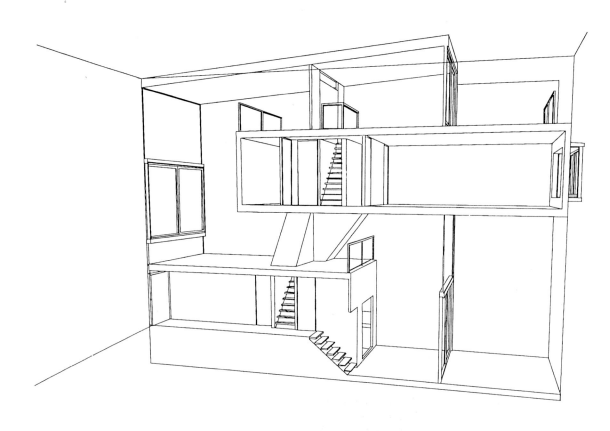

The interlocking system of suspended boxes is revealed in the sectional perspectives, seen from the side (left), canal (below left) and street (below right). This system allows daylight to penetrate into the heart of the house from both directions. It also creates a surprising number of levels through the house from bottom to top as revealed in the plans (opposite). From left to right are the garage and kitchen levels; the living-room level; the bedroom level, with void over the living room; the study level with gallery looking over living-room void; and roof level. The study opens through sliding French windows onto a terrace overlooking the canal (opposite below).

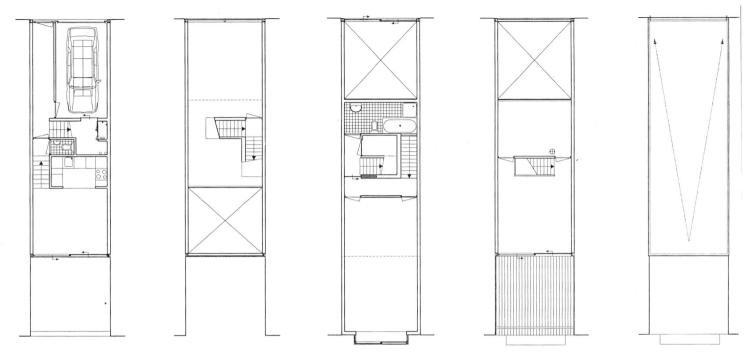

their particular needs, without any reference to a unifying, overall conception of urbanity.

One of the conditions of the development was that parking for each unit should be contained within the surface area of the plot. In the case of No 18, which is just under 4 metres wide, rather than 5 or 6 metres like most other developments, this required particularly careful organization. The garage occupies the front section of the ground floor area, with a narrow entrance passageway running alongside it to a central staircase wrapping around a service core. The sense of construction in the entry sequence is relieved by the sudden expansion into a kitchen set at a lower level at the back of the house, opening onto the garden and water through a full-height glazed wall. This creates a lofty, light-filled box at the rear of the house which is a marked contrast to the anticipated gloom of a traditional terrace-house interior.

The section of the house seems to be inspired by the interlocking Citrohan-based model used by Le Corbusier in his Unité d'Habitation at Marseilles, which creates a generous living space with a double-height window for each duplex apartment, by sliding back the floor-plate of the upper level, away from the facade, to create a gallery edge within the volume of the living space. The Borneo house section is based on the same principle, to generate a rich play of daylight from both sides throughout the house, and an unusual level of spatial variety and interconnectivity between the top and bottom of the house, maximizing the architectural possibilities within the constraints of the surface area. Hence the vertical volume is penetrated by a structurally self-contained box, containing the bedrooms, which is pushed away from the

street facade to project out over the garden on the canalside elevation. This allows the creation of a double-height glazed facade and void to the main living space, while the space between the top of the box and the roof, at the top of the house, accommodates a study looking out towards the street from a gallery over the living space, and towards the canal through French windows opening onto a terrace supported by the projecting structure of the bedroom. The gallery device is used again at the back of the main living space to create a similar interface with the kitchen/dining area on the level below, and a line of vision towards the canal which also allows light to filter through from this direction.

The achievement of transparency was a key principle in the design of the house, notwithstanding the high density of the surrounding development, which might have been expected to generate an emphasis on privacy and interiority. This should be understood as a manifestation of a conscious intention, in the cases of both Nos 18 and 12 Borneo, to establish a strong sense of interconnection between the public and private realms as the foundation for contemporary city life.

Project 222, designed by Future Systems for a site on the coast of Wales, 1998, frames vistas of the beach and sea through a glazed facade which has been compared to a 'lens' cut into the landscape. The house was prefabricated in transportable sections and assembled on site.

The commission to build a rural retreat has often been considered in the past as offering carte blanche to the architect to design a project of the imagination, unfettered by mundane functional requirements. There is a long architectural history of pavilions, casinos and rural villas fundamentally intended for pleasure, entertaining and relaxation, rather than as permanent residences for everyday life, or any deep involvement in the society and economy of the countryside. Among these buildings are some canonic works of architecture, notably Palladio's Villa Rotonda at Vicenza, or Mies van der Rohe's Farnsworth House outside Chicago, but many of them are follies created in the service of the whim and fantasy of the client, quite as much as the imagination and ideology of the architect.

It is precisely this lack of a functional programme to meet the day-to-day requirements of working lives, and provide an anchor for the client's and architect's desires, that can make a project of this sort a particularly awkward commission, and one that may well turn out badly. It can be argued that Edith Farnsworth's distressed response to her glass house and decision to pursue legal proceedings against the architect for fraud, was as much a result of her own lack of clarity about what she needed and expected in a weekend house as it was of Mies' total commitment to his own architectural ideology and lack of interest in developing a dialogue with his client.

The Farnsworth House was initiated on the basis of two ideas: that it should provide an escape from the city at weekends, and that it should make the most of the natural beauty of the site. Mies later said, 'we should attempt to bring nature, houses and human beings together into a higher unity. If you view nature through the glass walls of the Farnsworth House, it gains a more profound significance than if viewed from outside'. The same precepts can be seen as the driving force behind the 'rural retreats' commissioned during the 1990s. But, as a result of the revolution in mobility and communications during the latter half of the century, it is also increasingly common for clients to view these houses as potentially permanent, or at least primary residences, from which they can work and communicate with the world at large.

Hence the whole idea of the 'rural retreat' becomes increasingly an illusion or fantasy, as the very possibility of retreat from an efficiently networked, highly urbanized, speed-obsessed world becomes more and more difficult to achieve. Most of the traditional places of retreat associated with any big city have become near suburbs catering for communities of dislocated people who spend their lives constantly shuttling to and fro. Likewise, the

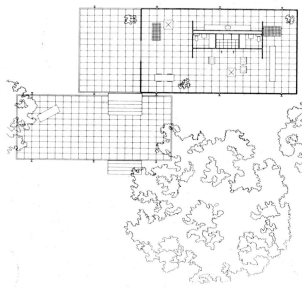

impossibility of being 'out of contact' has transformed the experience of being in even the most remote location. And as this situation evolves, the hankering for the elusive escape becomes ever stronger.

From an architectural point of view, the result has been the development of an ever more attentive concern for the construction of an exclusive relationship between a house and its surrounding natural context, even where a site may be surrounded by other houses built for precisely the same purpose. In contrast to the ambitions of any other kind of architectural project, the aim must be to ignore any neighbouring buildings and achieve a sense of freedom from the pressures of insistent human presence. This intense focus on the relationship between man and nature has opened the way in these types of projects for overlap with the aims and ideals of the environmental agenda. The gentle evolution of the classic 'rural retreat', designed essentially for the pursuit of culture within the contrasting context of nature, into an exemplar of environmental good practice is a distinct phenomenon of more recent times.

Of the houses featured here, those built on wooded sites have all been raised on pilotis above ground level, an approach common to various vernacular traditions, and enthusiastically explored by Le Corbusier, but comparatively rarely seen in

contemporary Western building today. This type of construction procedure embodies an ideal of building lightly on the land, minimizing the intervention of built form, particularly where the site is one of particular natural beauty, as all these are. It also seems to embody an ideal of the tree house as the ultimate retreat, out of the way of animals and also predatory human beings. Symbolically, the tree house occupies a plane above that of mundane human activity, suspended between the sky and the earth. Anne Lacaton and Jean-Philippe Vassal's house at Cap Ferret develops this form into a quite extreme version, where the trees actually pass through the house, invading the living space, before passing out through the roof on their lofty journey skywards.

In contrast to this approach, Will Bruder's Byrne Residence is a scheme intended to express an ideal of self-identification with the geology of the earth itself. The house appears to be deeply rooted in the ground, emerging as an extrusion of the geological strata beneath it, in a form which is conceived to reflect the natural formations of the landscape around it. Lightness and ephemerality are here dismissed in favour of an ideal of timelessness and ultimate fusion with the very substance of the earth.

In most of these cases, the organization of the internal space is under emphasized, even understated, taking second place in importance to the interfaces between interior and exterior and the transitional spaces. For example, the Reutter House by Mathias Klotz is designed to draw attention to the entry route, which carries the visitor through the trees towards the building on an elevated causeway. Large and prominent terraces, or other forms of viewing platform, constitute interfacing spaces from which to engage in a visual relationship with the context, as well as enjoy the physical sensation of being in the landscape without actually leaving the comfort and safety of the house. Finally, the window itself takes on an exaggerated significance and function as the primary architectural medium of communication between internal space and nature beyond. None of these houses develop this to the extreme that Mies van der Rohe did in his glass-walled Farnsworth House, recognizing the importance of contrasting solidity and transparency in dramatizing the relationship between man and nature; but all of them develop the use of the glazed surfaces in particular ways in order to frame, focus and edit the way the landscape is perceived from inside the house.

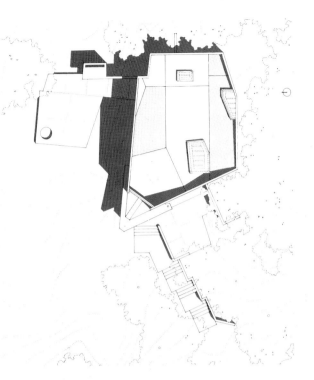

The house is conceived as 'a landscape focusing device', through which to experience the place. The site plan (top right) reveals the irregular geometry of the form, following the topography of the site, with the entrance located in the pointed prow of the building (above and right). The entrance is approached via a gently ascending path (opposite). A piece from the client's art collection is displayed along the route, authenticating the 'primitive' quality of the landscape setting.

As in the case of Will Bruder's Byrne House (pp196–201), the Barnes House, on Vancouver Island, embodies an ideal of escape from the 'civilized', developed east, to the wilder, uncharted landscapes of the west. The move from east to west may also evoke a sense of progress through life, and a developing maturity, following the course of the sun. Whereas in Glenn Murcutt's house for Marika Marmburra (pp32–9) this symbolism provided the basis for the programmatic organization of the sleeping quarters on the western side, with the children's bedrooms located to the east of the parents, it may also constitute a more subtle, less directly functional, influence on the design of many contemporary houses around the world, particularly those conceived in the nature of retreats.

Significantly, perhaps, John and Patricia Patkau's clients, Dave and Fran Barnes, have said that coming home from work each day to the Barnes House is like going on vacation, framing the house as an escape from the demands and routines of the world of work. The site on which it sits is the edge of a rocky outcrop within a generally forested area of land overlooking the Strait of Georgia and the mainland of British Columbia to the north, and the rocky shoreline of Vancouver Island to the northwest. The house itself is conceived, in the architects' words, as 'a landscape focusing device – a mechanism through which the experience of this place, from the small-scaled textural characteristics of the rock to the large-scaled expanse of the sea, is made manifest'.

This approach contrasts with that employed in the Byrne House, for example, in that the intention is explicitly not for the house to merge with, and become

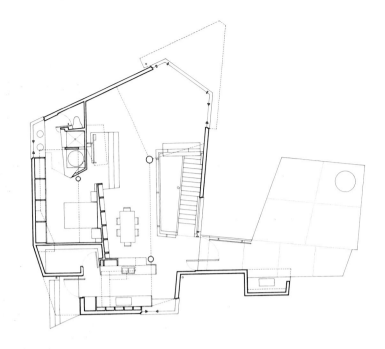

Generous openings cut into the walls reveal
views of the surrounding woodland and the
sea beyond (opposite). The main staircase leads
up the side of the house (opposite bottom left
and right) from the lower entrance level to the
main living level above (see floor plans: ground
level, below, and upper level, above). At the top
of the staircase there is an opening to the left
onto a terrace (opposite top). To the left lies the
open, multi-purpose living space, with a shallow
stair leading up to an adjacent bedroom
(opposite centre).

The cross and long sections (opposite) reveal
the outline of the weighty, over-arching roof.

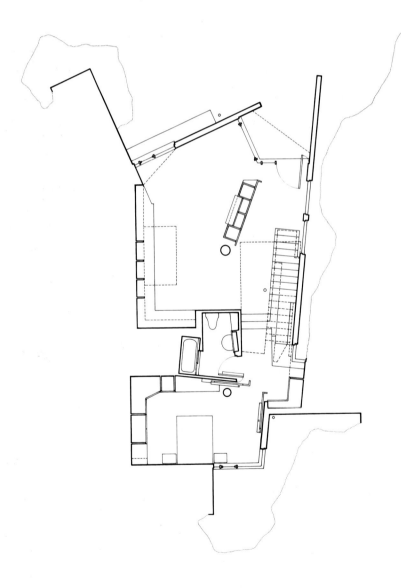

part of the physical make-up, or geology, of the
landscape, but in some way to capture it and distil its
essence. This difference is immediately apparent in the
materials and form of the building, which follows the
topography of the site, producing a somewhat irregular
geometry, rather than transforming particular
characteristics of the local landscape into a source
of architectural formal language and materiality. The
enclosing envelope of the building is simply constructed
out of conventional wood framing supported on a
reinforced concrete foundation and rendered with stucco.
The internal structure is somewhat naturalistic, being
supported by tree-like concrete columns rising to support
a heavy timber roof structure, the underside of which is
exposed within the lofty living space on the upper floor,
giving it a barn-like aspect. The house is firmly anchored
into the ground, as it probably needs to be in its coastal
position, conceived as something 'continuous with the
natural world', but also clearly manmade, and so not
of the landscape.

The creation of local particularity in the face of a
creepingly globalizing culture is one of the issues which
the Patkaus are particularly concerned to address. They
refer to the 'generalizing effect on our culture' of 'mass-
production and mass media'. Their concern has motivated
them to engage in a self-conscious 'search for the
particular' which 'begins with the givens ... of a project
... the "found potential".' In the case of the Barnes
House, this is identified as being most evidently the site,
'understood to be not only the rocky outcrop upon which
the house is situated and the surrounding vegetation
which encompasses it but the entire region centered on
the Strait of Georgia'. This involves, as a close correlation

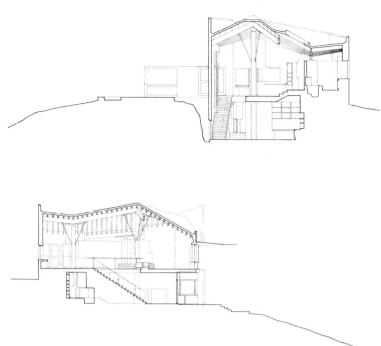

Views of the main living area, back towards the kitchen (opposite and above centre), and out over the entrance (top right) reveal the heavy timber roof overhead (see also drawing below), supported by tree-like concrete columns. The roof is like a dark protective carapace, in contrast to the lightness which pervades the house beneath it, revealed in the views of the upstairs bathroom (above), downstairs studio (top), and glimpsed across the downstairs bedroom (right)

the rejection of any architectural approach based on the principles of abstraction or idealism – be they classical or modernist. The universalism implied in these architectural ideologies is essentially at odds with the commitment to local particularity and distinction. The Patkaus identify their approach as being founded in a pragmatism which can accommodate irregularity and variability from project to project, and is inherently flexible. They point to these characteristics in the Barnes House, notably the conjunction of orthogonal and non-orthogonal geometries, the figural strength and weakness of the north and west, and south and east elevations respectively, and the pragmatic use of different materials to serve the different functions required of them most appropriately.

The original brief provided by the clients, who had had some experience of commissioning architect-designed houses in the past, was for standard living accommodation plus a guest bedroom and a studio to be shared by husband and wife – an amateur sculptor and landscape architect. This suggests a further reading of the house not simply as a retreat, but as a womb-like receptacle for nurturing personal creativity: the home as a focus for self-fulfilment. In this reading, the noticeably weighty, over-arching roof becomes redolent with meaning as a dark protective carapace high above the living space. By contrast, the interior as a whole is distinguished by a lightness produced by the continuity of space through the core accommodation, and the generous openings cut into the walls to reveal views of the surrounding woodland and the sea beyond.

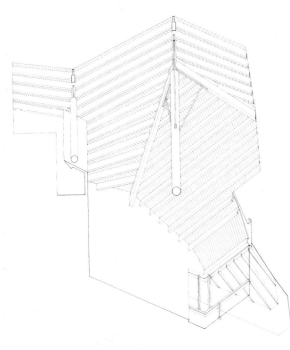

The architects adopted the traditional typology of farmhouse construction in Maine, which they describe as a 'house-town', offering a sense of conviviality and involvement. The house is not an object building, but a rich configuration of linked volumes, with a strong connection to nature (see site plan, right). This is underlined by the design of projecting vantage points, or 'porches' from which to look out into the landscape, as on the south-facing entrance elevation (below) and sharply angled living-room wing (opposite).

This house is the result of an unusual relocation from West to East, and North: from Venice Beach, California, to Horseshoe Pond in Lovell, Maine, north of Toronto. The client's decision to move was in part prompted by the wildness and unpredictability of a Western landscape prone to earthquakes, mudslides and forest fires, and a desire to establish a home and artist's studio in close connection with a less extreme, more stable and greener natural environment.

In their design of the house, the architects evoke a traditional model of domestic construction in Maine, the 'big house, little house, back house and barn'. This typology, which they describe as that of a 'house-town' offers complete connection of domestic and farmhouse activities during winter months as well as a sense of conviviality and involvement even in the more remote locations, establishing a resistance to feelings of isolation. Hence this house, while embodying in many ways the ideal of the rural retreat, distanced from the pressures of contemporary life, also demonstrates an awareness of the continuing depth of ancient human fear when brought face-to-face with nature and solitude.

Nomentana, a painter and interior designer, 'wanted to be as close to nature as possible', but her past experiences had also shown her that nature cannot always be relied upon as a friend and companion. The architects took pains to design a house that was not 'an object building looking out exclusively to the landscape', but a rich configuration of linked volumes and internal and external spaces, that would allow the inhabitant to keep parts of the house, and its lights, in constant vision from wherever she might be in the house at a particular moment. Mack Scogin has

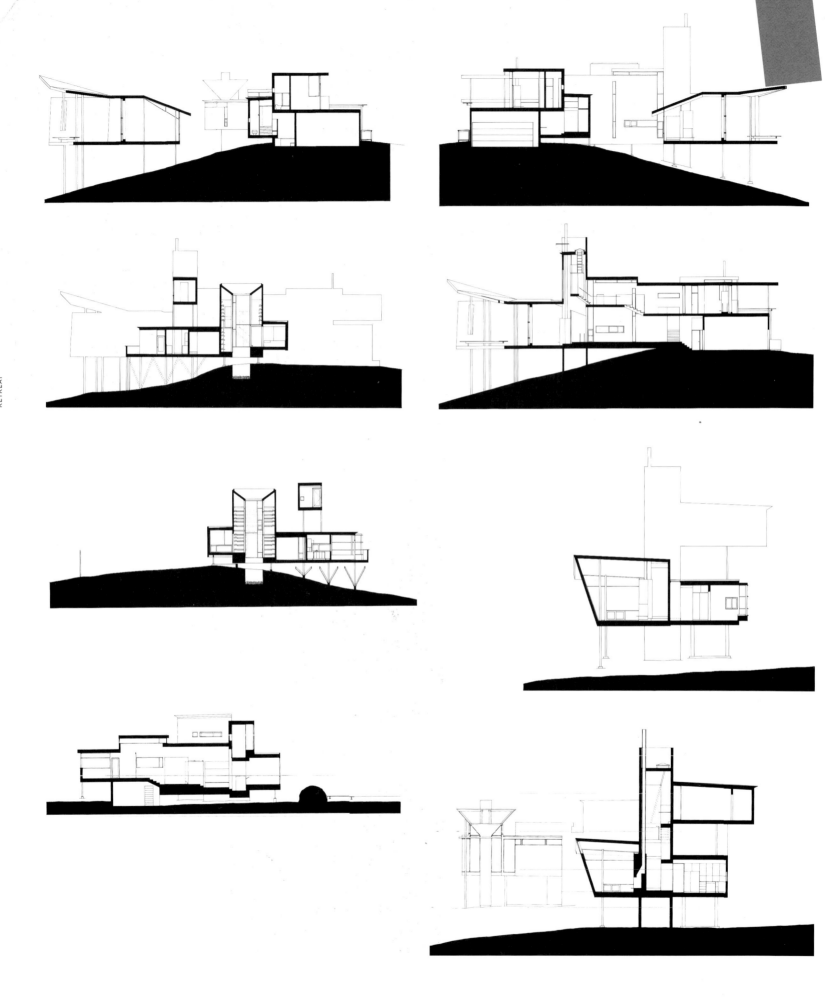

observed that 'the house is about a forced movement that becomes a companion you constantly have to deal with as you move through it.'

The critic Joseph Giovannini has drawn an interesting comparison between the Nomentana Residence and Le Corbusier's Villa Savoye, outside Paris – a link easily made by virtue of the use of pilotis in the Nomentana scheme, which elevates most of the living accommodation above ground level. He defines the Villa Savoye as the classic 'object building' which the Nomentana house is not. Indeed, the use of pilotis, the light grey external walls and manipulation of transparent and solid planes in the latter, suggests a reading of the house as a curious distortion of the Savoye model. The multiplicity of volumes presents a stark contrast with the compact plan and internal organization of the Villa Savoye, which has the advantage of limiting the extent of the intervention on the site.

The Nomentana House is a rambling structure by comparison, although the use of pilotis emulating the surrounding slender tree trunks serves to minimize its footings on the ground and create an apparently lighter intervention. The plan is described as pinwheel-shaped, creating a series of distinct vantage points, formally articulated as 'porches', from which to look out on the surrounding landscape and forming an embrace around an open area at the centre of the site. Each element of the plan, which comprises a living room, sitting room, dining room, kitchen, library, two bedrooms, drawing studio, garage and detached painting studio, is expressed volumetrically within the external massing of the building, creating a complex, abstract form, which seems to be in a constant state of movement, against the backdrop of the woods and mountain.

The architects' notion was one of 'wrapping the house around nature'. The result is a complex, abstract form which seems to be in a constant state of movement, and gives volumetric expression to each element of the plan, as shown in the images and sections. Clockwise from top left: oblique view across the living room porch, north elevation, two views of south-facing entrance elevation.

Sections in pairs from top to bottom (opposite): east–west sections at the living room and guest room looking north (left) and south (right); east–west section at the stairwell/library, looking north (left) and through the living room, chimney tower also looking north (right); section through the library, sitting room and drawing studio (left) and through the sitting room and kitchen porch looking east (right); section through the sitting room, master bedroom and hall looking east (left) and through the living room, kitchen, chimney tower and drawing studio looking east (right).

The living-room 'porch' is designed to allow
'snow and rain and light to come through the
house, nature comes in and falls out'.

This approach is a result of the client's express wish
not to have open, generic, 'loft-type' living spaces, but a
series of small, differentiated rooms, each with its own
clear identity. Perhaps this can also be understood as a
response to the wide expanses of nature outside the
windows, in the sense of an intention to draw nature into
the embrace of a more protective living environment,
rather than open up, or expose, the interior space of the
house itself to nature.

The architects refer to a notion of 'wrapping the
house around nature', which is a rather different concept
from that of the classic, modernist picture window, with
its implication of framing and distance. They point in
particular to the design of the jutting, angular living-
room porch, with one sheltering wall in which a large
opening is punched to allow 'snow and rain and light [to]
come through the house; nature comes in and falls out'.
Comparable aspects of the design include the two-and-a-

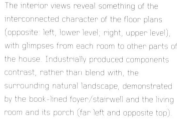

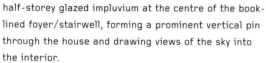

half-storey glazed impluvium at the centre of the book-lined foyer/stairwell, forming a prominent vertical pin through the house and drawing views of the sky into the interior.

The structure consists of timber and steel frame, the main body of the house clad in cementitious fibre-board, and the detached painting studio in zinc. This represents an interesting disavowal of obviously 'natural' materials in the conception of the house, and an embrace of industrially produced components which contrast, rather than blend, with the surrounding landscape. The clear distinction between the natural and the manmade is emphasized by the use of perforated metal for the stairs, and plate aluminium for the balustrades, and the predominant use of light grey and white walls throughout the interior and exterior. Significantly, a strong argument against whiteness and abstraction as being 'unnatural' was formulated by the nineteenth-century German architectural historian Gottfried Semper, who proposed that polychromy actually clarifies form, by bringing the eye back to a natural way of seeing. Semper suggested that the origins of internal walls lay in the use of moveable, textile partitions in which colour would have been inherent. But his views were cast out and largely forgotten as a result of Modernism's institutionalization of the white wall, signifying the supremacy of contour and outline.

To a great extent, the Nomentana residence also emphasizes the importance of those values. By placing itself firmly within a cultural context of Modernist referents, it provides a consistent reminder to its inhabitant and visitors of a sustained cultural connection with urbane, urban society, even when submerged in the depths of the rural landscape.

The interior views reveal something of the interconnected character of the floor plans (opposite left, lower level; right, upper level), with glimpses from each room to other parts of the house. Industrially produced components contrast, rather than blend with, the surrounding natural landscape, demonstrated by the book-lined foyer/stairwell and the living room and its porch (far left and opposite top).

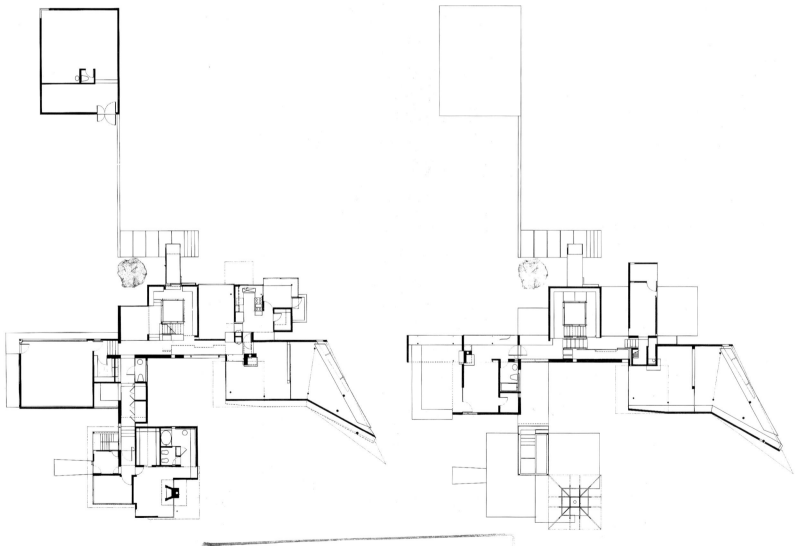

House at Cap Ferret
Arcachon, near Bordeaux, France
1998
Lacaton Vassal

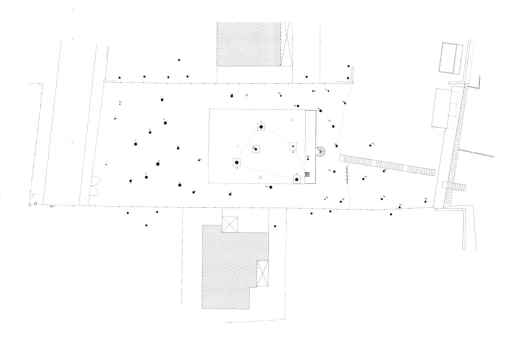

This is another example of a house elevated among trees, to preserve and make the most of the natural features and qualities of the site, and approach the realization of a dream of living in close communion with nature and one's inner self.

The house at Cap Ferret is built amongst pine trees on a sand dune 15m above sea level, overlooking the Bassin d'Arcachon – one of the most important expanses of wetlands remaining in France. Insofar as the whole of the Bassin is ringed with small settlements, the site is not strictly speaking a 'rural retreat'; on the other hand, in symbolic terms, it is. Arcachon, on the southern edge, is the oldest resort on the Côte d'Argent, a long coastal strip of sandy beaches, pine forest, and remarkable sand dunes, which embodies a romantic ideal of untamed nature and escape from city life in the minds of the French, and is still comparatively little visited.

The architects set out to preserve all the trees on the site of the house by the simple, but startling, recourse of allowing six trees to pass through the structure, designed with sufficient leeway to accommodate movement in the wind. This unusual approach evokes a classic image: Le Corbusier and Pierre Jeanneret's Pavillon de l'Esprit Nouveau, constructed for the International Arts and Crafts Exhibition held in Paris in 1925, which became a manifesto of modernity, providing a model for standardized dwelling. One of its most striking features was the large terrace, or 'hanging garden', with a mature tree growing up through a large circular hole cut in a canopy-style roof above.

It is Lacaton and Vassal's reconceptualization of this image in the context of contemporary culture and concerns which makes it interesting. In a sense, the house is the antithesis of the ideal of standardization embodied in the

The design approach hinged around the importance of preserving the trees on the site, a 15 metre-high sand dune overlooking the wetlands (see section above). As a result, six trees actually pass through an elevated structure (see site plan below, with location of trees marked, and opposite bottom left).

The views across the roof (opposite top) show how the trunks pass through skylights covered in plastic sheeting, to which they are attached by rubber strips. These allow for movement in the wind without risk of the structure being dislodged. The house is a single-storey steel-frame box supported on steel piles, and clad in corrugated aluminium (opposite centre left and bottom right).

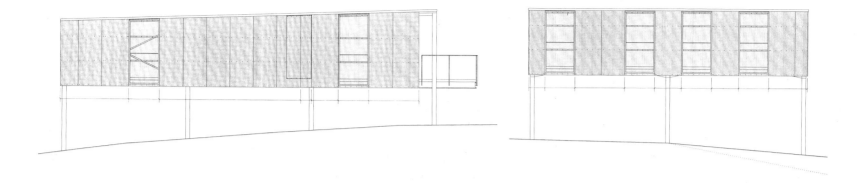

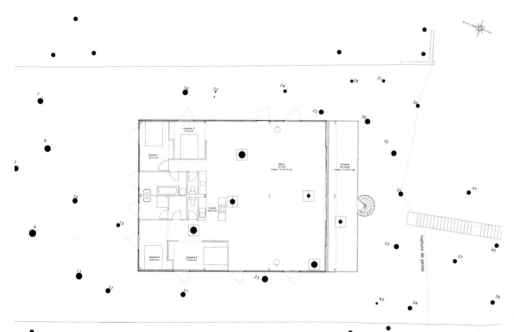

The underside of the house, clad in aluminium,
is illuminated by the sun's rays reflected off the
water at different angles according to its level
(opposite). The east and north elevations (top
left and right) show details of the arrangement
of the piles, varying in height according to
changes in the ground level, and of the
disposition of panels of translucent
polycarbonate within the external aluminium
cladding system. The floor plan (above) shows
the location of the individual tree trunks within
the main living space and terrace, with the
bedrooms and services grouped towards the
rear of the house.

1925 pavilion, being designed as a one-off, part-time
residence on a unique site. There is little indication of any
ambition, as in the Acayaba House for example, to produce
a prototype for a structural system capable of widespread
application. Although the materials themselves are
industrial products – a lightweight steel frame, corrugated
aluminium, and transparent corrugated plastic sheet –
which would be available more or less anywhere, they are
put together with a minimum of artfulness, and even a
suggestion of improvization. This suggests a reluctance to
impose the values of the manmade on the natural
environment, and a desire to evade the seductive,
persuasive qualities of the photographic image and
manifesto, so close to Le Corbusier's heart.

Inevitably, these very characteristics have made the
house an object of architectural curiosity, in much the
same way as the earlier house built by the architects at
Floirac, in the suburbs of Bordeaux, which attracted
attention because of its corrugated fibrecement street
facade. But it maintains an elusive quality, screened by
trees, floating above the uneven ground plane, and clad in
materials which shimmer in the light and merge with the
sky behind so that the structure becomes almost invisible.

The steel framed, single-storey house comprises a
210m-square concrete platform raised on steel piles
between two and four metres high, depending on the
ground level. The site slopes down towards the water,
with a long staircase leading to the water's edge. The
house thus provides a viewing platform from which to
contemplate the boats and other activity in the Bassin,
and the changes to the water and sky that occur through
the day and from one season to the next. A steel, spiral
staircase dropping down through the trees and shrubs

The house provides a viewing platform from which to contemplate the Bassin, with a spiral staircase dropping down through the trees from the terrace to ground level (left and below). The front of the house is fully glazed, blurring the boundary between the surroundings and the internal, open-plan living space (below left). This impression of ambiguity is reinforced by the literal invasion of nature in the form of living trees passing through the house (opposite, view towards back of house across bedroom).

The section (bottom) shows how the structure is detailed at the points where the trees pass through the floor plate and roof, in order to ensure it remains weathertight.

provides direct access from the open terrace at the front of the house to the ground below.

The plan is very straightforward: an open, rectangular box, with the services and sleeping quarters (four bedrooms and two bathrooms) clustered together at the rear, and an extensive living area filling the rest of the space. The external envelope of the structure, including the underside of the floor-plate, is made predominantly of corrugated aluminium, with opening panels of transparent corrugated polycarbonate for light and air, although the front elevation is constructed out of sliding glass panels, to allow for complete transparency. Yet the perception of this industrial construction is forcefully altered by the natural invasion of the internal space, in the form of the rough, irregular bodies of the tree trunks.

All the trees rise up through the main living space and terrace, in tacit acknowledgement, perhaps, of a desire to preserve a boundary between culture and nature within the more private domains of human life. The trunks pass through wood-lined openings marked by steel plates in the polished concrete floor. Underneath the floor, the trunks are held apart from the structure in metal rings and protective bands of soft rubber. At roof level the trunks pass through generous skylights covered in plastic sheeting, to which they are attached by rubber strips allowing them to move in the wind without dislodging the structure. The high level of ventilation and lack of humidity within the interior enables them to live. These features of the design seem to embody an explicit dialectic between nature and culture, brought together in a poetic statement about the possibility of a symbiotic coexistence, at the most precise level of architectural detailing.

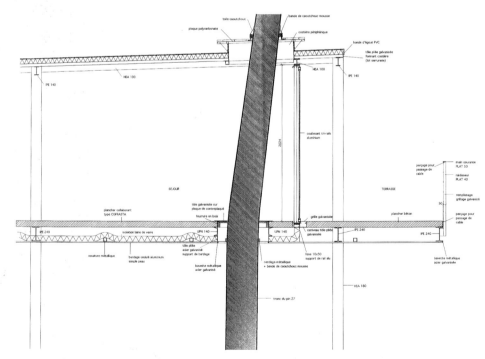

Byrne House
Scottsdale, Arizona, USA
1998
Will Bruder

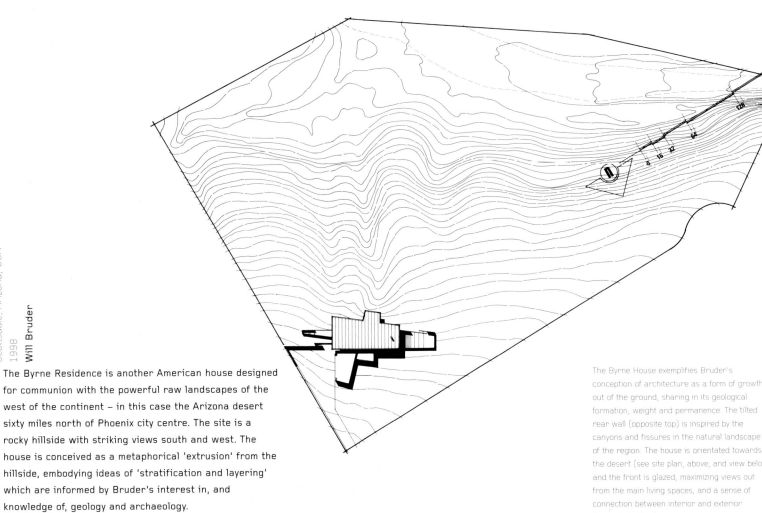

The Byrne Residence is another American house designed for communion with the powerful raw landscapes of the west of the continent – in this case the Arizona desert sixty miles north of Phoenix city centre. The site is a rocky hillside with striking views south and west. The house is conceived as a metaphorical 'extrusion' from the hillside, embodying ideas of 'stratification and layering' which are informed by Bruder's interest in, and knowledge of, geology and archaeology.

The project was commissioned by a couple, Bill and Carol Byrne, as a primary residence in the desert. They had moved from the East Coast to Arizona some time before, evidently drawn by the promise of its wide open, wild spaces. The house represents the deliberate pursuit of an 'organic' ideal which originally came out of the Byrnes' brief, and is embodied in an emphatically material architectural aesthetic in order to emphasize an integral relationship between the building and the natural landscape. In the architect's words, 'the architecture possesses a mysterious quietness and power in the landscape'.

Bruder's is a design approach which produces a very different type of building from the houses of, say, Murcutt or Poole, which come out of an ideal of lightness on the ground, and have an almost ephemeral quality within the landscape – as if they could be blown away and forgotten at any moment, without trace. While these houses are consciously designed as interventions in the superstructure of the landscape that should disturb and alter it as little as possible, Bruder's work is conceived as a form of growth out of the ground itself, sharing in its geological formation, weight and permanence. This distinction is also indicative of the contrasting

The Byrne House exemplifies Bruder's conception of architecture as a form of growth out of the ground, sharing in its geological formation, weight and permanence. The tilted rear wall (opposite top) is inspired by the canyons and fissures in the natural landscape of the region. The house is orientated towards the desert (see site plan, above, and view below) and the front is glazed, maximizing views out from the main living spaces, and a sense of connection between interior and exterior (opposite bottom)

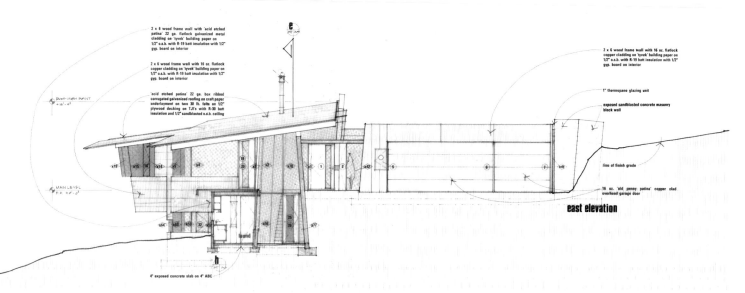

2 x 6 wood frame wall with 'acid etched patina' 22 ga. flatlock galvanized metal cladding on 'tyvek' building paper on 1/2" o.s.b. with R-19 batt insulation with 1/2" gyp. board on interior

2 x 6 wood frame wall with 16 oz. flatlock copper cladding on 'tyvek' building paper on 1/2" o.s.b. with R-19 batt insulation with 1/2" gyp. board on interior

'acid etched patina' 22 ga. box ribbed corrugated galvanized roofing on craft paper underlayment on two 30 lb. felts on 1/2" plywood decking on TJI's with R-30 batt insulation and 1/2" sandblasted o.s.b. ceiling

2 x 6 wood frame wall with 16 oz. flatlock copper cladding on 'tyvek' building paper on 1/2" o.s.b. with R-19 batt insulation with 1/2" gyp. board on interior

1" thermopane glazing unit

exposed sandblasted concrete masonry block wall

ROOF HIGH POINT

MAIN LEVEL

line of finish grade

16 oz. 'old penny patina' copper clad overhead garage door

laund

4" exposed concrete slab on 4" ABC

east elevation

The main floor plan (below) and east elevation (above) show the organization of the internal space around a linear 'spine', made of concrete-block walls leaning at varying degrees from the vertical and horizontal (opposite right, above and below). A steel-framed roof is cantilevered off the 'spine' and juts out over the main living spaces towards the front of the house (see elevation).

The accommodation to the rear of the spine comprises a garage and secondary bedroom, while the master bedroom opens onto a long terrace running parallel to the primary axis. The entrance is located at the same end of this axis, tucked between the tilting structural elements and colliding roof plates as if at the centre of a momentous geological event (opposite left).

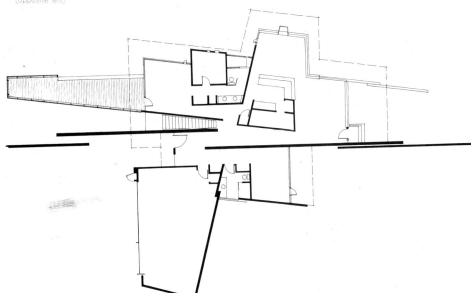

architectural genealogy of the architects' work. While the two Australians can be linked to an essentially European tradition dominated by the influence of Le Corbusier and his ideal of buildings 'liberated from the soil' through the use of pilotis, Bruder represents a line of descent from the great American master of what has been called the 'organic tradition' – Frank Lloyd Wright, and his ground-hugging Prairie Style houses. He explicitly relates the Byrne House to Wright's Price House of 1954 in the suburbs of Phoenix, and the similarity between the two, in terms of form and materials, is evident.

The striking character of the Byrne House derives from the angular geometry driving the plan, and the use of concrete-block walls leaning at varying degrees from the vertical to form the spine of the house. The hefty cantilevered steel-framed roof juts out over the main living spaces of the house, which are enclosed by glazed walls of clear and 'solex' green, non-reflective glass, maximizing views out over the landscape, and the sense of connection between interior and exterior. The weight of the roof is somewhat disconcertingly held off and away from the back wall by steel brackets, the glazed gap allowing sunlight to filter into the spinal circulation zone of the plan, where there are few windows.

Bruder attributes the inspiration for the tilted walls to the canyons and fissures in the natural landscape of the region, and the entrance to the house, located at one end of the linear axis, is tucked in between the tilting structural elements and the colliding roof plates as if at the centre of a momentous geological event – a reminder that the forces of nature can be both dramatic and unpredictable in their physical impact. By contrast, the steel and timber deck which stretches out beyond it

along the same axis, exaggerating the attenuated linear quality of the plan, evokes a landscape of leisure and peaceful enjoyment.

In fact, the possibilities of outdoor living are limited by the sheer force of the sun. Considerable effort was made to protect the interior of the house from its rays, while also allowing enjoyment of landscape views. Precautionary measures included the deep overhang of the roof over the glazed living-room walls and the use of solar glass, fitted with operable perforated metal screens. The rest of the house was designed to allow as little sunlight to enter as possible, set on the level below the main living space, with narrow horizontal strip windows, so forming a cool underbelly to the building.

The house was, most unusually, constructed by the client. Bill Byrne was a general contractor with considerable experience in domestic work, but none in the sort of structure and materials which the scheme required. This entailed a process of learning in new fields of experience which proved 'exhilarating'. Carol Byrne was herself a textile and interior designer, working as a colour consultant to the car industry, and the house provided her with an opportunity to explore her sensibilities and talents in a joint project with her husband and their architect. Hence, in a very real sense, the project of the house embodied a voyage of personal self-development and discovery for the pair, both as individuals and as a couple, leading to an expression of self-identity facilitated and mediated by the architect.

The main internal spaces, including the master bedroom (top left), dining area (top right and bottom) and living room (above left and left) are enclosed by 'solex' green non-reflective glass, shaded from the glare of the sun by the deep overhang of the roof, and framing inspiring views of the landscape. The entrance (opposite), by contrast, is located at the side of the house in a more sheltered position, opening into the deeply shaded main circulation space along the back wall

Reutter House
Zapallar, Chile
1998
Mathias Klotz

The house is situated on a sloping site near the beach, decisively orientated in one direction towards the ocean (opposite). The approach to the house is via an elevated walkway which crosses the roof (opposite and below, see also elevations and long section below). The bedrooms and open-plan living space are located on the level below (see plan), reached via a descending staircase from the roof, and opening onto a large terrace (below left). The east and west elevations, and the cross section, clarify the conception of the house as 'two rectangular boxes floating on a wall', with a third volume of reinforced concrete passing through the larger box vertically.

In most, if not all, of the big cities of the world, there is a cultural assumption that those citizens of elevated social status will enjoy some form of regular access to the countryside or coast as a natural extension of urban life. The concept of the house in the hills, the weekend cottage, or the beach house, is firmly written into the ideal of city existence as a necessary escape from its pressures, heat and dirt. However, the rapid urban expansion of the last decades and growth of the peripheral areas has had the effect of making cities less permeable, in the sense of being less open to easy inward and outward movement, while the traditional destinations – the typical hill stations and beach resorts within hailing distance of the city centre – are themselves being increasingly suburbanized, forcing city dwellers to travel across longer, less convenient distances in search of peace and fresh air. These developments could threaten the whole institution of the urban-rural relationship and symbiotic economy; certainly, they force a reconsideration of the concept of the 'rural retreat' as an extension of city life.

The Reutter House, located at Cachagua Beach near Zapallar, a town 200 kilometres north of Chile's capital city Santiago, is typical of this institution. Cachagua is a destination enjoyed by many from Santiago's wealthy business community who have houses there overlooking the Pacific Ocean. Mathias Klotz's client is one such, an exporter of salmon, who wanted a holiday home in which he could also work, taking advantage of the new de-territorialization of working practices.

The house is decisively orientated in one direction towards the ocean, situated on a sloping site covered with pine trees next to the beach, but it is hardly isolated.

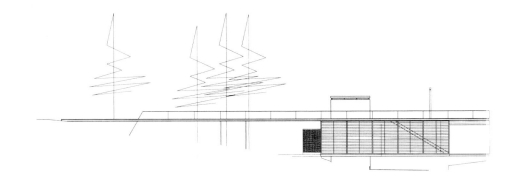

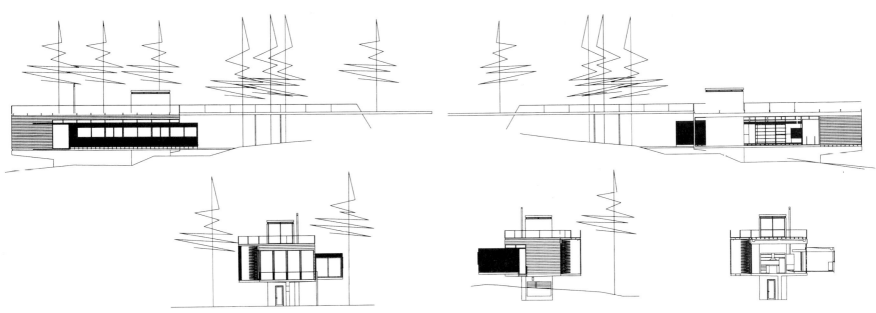

The south elevation has a continuous horizontal line of fenestration lighting the bedrooms and giving views out to the trees. The bedrooms and bathrooms are located in the smaller volume of the two, elevated above ground level, and clad in copper. The larger box is clad in timber, with a glazed facade and fixed slatted screen facing north.

Two roads delimit the eastern and western boundaries of the site, from which access to the house is obtained via a 30-metre long bridge. But the conception and presentation of the project is designed to emphasize a quality of isolation, remoteness and privacy, playing on a romantic ideal of apartness and communion with nature.

In the architect's own words: 'the idea towards the landscape was to build a house in the trees, and for the inside, a house into the house'. Hence the exterior of the house was to be read predominantly in relation to the trees and the ocean, while the architectural conception of the interior was to be highly internalized, or self-referential, except at the point where it opens out towards the ocean across a large terrace, forming a controlled intermediary space between the interior and the landscape beyond.

Klotz describes the architectural approach in almost formulaic terms, as consisting of 'two rectangular boxes floating on a wall, to elevate the living space and insert it into the trees'. The larger box, clad in timber, contains the main living accommodation, and the smaller one, lodged alongside it, and clad in copper, contains the bedrooms and bathrooms. The edges of the two volumes interpenetrate so that the bedrooms can be opened up, by means of sliding partitions, onto the open living space. Both are compact, partially elevated, single-storey structures. A third volume built of reinforced concrete passes through the larger box vertically, containing the core 'service' functions on three levels: laundry and staff bedroom on the ground floor, kitchen and TV room on the first and a study on the second.

Once again, it is difficult not to see the influence of a classic Corbusian model at work in this house: the Citrohan Houses of 1920–2, conceived as a box partially,

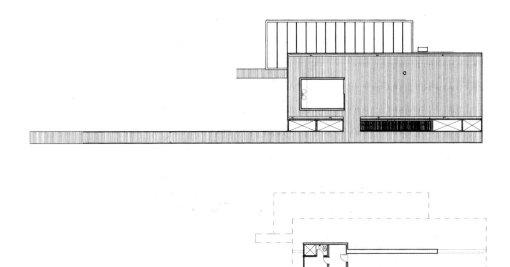

Views of the interior show the unified nature of the main living space, looking towards the kitchen (below left) across the seating and dining areas, and out towards the ocean (opposite centre). The view of the dining area through the glazed north elevation (opposite top) shows the staircase leading into the space from the roof, and the sliding timber screens behind, which partition the bedrooms from the central space (see also below). The close-up view of the kitchen (opposite bottom), with its freestanding hob surrounded by high stools, reveals the concrete structure of the vertical volume through the house which contains the 'service' functions on three floors. It also shows a detail of the glazed façade, with the external slatted timber screen set back from it.

The plans (left) show the ground level of the house (bottom), occupied only by the lowest level of the vertical service structure, and the entrance, or roof, level (top), reached by the elevated walkway, which represents a deliberate infusion of drama into the design of the house.

and ultimately fully, elevated on pilotis, with a roof garden and access to the main entry level by a raised walkway – a model which in its final phase of evolution becomes an amphibian structure projecting out into the water. The Reutter House does not quite meet the water's edge, but its attenuated linear form, in contrast to the more compact Citrohan block, serves to emphasize the impression that it is straining to do so. This quality of linearity or horizontality is dramatically heightened by the extended, high-level boardwalk which runs for 30 metres through the trees from the road, and across the roof. The visitor enters the house with a theatrical flourish from the level of the tree tops, dropping down into the main living space via a staircase against the external wall. A small, external, secondary staircase gives separate access to the ground floor level.

It is the deliberate sense of drama in this house which constitutes a key difference from the Corbusian model, despite the similarities in the organization and handling of the architectural components and their relation to the ground level. The structure, geometries and massing are simple and straightforward, adhering to a rigurously linear and grid-based architectural approach, but the overall composition infuses a sense of theatre into the relationship between humans, their emotions and the landscape.

Klotz describes the project as an evolution of his work combining two strands of development which until now have run in parallel, but separately. He refers to one as 'a series of wooden boxes', and the other as 'projects in which the structure plays an important part'. The fusion of these two conceptions of architecture can be clearly seen in the Reutter House, as the latest manifestation in a developing typology of the urban–rural retreat.

Project 222
Pembrokeshire, Wales, UK
1998
Future Systems

The view out west across the sea is unobstructed as far as the Statue of Liberty. Project 222 is wholly orientated towards the view (see site plan left) and designed to merge into the contours of the cliff-tops in the course of time (opposite). The glazed west-facing elevation is the primary architectural element (see sketches below). It also makes explicit technological references.

This house represents perhaps one of the most extreme examples of a landscape strategy, embodying the ultimate ideal of the rural retreat. It is designed to disappear almost completely from sight over the course of time, its physical dimensions merging into the contours of the Welsh cliff-tops, and its architectural identity being subsumed into the vision of the Atlantic ocean which is its raison d'être.

It is no surprise to find that the site is located in one of the most westerly parts of the British Isles, on the coast of Wales, long favoured by those in search of rural solace amidst the pressures of over-development and urbanization. The main reason for its appeal was that, in the words of the architect, the view out west across the sea is unobstructed as far as the Statue of Liberty. The new house replaces an old army barracks which occupied the land, following a number of schemes designed by others which, because of the site's exposed nature, posed potential planning problems.

Future Systems has created a body of work over the years which succeeds in disrupting the familiar building typologies and creating alternative images of shelter out of a curious fusion of organic and technological forms and references. Project 222 follows that trajectory of development in being emphatically 'not a box sitting in beautiful surroundings' in the classic modernist tradition, but 'part of the landscape'. This earthy ideal is realized through a combination of materials and construction that are essentially very simple, so that the house could scarcely be described as high-tech; nevertheless the technological references are made quite explicitly through the primary architectural element of the glazed west-facing elevation.

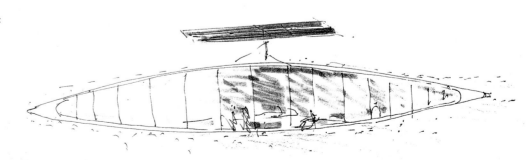

The ellipse-shaped glass facade (opposite) has been described as a 'lens' cut into the landscape (see also section, below), evoking the imagery of camera and telescope. The porthole openings provide for cross-ventilation, but are also suggestive of the the technology of ship design. The house itself is relatively 'low-tech'. The aerial perspective (right) reveals a simple space contained by an arc-shaped retaining wall, banked up with earth, which supports a steel ring beam holding a plywood roof (below) overlaid with turf. The internal layout is roughly divided between bedrooms at each end, and living-space in the centre, with kitchen and bathroom services contained in free-standing, prefabricated 'pods' (right).

Overleaf: The facade, illuminated by night, embodies the purpose of the house as a framing device for views out to sea.

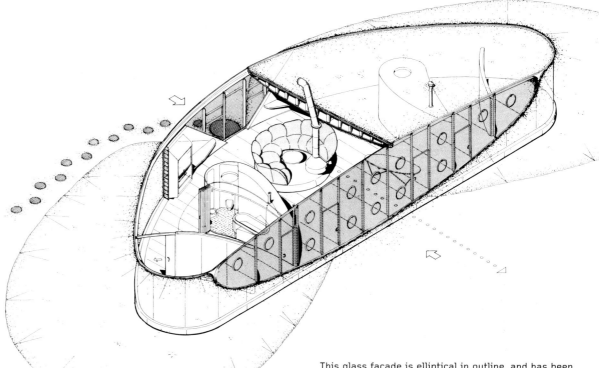

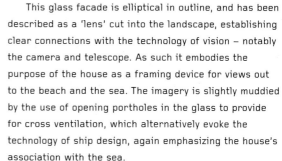

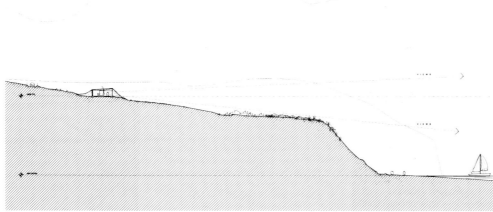

This glass facade is elliptical in outline, and has been described as a 'lens' cut into the landscape, establishing clear connections with the technology of vision – notably the camera and telescope. As such it embodies the purpose of the house as a framing device for views out to the beach and the sea. The imagery is slightly muddied by the use of opening portholes in the glass to provide for cross ventilation, which alternatively evoke the technology of ship design, again emphasizing the house's association with the sea.

On the other hand, the structure consists of a simple blockwork retaining wall, banked up with earth, which describes an arc around the 'back' of the house now submerged by the grass-covered banks. The retaining wall supports a steel ring beam running around the top and across the front to hold a plywood roof overlaid with turf. These basic elements were prefabricated in transportable sections and assembled on site, while the two plywood shell 'service pods' were fully prefabricated and fitted out with bathroom and kitchen appliances before being transported to the site and installed. It would, say the architects, have been impossible to have had this type of precision work carried out on site, due to lack of local experience. The soil for banking up the house had also to be imported, in the absence of any major excavation work on the site.

The entrance to the house is located at the 'back' between the grass banks, providing the only evidence of an architectural and domestic presence on the approach to the site. Thus the complete transparency of the west facade, clearly exposing the internal, earth-sheltered, volume, is all the more surprising. Although the earth-sheltering of almost half of the external perimeter of the

The interior space is dominated by a specially designed circular sofa, embracing the view (opposite bottom). The entrance is located directly behind it, approached from the 'back' of the house between the grass-covered retaining banks (opposite top left). The kitchen appliances and storage are located to one side, built into the external surface of one of the bathroom pods (opposite top right). The section (right) shows the tilt of the roof from back to front, and the key elements of sofa and stove.

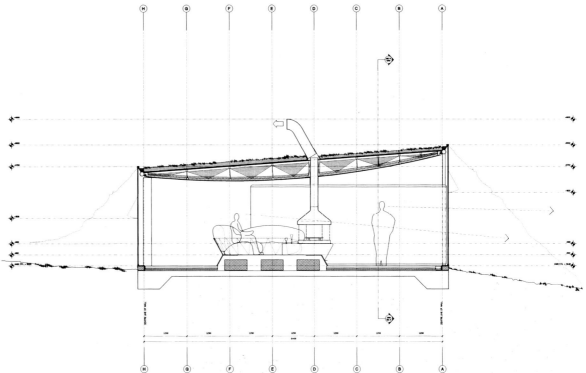

house generates high thermal capacity, the extent of the glazing to the final section also exposes the interior spaces to the fluctuations in the external temperatures, so while at first sight it might look like an experimental environmentally sustainable dwelling, the house is not technically 'green' in that sense, and neither was this a priority on the design agenda.

It is important to be aware that the house is not actually dug into the ground; on the contrary, it is the ground itself which has been raised up around it, representing a considerable reshaping of the landscape which is, from an essentialist point of view, the reverse of the policy of minimal site intervention and impact cited in some of the other projects featured here. A case such as this, then, raises the interesting 'eco-ethical' question of what strategies can be permitted to maintain the appearance of the natural, unconstructed landscape, even when this involves allowing substantial, transformative, human intervention on site. The question can also be extended to embrace the issue of visual and physical disruption of the landscape caused by ecological interventions aimed at the long-term conservation of the natural environment – for example, wind farms on Welsh hilltops. But the entire history of the 'natural landscape' in a small country such as Britain is deeply entangled with projects of human intervention, often designed to improve its natural beauty, as in the picturesque landscaping schemes carried out by Capability Brown for many of the big landowners in the eighteenth century.

The very concept of the 'untouched' (or unspoiled) landscape is relatively recent, enshrined in the institution of the National Parks. Project 222 sits just outside the edge of the Welsh National Park, and within the protected coastal zone, which facts provided the basis for the planners' concern that any construction on the site should primarily have low visibility, rather than – as is so often the case – that it should conform to any stereotype of traditional regional architecture. They further stipulated that no garden should be planted around the house at any time, because such a construction of artifice would be out of character with the rough, uncultivated cliff-top landscape.

The result then is a site-specific, rather than culture-specific response – or, at least, not in terms of a locally rooted culture. The culture which this house speaks of is liberal, forward-thinking, and fundamentally connected with metropolitan values, and although the clients hope eventually to take up permanent residence there, their relationship with the house and the site for the time being is very much based in the ideal of leisure and escape from the city as the real domain of social action and public life.

Many of the architectural ideas which are subsequently recognized as being most influential on later developments in the history of architectural practice are developed in the conceptual realm, on paper, and never actually realized as buildings by the author. The construction industry is, as a rule, slow in implementing new ideas, so that the buildings which get built are very rarely at the cutting edge of architectural ideas in circulation at any given time. The construction procedure can be seen, then, as a conservative force which effectively holds back changes in the built environment and the way people live. While there may be some exceptions to this rule, the whole concept of 'research and development', particularly in a highly charged, emotive area like housing, which affects every aspect of people's day-to-day lives, is virtually non-existent in the construction industry.

For several of the architects featured in this book, one answer to the problem has been to take on the role of client and construction manager themselves, in order to realize a built prototype which might serve to convince a wider audience. But for many others, where finance and other issues present obstacles, the 'paper project', developed in response to a competition brief or a specific invitation, remains an extremely important vehicle for the development of new ideas which might pave the way for the future.

The house has always been a popular subject of the 'hypothetical' architectural brief, precisely because of its universal relevance and meaning, and its very direct relationship with social structure, conditions and ideals at any particular historical moment. In this sense, there is a parallel to be drawn with the popularity of the doll's house as a children's toy through much of modern history. The conceptual house design stimulates a process of vivid self-identification and imagination of day-to-day life which is highly engaging for a wide audience.

The conceptual houses featured here embody many of the issues which have been raised for discussion, projected into architectural form through a process of speculation and intent to challenge the status quo. Embedded within each project is the potential for the ideas to become part of the mainstream at some point in a future which might be close at hand or more distant. They range from being quite closely focused on the immediate possibilities for discussion and implementation, to being essentially abstract in quality, designed for a more limited audience within the architectural world itself.

The Concept House competition in the UK is the interesting case of an architectural competition organized by an essentially populist national newspaper in conjunction with the professional architectural body, the Royal Institute of British Architects. This

unusual coming together of interests resulted in the development of a serious architectural brief intent on addressing some of the most pressing concerns surrounding the design of new homes in the future, particularly the ecological issues. An exceptional aspect of the competition was that the winning entry was to be constructed as a show house at a big national trade and retail fair devoted to homes and gardens. Thus the design was expected to speak to a very mixed audience of intellectually engaged architects, representatives of the construction industry who would visit the fair in a professional capacity, and a 'middle-brow' audience of home-lovers attracted to the show by their 'dreamhouse' fantasies. The resulting scheme was driven by the desire to present a forward-looking, but highly plausible, model of new housing for the future which could be taken up immediately by the construction industry for further development as a prefabricated system of parts.

By contrast, the Glass House in the Sky and the Suburban House projects created for Time magazine were essentially designed as a media tool to provoke discussion about new patterns of domestic living in the future as part of a wider debate about social change in the twenty-first century. Although Time is a magazine with an international, though Western-orientated, readership, both schemes, particularly the latter, evoke a specifically American context and response.

It is possible to draw a parallel between these projects and the products of the American film industry, with their emphasis on a readily consumable image generated by technology and style, as opposed to a finer-grained level of detail. But by the nature of the commission, both schemes were designed to strike a more obviously 'futuristic' note than, say, the Slim House.

At the turn of the century, the concept of the 'House of the Future' has been particularly in circulation, even focusing a need for clarification of what is meant by the term 'the future'. Many theoretical projects have embraced an under-considered agenda based on sci-fi fantasy and imagery, conforming to a long Western history of ideas which has placed technological progress at the heart of a linear conception of human social history marching on towards an ideal of final technological supremacy over the earth. Now that the true and horrifying potential of that situation has become clear, the need for global society to reconsider its ideals for the future, and shift the emphasis towards non-material, unquantifiable values, has been recognized.

For this reason, it is interesting to include in this section the 1998 winner of the long-standing and highly regarded Shinkenchiku Residential Design Competition, run under the auspices of Japan Architect magazine. The title for that year's competition, judged by

Frank Lloyd Wright's Broadacre City, 1934–5 (opposite), was a conceptual project for a contemporary city, in which the fundamental unit was the single-family house: it ranged in size and type from the 'minimal', one-can, DIY prefab to 5-car dwellings of 'machine-age luxury'.

The Township of Ideal Homes at the 1924 British Ideal Home Exhibition, contained thirteen 'modern' houses in as many different styles (below). In 1928, a House of the Future, designed by S Rowland Pierce and R A Duncan, was also included in the show for the first time (below right): one of the most daring and original homes in the Exhibition's history.

Branson Coates' Oyster House (right) won the Concept House competition in 1998.

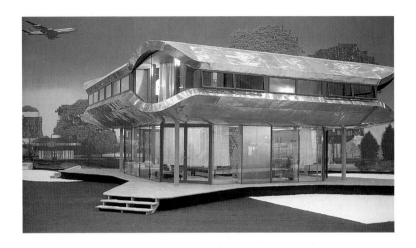

Shin Takamatsu, was The House of Poetic Space, and the 'brief', insofar as any brief can be said to exist, was to achieve a conceptualization of 'poetic space'. The winning scheme, described as a process in which 'light undergoes variations and dislocations and becomes architecture', embodies a vision of the future based on immateriality and transcendence which is in stark contrast to the prevailing discourse of 'the future' throughout the West. Although it is important not to disregard issues of material and physical comfort as vital factors in the construction of social and political equality throughout the world, it seems fitting to end with a reminder encapsulated in Takamatsu's thanks to the Shinkenchiku competitors, 'who were prepared to embark upon a poetic adventure into the unknown territory of their own awareness. It gave me a deep understanding that poetry is simply another name for hope.'

House of Poetic Space (Dream House)
Shinkenchiku Residential
Design Competition 1998
Kyna Leski

The drawings of the house were made after the walls had been first built in model form. The section along the north–south axis (below) shows the trajectory of light entering the house through a large square opening in the south wall, passing through the lens and refracting onto the rear wall of the stairwell, or 'retinal wall', which thus receives the projected image from the outside.

The walls were developed by casting light beams onto cones (opposite top), and using the petal shapes (compare with flower, far left) so derived to construct screens around a central 'blind spot' (see models, following page). The shadows cast by the screens became the rooms (left).

The Generative Light Plan (opposite below) shows a plan view of the projections of light that generated the architectural elements.

This project, designed by an architect based on the east coast of America, can be seen as the antithesis of the technologically orientated, narrative proposals typically engendered by conceptual discussions about the nature of the house on the threshold of a new century. The competition judge, Shin Takamatsu, describes the architecture as 'a topography of light. The process undergoes both interruptions and leaps forward. Each moment it becomes more complex and attains a new depth of beauty. The architecture is woven into it. It is true poetry.'

The Shinkenchiku competition has generated over many years a substantial tradition of theoretical ideas about the house, conceived with little or no reference to the possibilities of actualization, or embodiment and human inhabitation. Thus it represents a valuable counterpart to both the Daily Mail/Ideal Home competition and the Time commission. Kyna Leski's response has virtually no programmatic content in terms of the day-to-day use of the house, beyond a schematic schedule of rooms. Neither does it have any materiality to speak of: the sole material explicitly referred to, in relation to the objectification of the house itself, is the most elusive, or transcendent, of all – light. But paradoxically, the process of generating abstract, poetic three-dimensional form grew very much out of the architect's embodied experience of living in a glass house as a child. Furthermore, the investigation itself was profoundly physical in character, involving the intensive working and detailed manipulation of various materials.

Leski calls the project 'Dream House', evoking its relationship to a series of 250 watercolours which she

   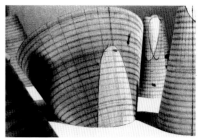

made of dreams she had; but there is a severe disjunction between her conception and the materialistic 'dreamhouse' fantasies of domestic life in the future woven and purveyed by the mass media. Leski's vision has the quality of a true dream – evanescent, immaterial, and elusive, but always in a close, meaningful and transformative relationship with reality.

The Dream House proposal starts from a scientific-philosophical proposition, as summed up in a statement by Alan W Watts: 'Theoretically, many scientists know that the individual is not a skin-encapsulated ego, but an organism-environment field. The organism itself is a point at which the field is "focused", so that each individual is a unique expression of the behavior of the whole field, which is ultimately the universe itself.' Leski proposes that this concept of the distinction between individual and environment as essentially fuzzy is manifested through the operation of vision: 'Somewhere along the passage through the eye the "self" seems to begin and the "all" ends. The threshold is ambiguous – even in our sense of it...' The literal form and metaphorical significance of the eye and lens is then used as the basis from which to construct the edifice of the house as an authentic expression of this understanding of the nature of existence: it is 'a phenomenal study of how the "self" exists in the world through a house'.

The architectural organization and form of the house is generated by the construction of a 'blind spot, a specific space that needs to be obscured from view', as a three-dimensional geometric diagram, surrounded by concentric layers of screens that block light from entering it. These screens were modelled as petals

Three-dimensional models were used to explore the form and geometry of the house.

The 'blind-spot' was modelled first as a piece of three-dimensional geometry (below left centre), and then as a Phenomenal Model (below left top). The intersections between vaults (the shadows cast from petals, forming rooms) were explored in three-dimensional form (below left bottom and below right), and drawn (right) as projections from the petals stretching out to touch secondary walls. The configurations of internal planes and spaces were also rendered as interior perspectives in watercolour (opposite)

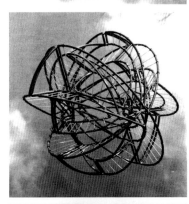

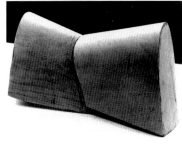

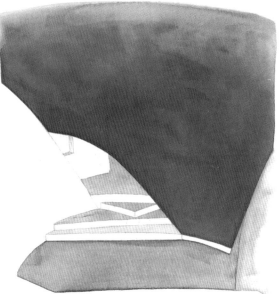

derived from the shape made by light-beams cast on cones, and the petals became the walls of the house. The 'rooms' are located under the 'vaults' formed by projections from the top of the petals in a particular direction. The rooms themselves are listed in order, following the passage through the structure of the eye from the outside, as Blink (entry), Floaters (living room), Sunrise Room (kitchen), Sunset Room (bathroom), Pineal body (TV room), Insomnia Room (library), Deep Sleep Dream Room (bedroom), Fuse with the All and Drawing Out Room (studio). Thus at each stage of the journey from the external world to the self within, and the ultimate realization of the indissolubility of self and world, metaphors are drawn between the everyday functions of living and the proposed cosmology of daily life, culminating in the creative heart of the house, the studio. The blind-spot 'is located centrally in the house, behind the lens wall and in front of the retinal wall', as a sort of still point that generates changes in level.

Thus the architectural form of the house is generated by a detailed study of the fall of light onto the structure of the human eye, or spherical lens, as a poetic metaphor for the conundrum of existence – but also a literal structural framework of curved planes. The lens itself is incorporated into the final design of the house, projecting an image of the outside onto an interior wall, located at the lens' focal length, in the 'stairwell' of the house. This is in no sense a 'house of the future' as popularly conceived, but it is a house of the imagination, of the mind's eye, which gives expression to important philosophical and scientific ideas for the next century.

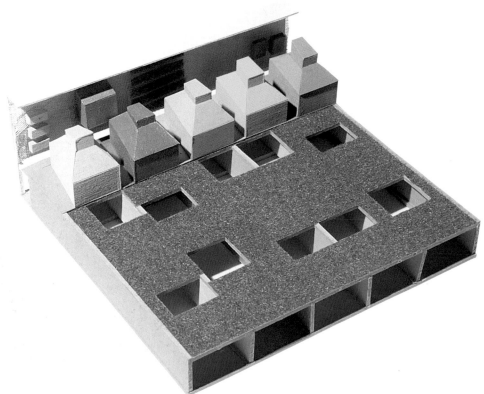

Slim House offered a reinterpretation of the traditional British terrace, in which the gardens were placed on the roofs and provided the potential for communal use (left, aerial perspective of model). The section through the model (opposite) shows the internal courtyards providing more intimate outside space for each household.

Most of the linear volume is one storey in height, with a two- or three-storey pavilion at the front, and an 'active façade'. For the show house, this was rendered as an inflatable (below and opposite, detail). The interior view (opposite bottom) shows a perspective through the main, double-height living space at the front of the house, towards the first glazed courtyard.

Concept House 1999 was the second in a newly launched, five year competition series organised by the Daily Mail newspaper in association with its annual Ideal Home Show. Since 1908, when it was founded, this event has provided a remarkable national showcase in the UK for popular dreams and fantasies about the home, as well as a lively fair for 'labour-saving' domestic gadgets and appliances of all shapes and sizes. The Show was originally conceived as a publicity vehicle for the newspaper, which, from its beginnings in 1896 had targeted middle-class office-workers and women as its primary readership. It continued in the tradition of the World Fairs, but it was the first of its kind to focus on domestic life, and a specifically national audience, and during the course of its evolution had a significant impact on shaping English taste and ideas in domestic matters.

The crowd-pulling centrepiece of each exhibition was always the themed 'village' of show-houses in a variety of styles, including an 'Ideal Home' designed by an architect. Until the 1980s, the village of homes usually embodied some forward-looking ideas about architecture alongside more traditional models. In 1928, for the first time, a House of the Future was also included in the show (see the introduction to this chapter), but by the 1930s this had fizzled out, not to be revived until 1956, the Jubilee Year of the Daily Mail. This house, designed by the radical young architects Alison and Peter Smithson, attracted widespread architectural attention. But by the 1980s, the emphasis of the show had become overwhelmingly nostalgic, and increasingly controlled by banal commercial interests.

The Concept House architectural competition was launched in 1997 to revive the exhibition through a re-injection of some newsworthy architectural novelty, following the precedents of the past. The first competition was for a detached, suburban-style 'ideal home' intended to appeal to the exhibition's core audience. But the second competition represented a move away from that kind of mass-market appeal. The brief asked for a serious, thoughtful response to the redesign of the 'speculative British urban terraced home'; to produce a building which describes a new environmentally sustainable model for the mass-produced or factory-built contemporary urban house'. In other words, it crystallized the most pressing concerns about demographic trends, ecological impact, and the implications of technology, within a framework that implicitly discouraged the use of conventional 'futuristic' images and ideas.

Pierre d'Avoine Architects' winning scheme, Slim House-Model Terrace, was constructed as a show house at the 1999 Ideal Home Show – a life-size, timber-built maquette of a simple, linear (5m x 25m), self-contained steel-frame and timber-stud panel structure, in which the only 'futuristic' element of the design was the translucent inflatable facade. A spokesman for the jury commented, 'over the course of the judging a clear winner emerged with a simple yet ingenious solution to the brief, spreading the terrace house across the entire dimension of the site. We all believe this scheme works as a show home and as an alternative prototype for urban living.'

The design is based on five fundamental principles, conceived as a response to social change and contemporary patterns of urban and suburban home and work life: loose-fit/flexible accommodation; raised threshold; roof garden; active facade with urban(e) front and DIY back; and vertical extension. The main, double-height living space, incorporating a kitchen range, is located at the front of the house, with a large window-opening onto a front verandah and out to the street beyond. Three bedrooms, a bathroom, shower room, and two internal courtyards are laid out across the length of the plot behind it in a one-storey structure with a garden on the roof. The principle is that when terraces of the house are built, the gardens could be opened up to form a large, green communal area for relaxation and safe children's play above the level of the street. By contrast, the internal courtyards would provide more intimate open areas dedicated for household use, which also perform the function of providing acoustic buffer zones and lightwells between the different rooms.

The roof garden is designed to be accessed from the upper level of the two-storey pavilion comprising the front section of the house, facing the street.

The proposal suggests a number of variations on how the first floor level of this double-height, skylit volume might be used: for example, as a gallery looking down into the living area, accommodating a work-station; or as a fully segregated office; or as a living-room over a ground-floor shop unit. In both the latter cases, the open staircase constructed for the show house could be fully enclosed with a separate street entrance. It is also suggested that the volume could be extended vertically by another storey if required. Hence the model is explicitly conceived to accommodate

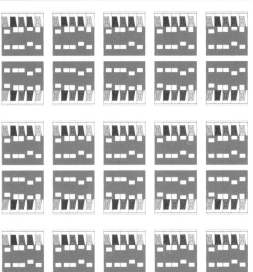

Slim House constitutes the basic unit of Model Terrace (see facade, bottom). Within the terrace, the layout of each house can be varied according to household requirements. The plans of the ground and upper levels (right, bottom and top) show a number of possible variations, including retail and office use of the front of the house in conjunction with domestic use. The aerial photomontage (above left) shows the terrace superimposed onto the existing urban fabric of south-west London; the plan (left) demonstrates how the terrace can be configured to generate urban blocks

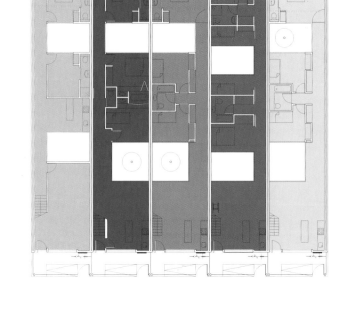

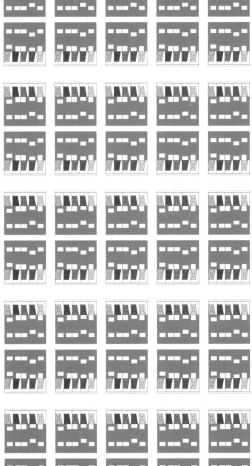

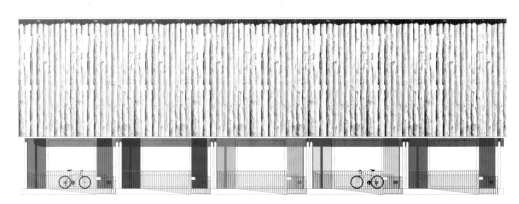

Slim House: Model Terrace
Pierre d'Avoine Architects

The 'active facade' has an 'urbane' front and a 'DIY' back, which can be used as a vertical backyard (see section, left). The 'pavilion' behind it houses the main living space and potential office or retail use, while the bedrooms and bathrooms are organized at ground level around the internal courtyards in the one-storey volume extending the length of the site. The two interior perspectives (below) give a sense of the vistas through the house and lightness of the interior, which are achieved through the use of the glazed courtyards.

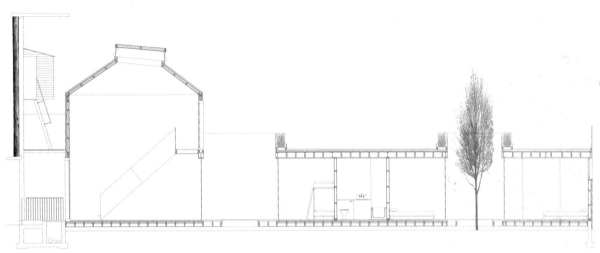

changing working patterns, producing a greater emphasis on the home as a centre of production.

The flexible, or 'active' facade of the house, represented by a translucent plastic inflatable, is conceived as a resolution of the problem of building in different physical and cultural contexts, which also presents the possibility of exploring the use of new technologies within the public realm. The structure is independent of the front of the house, forming the outer edge of the verandah at ground level, and rising to a total of three storeys in height. It is tied back to the eaves level of the front pavilion, creating a space between the facade and the structural front of the house which is intended for use as a vertical back-yard. The back of the facade structure is designed for customisation as garden-shed, cold-frame, grey-water storage, or vertical garden, as desired, while the front could be developed as a hoarding for signage, advertising or artwork, a source of street-lighting, a solar-panel installation, a topiary wall, an acoustic buffer against street noise, or in a more traditional way, with the flexibility to change in response to surrounding environmental conditions through time.

The Slim House is essentially a modest proposal, designed for prefabrication, ease of transport, adaptability, energy-efficiency, and potential re-cycling, for less than £50,000/$80,000. But within that framework it offers a reconceptualization of everyday, domestic life for the future which is bold and inspired in its architectural ambition, and as such provided the Ideal Home Show with fresh credibility as a forum for architectural ideas.

The Glass House in the Sky is a reaction against the dream of suburbia, which creates a new layer of inhabitation above the old, by building on the rooftops (left). As architect Bernard Tschumi states, it satisfies a 'desire for infinite space in the dense metropolis', allowing expansive views out across the city (below). The organization of the interior is conceived as a play on the 'opposition between its industrial looking rectangular envelope and the lush curvature inside', as described by the exploded perspective (opposite right).

The section (opposite left) and plans (below) show how the internal 'guts' of the house are contained with an undulating sandwich wall, that serves at the same time to define the shape of the living spaces on two levels (first floor plan below, second floor plan above). A 'digital wall' contains a projection system for domestic use (below, and section opposite left).

The American magazine Time dedicated one of its weekly issues in February 2000 to a wide-ranging consideration of 'How We Will Live' in the 21st century, which included an invitation to two American architects to formulate proposals for houses of the future. These conceptual projects encapsulate many of the current ideas about the development of domestic architecture in response to technological advances, environmental considerations and social change, in a form specifically intended to make a strong visual impact on the pages of a magazine.

The editorial claims that the architecture of the new century will realize the final dissolution of the modernist box, through an 'eruption' of fractured, tilted, sliced and shredded forms, and building surfaces overwhelmed by all-over ornamentation and illuminated signage. This shift is attributed to 'the spirit of the age', as expressed through French literary criticism or chaos theory, and to 'sheer boredom with the slabs of Modernism and disenchantment with the mild remedies of postmodernism.' But these are characteristics not to be found in either the Tschumi project for a Glass House on the city skyline, or the Jones project for a house in the suburbs. The latter conforms to a recognizable outline determined by right angles and linearity, solid and void, while the former plays on what the architect describes as 'an opposition between its industrial-looking rectangular envelope and the lush curvature inside.'

Bernard Tschumi defines his scheme as a potential realization of 'the timeless desire for infinite space in the dense metropolis.' In this sense, it constitutes a direct response to the move away from the garden city model in urban planning terms, and towards a determined densification of existing urban areas: a

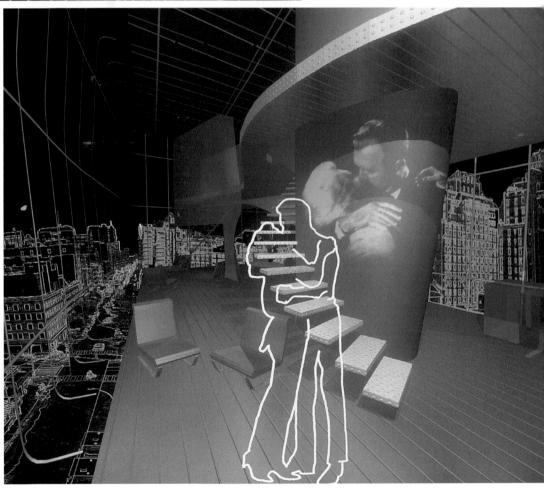

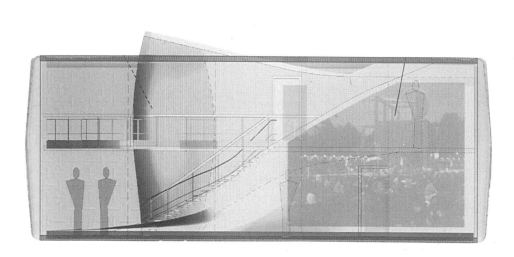

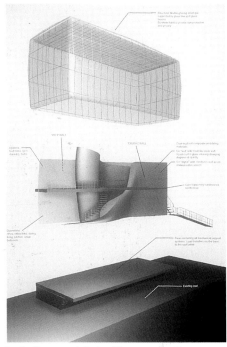

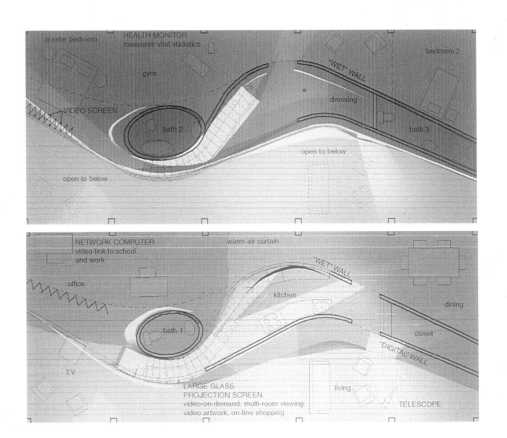

process historically associated with overcrowding, urban tension and insanitary conditions, and one essentially at odds with American suburban and pioneering ideals. Tschumi describes his house as 'a reaction against the dream of suburbia; rather than abandoning the city and re-creating an artificial urban experience outside it, the house addresses the city by existing both within and above it.'

He proposes a strategy of building on the rooftops of city buildings, creating a new layer of inhabitation above the old. The idea makes sense in the light of the shortage of land at ground level, offering the possibility of vertical expansion as an alternative to horizontal. In the case of New York, where Tschumi is based, the concept is enshrined in the historical typology of the city; but it presents for many other cities the possibility of a radical transformation.

The scheme is presented as an idea rather than a prototype, but it suggests the development of a model of a prefabricated dwelling unit which could be assembled and dropped into place on a wide range of rooftop sites. The internal 'guts' of the house are contained within an undulating sandwich wall, that serves at the same time to define the shape of the living spaces on two levels. These include living room, dining room and office spaces on the first floor, with a kitchen, bathroom and staircase contained within the core wall, and three bedrooms and a gym on the second floor, with two further bathrooms and a dressing room within the core.

Tschumi's scheme presents an interior which is materially rich – 'with velvet or silk curtains, rounded and polished composite surfaces and translucent glass.' These aspects demand a sensuous, bodily response and

The new model for suburban living plays heavily on technological imagery, extending to household use of ELOVS, or 'electric, low-occupancy vehicles' (opposite top). But it also proposes new, more efficient patterns of land usage, including interlocking layouts with private courtyards, gardens and parking on the rooftops (opposite top and bottom).

Within the house (right) the traditional codification of rooms is replaced by one large multi-purpose space in which moveable 'activity pods' accommodate different activities, and a battery of ceiling-mounted sensors, scanners and regulators controls the internal environment.

seem intended as an antidote to the perceived 'coldness' of the anti-corporeal technological emphasis often found in hypothetical schemes for homes of the future, and understated by comparison in the conception of the Glass House in the Sky. The only explicit technological references are to a digital wall containing a projection system for domestic use, and the 'network computer with videolink to school and work'.

By contrast, Wes Jones' proposal for a new model of suburban living in the 21st century is fundamentally generated by an interest in the potential of new technology for the reconceptualization of the management of domestic life, both within and outside the home. He suggests, 'the cyberrevolution and the environmental movement promise to alter the landscape ... as the vastness of cyberspace increasingly satisfies the craving for more space, the house and yard will shrink to a more supportable size .... As cyberspace becomes the kind of space that matters, the primitive territorial need for fixed rooms will fade...'

Jones proposes that the suburban houses of the future will be more closely interlocked, by building to the edges of the individual plot, putting gardens on the rooftops and creating private internal courtyards, much as in the Slim House scheme, and as discussed in the case of the C House (pp150–57). This strategy for a more efficient use of space frees up extensive areas beyond for use as parks and other community facilities, and opens vistas of the landscape. Within the house, the traditional codification of rooms is replaced by one large open, multi-purpose space, in which different activities are accommodated within moveable 'activity pods'. The kitchen is pared down to the minimum in terms of space,

reflecting its vastly reduced role in the house and family life – little more than a galley for opening and heating deliveries of pre-cooked food. Moveable work-stations around the house, and built-in videoconferencing facilities allow people to work from home as a matter of course. Bedrooms become smaller, with fold-down beds to save on space, and reduced storage, 'since cyberspace will be the arena for personal display'.

The technological infrastructure of such houses includes an automated waste-management system, safety features (wheelchairs which can climb stairs, airbags to replace balustrades), a battery of ceiling-mounted devices including medical and security scanners, heating, ventilation and air-conditioning sensors, and environmental regulators, and a full range of domestic machinery that could be partially powered by the exercise activities of the homeowner. Energy is be provided by neighbourhood generators, thermal-mass cooling ponds and solar collectors in the streets, and windows will become display surfaces allowing views to be replaced by alternative, imaginary vistas as desired. The family car becomes an ELOV, or electric, low-occupancy vehicle, which can be enlarged when necessary by coupling two together.

Both the Glass House and the Suburban House represent a projection of ideas about the design of houses in the future, at a broad conceptual level. They are not intended as a real-life prototype for general implementation, like the Slim House, which was addressed as much to the construction industry as to a general public audience, but to provide a provocative starting point for public debate within the forum of the mass media.

CREDITS

Charlotte House
Stuttgart, Sillenbuch
Germany
1992–3
Architect Behnisch & Partner
Büro Sillenbuch
Gorch-Fock-Straße 30
70619 Stuttgart, Germany
Client Charlotte Behnisch

Marika Alderton House
Yirrkala, Northern Territory
Australia
1993–4
Architect Glenn Murcutt Architect
76a Raglan Street, Mosman
Sydney 2088, Australia
Client Yirrkala-Dhanbul Community
Association Inc:
Community House for
Marmburra Marika
Engineer James Taylor & Associates
Contractor Simon Thorpe &
John Colquhoun

Mexican Whale House
Mexico City, Mexico
1992–4
Architect Javier Senosiain
Calz. Legaria No 7,
79 5-2 Col. Irrigacion CP
11500 Mexico City, Mexico
Design team and structural engineer
Javier Senosiain
Luis Raul Enriquez
Client Ricardo Torres Nava
Flor Berenguer
Contractor Juan Sanchez Torres

Poole House
Lake Weyba, Queensland
Australia
1996–7
Architect Gabriel Poole
50 Paradise Drive, Doonan
Queensland 4562, Australia
Design team Elizabeth Poole, Gabriel Poole
Client Elizabeth Poole, Gabriel Poole
Structural engineer
Rod Bligh, Bligh Tanner
Contractor Barry Hamlet

Acayaba House
Guaruja, São Paulo, Brazil
1996–7
Architect Marcos Acayaba
Rua Helena, 170-cj 143
04552-050 Vila Olimpia
São Paulo, Brazil
Design team Marcos Acayaba
Mauro Halluli, Fabio Valentim
Suely Mizobe
Client Marcos Acayaba
Structural engineer
Helio Olga de Souza Jr
Electrical engineer, plumbing
Sandretec
Construction Marcos Acayaba
Ita Construtora

Crescent House
Wiltshire, UK
1997
Architect Ken Shuttleworth,
Foster and Partners
Riverside Three
22 Hester Road
London SW11 4AN, UK

Client Ken and Seana Shuttleworth
Structural engineers
Ove Arup & Partners:
Tony Fitzpatrick
Adrian Faulkner
Mechanical engineers
Roger Preston & Partners:
Trevor Farnfield, Chris Munn
Quantity surveyors
Everest: Paul Morrell
Erland Rendell Davis Langdon
Contractor O'Rouke Group:
Ray O'Rouke, Andy Holt

Lannoo House
Sint Martens Latem, Belgium
1991–3
Architect Robbrecht & Daem
Kortregksastee 777b
900 Ghent, Belgium
Collaborator Sofie Delaere
Client Unnamed
Landscape architect
Erik Dhondt
Engineer Jan Vangheluwe
Contractor Verkest

Villa Anbar
Dammam, Saudi Arabia
1992–3
Architect Peter Barber Architects
11/12 Great Sutton Street
London EC1V 0BX, UK
Client Unnamed

Corson/Heinser Live-Work
San Francisco, California, USA

1992 (addition to rear 1996)
Architect TLMS (Tanner Leddy
Maytum Stacy) Architects
444 Spear Street
San Francisco, CA 94105, USA
Client Thomas Heinser
Madeleine Corson
Structural engineer
Tennebaum-Manheim
Contractor Fine European
Construction Service

House at Shiloh Falls
Tennessee, USA
1994–6
Architect Mockbee/Coker Architects
431 S Main Street
Second Floor
Memphis, TN 38103, USA
Client Drs James and
Rushton Patterson

House near Bordeaux
Bordeaux, France
1994–8
Architect Office for Metropolitan
Architecture
Reer Bokeweg 149
NL 3032 AD Rotterdam
The Netherlands
Design team Rem Koolhaas, Maarten van
Severen, Julien Monfort
Jeanne Gang, Bill Price
Jeroen Thomas, Yo Yamagata
Chris Dondorp, Erik Schotte
Vincent Costes
Client Unnamed
Engineer Ove Arup & Partners:
Cecil Balmond, Robert Pugh

Consultants Robert-Jan van Santen
Gerard Couillandeau
Petra Blaisse
Fitted furnishing and mobile platform
Maarten van Severen
Raf de Preter
Coordination and technical assistance
Michel Régaud

Check House 2

Cluney Park, Singapore
1997–9
Architect KNTA Architects
154A Rochor Road
Singapore 188429
Design team Tan Kay Ngee, Tan Teck Kiam
Vijay Ahuja, Akira Koyama
Jason Ong, Jonathan Rowley
Bradley Starkey, Daniel
Statham, Francesco Zafarana
Client Unnamed
Structural engineer
Ronnie & Koh Partnership
Landscape designer
Cicada Landscape Architects
Contractor Patson Marketing
& Construction

Craig House

Christchurch, New Zealand
1998–9
Architect Thom Craig,
Architecture Warren
& Mahoney
131 Victoria Street
Christchurch, New Zealand
Client Mr and Mrs T Craig
Design team Thom Craig, Tim Devine
Maurice Paton

Carlo Heeman
Interior and landscape design
TC/AW&M
Structural engineer
Dick Cusiel, Lovell-Smith
& Cusiel Ltd
Contractor Clive Barrington
Construction Ltd
Interior lighting
Accent Lighting
Sculptural lighting
Metaform Industries Ltd

Nalin Tomar House

New Delhi, India
1992
Architect Revathi and Vasant Kamath
301 N 19
Green Park Extension,
New Delhi 110016, India
Client Nalin Tomar

Koechlin House

Basel, Switzerland
1993–4
Architect Herzog & de Meuron
CH-4056 Basel
Rheinschanze 6
Switzerland
Design team Jacques Herzog, Pierre de
Meuron, Christine Binswanger
Jean-Frédéric Lüscher
Client Domenik and Stephanie
Koechlin
Landscape Dieter Kienast, Zurich
Plantago, Basel
Structural engineer
Helmut Pauli, Basel

New York City House

New York, USA
1994–6
Architect Tod Williams and Billie Tsien
222 Central Park South
New York, NY 10019, USA
Design team Tod Williams, Billie Tsien
Vivian Wang, Peter Arnold
Christopher Haynes, Matthew
Pickner, Marianne Shin
Client Unnamed
Structural engineer
The Cantor Seinuk Group
Mechanical engineer
Cosentini Associates
Contractor Turner Interiors

M House

Tokyo, Japan
1996–7
Architect Kazuyo Sejima
& Ryue Nishizawa,
SANAA7 – A,
Shinagawa-Soko, 2-2-35
Higashi-Shinagawa
Shinagawa-Ku, Tokyo 140
Japan
Client Unnamed
Structural engineer
ORS Office
General contractor
Heisei Construction

Ozone House

Venice, California, USA
1997–8
Architect Koning Eizenberg Architecture
1454 25th Street, Santa
Monica, CA 90404, USA

Client Judy and Michael Israel
Design team Hank Koning, Julie Eizenberg
Tim Andreas, Fernando Bracer
Contractors Charles Kuipers, Judy Israel
& Blue Heron
Landscape designer
Landscape

C House

Brisbane, Queensland
Australia
1991–8
Architect Donovan Hill Architects
112 Bowen Street, Spring Hill
Queensland 4000, Australia
Design team Brian Donovan, Timothy Hill
Fedor Medek, Michael Hogg
Client Unnamed
Structural and civil engineer
Mattefy Perl Nagy
Landscape architects
Donovan Hill Architects
with Butler & Webb
Carpentry Jim Evans

Film House

Paris, France
1998–9
Architect Atelier Lab
15 Rue de Minemes
75003 Paris, France
Client Unnamed
Landscape architect
Guillaume Sevin

Borneo Sporenburg 18

Amsterdam, The Netherlands
1996–9

Architect MVRDV
PO Box 63136
Schiehaven 15
3024 EC Rotterdam
The Netherlands
Design team Winy Maas, Jacob van Rijs
Nathalie de Vries, Joost
Glissenaar, Bart Spee, Alex
Brouwer, Frans de Witte
Client C Wiersema, P Fröhlich
Structural engineer
Pieters Bouwtechniek,
Haarlem
Building physics
DGMR, Arnhem

Barnes House
Nanaimo,
British Columbia, Canada
1992–3
Architect Patkau Architects
L110 560 Beatty Street
Vancouver, Canada
Design team Tim Newton, John Patkau
Patricia Patkau, David Shone
Tom Robertson
Client Unnamed
Structural engineer
Fast & Epp Partners
Contractor RW Wall Ltd

Nomentana Residence
Lovell, Maine, USA
1997
Architect Scogin, Elam and Bray
75 JW Dobbs Avenue,
NE Atlanta, GA 30303, USA
Design team Mack Scogin, Merrill Elam
Lloyd Bray, Denise Dumais

Martha Henderson Bennett
Jeff Atwood, Tim Harrison
Ned Frazer, Elizabeth Pidcock
Kathy Wright, Dustin
Lindblad, Juan Du
Client Margaret Nomentana
Structural engineer
Uzun and Case Engineers
Landscape architect
Michael van Valkenburgh
Associates
Contractor Mark Conforte
Conforte Builders

House at Cap Ferret
Arcachon, France
1997–8
Architect Anne Lacaton, Philippe Vassal
Palais de Tokyo, 2 Rue de la
Manutention, 75016 Paris
France
Collaborators Lawrence Baggett, Sylvain
Menaud, Emmanuelle Delage
Christophe Hutin
Pierre Yves Portier
Client Unnamed
Structural engineer
Mr Stanik, CESMA
General contractor
Enterprise DEGAS

Byrne House
Scottsdale, Arizona, USA
1994–8
Architect Will Bruder
1314 West Circle
Mountain Road, New River
AZ 85027, USA
Project team Will Bruder, Tim Christ

Jack DeBartolo
Client Carol and Bill Byrne
Structural engineer
Rudow & Berry
Mechanical engineer
Otterbein Engineering
Electrical engineer
CA Energy Designs
General contractor
Bill Byrne

Reutter House
Zapallar, Cachagua, Chile
1998
Architect Mathias Klotz
Isidora Goyenechea 3356
Officina 60, Las Condes, Chile
Design team Mathias Klotz, Liliana Silva
Client Unnamed
Structural engineer
Patricio Stagno
Contractor Estructuras Cordillera

Project 222
Pembrokeshire, Wales, UK
1994
Architect Future Systems
The Warehouse
20 Victoria Gardens
London, W11 3PE, UK
Client Bob and Gill
Marshall-Andrews
Structural engineer
Techniker
Environmental engineer
BDSP
General contractor
Young Construction

House of Poetic Space
Shinkenchiku Residential
Design Competition
Japan, 1998
Architect Kyna Leski
Studio 360, 112 Union Street
Suite 303, Providence
RI 0293, USA

Slim House
Daily Mail/Ideal Home
'Concept House' Competition
UK, 1999
Architect Pierre d'Avoine Architects
6A Orde Street
London WC1N 3JW, UK
Design team Miraj Ahmed, Pierre
d'Avoine, Alex Evy, Tom
Emerson, Kim Fichter
Talar Kouyoumdjian, Noemie
Laviolle, Zachary Marshall
Environmental services engineer
Max Fordham and partners
Structural engineer
Jane Wernick Associates

House for the Suburbs, House for the City
Time Magazine:
Visions 21: How We Will Live
USA, 2000
Architects **Wes Jones**
(House for the Suburbs)
Jones Partners, Architecture
141 Nevada Street
El Segundo, CA 90245, USA
Bernard Tschumi
(House for the City)
227 West 17th Street
New York, NY 10011, USA

The following titles are divided into three sections: books on building design and construction; theoretical books on society and culture; books on and by the architects featured in this volume.

Design and Construction

Cerver, Francisco Asensio. House Details (Arco Editorial Team, Plans of Architecture series, 1997).

Frampton, Kenneth. Studies in Tectonic Culture: the Poetics of Construction in Nineteenth and Twentieth Century Architecture (Cambridge, MA: MIT Press/Graham Foundation, 1998).

Friedman, Alice T. Women and the Making of the Modern House (New York: Harry N. Abrams, 1998).

Gollings, John and Michell, George. New Australian Style (Australia: Thames and Hudson, 1999).

Herbert, Gilbert. The Dream of the Factory Made House (Cambridge, MA: MIT Press, 1984).

Melhuish, Clare (ed). Architecture and Anthropology, AD Profile 124 (London: Academy Editions, 1996).

Oliver, Paul. Dwellings: the House across the World (London: Phaidon Press, 1987).

Rapoport, Amos. House Form and Culture (1969).

Russell, Barry. Building Systems, Industrialization and Architecture (John Wiley and Sons, 1981).

Spiller, Neil. Digital Dreams, Architecture and the New Alchemic Technologies (London: Ellipsis, 1998).

Riley, Terrence. The Un-private House (New York: Museum of Modern Art, 1999).

Ryan, Deborah S. The Ideal Home through the Twentieth Century (London: Hagar Publishing, 1997).

Sudjic, Deyan. Home: the Twentieth Century House. (London: Laurence King, 1999).

Venturi, Robert. Complexity and Contradiction in Architecture. (New York: Museum of Modern Art, 1966).

Waterson, Roxana. The Living House (Oxford: Oxford University Press, 1991).

Society and Culture

Bachelard, Gaston. The Poetics of Space (Boston: Beacon Press, 1969). Originally published in French, 1958.

Bourdieu, Pierre. Outline of a Theory of Practice (Cambridge: CUP, 1977); and Distinction: A Social Critique of the Judgement of Taste (London: Routledge, 1984).

Buchli, Victor. An Archaeology of Socialism (Oxford: Berg Publishers, 1999).

Carsten, Janet and Hugh-Jones, Stephen. About the House (Cambridge, MA: CUP, 1995).

Chapman, Tony and Hockey, Jenny (eds). Ideal Homes?: Social Change and Domestic Life (London: Routledge, 1999). See essay by Tim Brindley 'The Modern House in England'.

Chakrabarty, Dipesh. Postcoloniality and the Artifice of History: Who Speaks for 'Indian' Pasts? (Representations 37, University of California, Winter 1992).

Colomina, Beatriz. Privacy and Publicity (Cambridge, MA: MIT Press, 1995).

Damluji, Salma Samar. The Architecture of the United Arab Emirates (Reading: Garnet, 2000).

Hiddenobu, Jinnai. Tokyo: A Spatial Anthropology (California: University of California Press 1995).

Kant, Susan. Domestic Architecture and the Use of Space (Cambridge: Cambridge University Press, 1990).

Lovins, Amory. Natural Capitalism: Creating the Next Industrial Revolution (New York: Little Brown & Company, 1999).

Mackay, H (ed). Consumption and Everyday Life (London: Sage, 1997).

Mernissi, Fatima. Beyond the Veil (London: Al Saqui Books, 1995).

Mitchell, William. City of Bits (Cambridge, MA: MIT Press, 1995); and E-topia (MIT, 1999).

Miller, D. 'Household as Cultural Idiom' in Modernity: an Ethnographical Approach (Oxford: Berg Publishers).

Ravetz, Alison and Turkington, David. English Domestic Environments 1914–2000 (E & F N Spon, 1995).

Reed, Christopher. Not at Home: the Suppression of the Domestic in Modern Art and Architecture (London: Thames and Hudson, 1996).

Silverstone, Roger and Hirsch, Eric (eds). Consuming Technologies: Media and Information in Domestic Spaces (London: Routledge, 1992). See essay by Sonia Livingstone 'The Meaning of Domestic Techologies'.

Tilley, Christopher. A Phenomenology of Landscape (Oxford: Berg Publishers, 1994).

Tilley, Christopher. Ethnography and Material Culture, from The Sage Handbook of Ethnography, Atkinson, P, et al (eds) (London: Sage 2000).

Virilio, Paul. Open Sky (London: Verso, 1997).

Wilson, William Julius. 'The State of American Cities', from Social Exclusion and the Future of Cities (CASE paper 35, London School of Economics, 2000).

Architects' Monographs

Balau, R&M. 'Documenta 9: Architecture in its Place. Displacement. Interview with Paul Robbrecht' (A+U Japan, 1992).

Betsky, Aaron and Mitchell, Willaim J. Koning Eizenberg: Buildings (New York: Rizzoli, 1996).

Blundell Jones, Peter. Gunter Behnisch (Basel: Birkhäuser, 2000).

Carter, Brian. Patkau Architects: Selected Projects 1983–1993 (Nova Scotia: Tuns Press/Dalhousie University, 1994).

Cassiman, Bart. 'Paul Robbrecht and Hilde Daem. Architecture in Sculpture' (Antwerp: deSingel, 1989).

Field, Marcus. Future Systems (London: Phaidon, 1999).

Fromonot, Françoise. Glenn Murcutt: Buildings and Projects (London: Thames & Hudson, 1995).

Gauzin-Muller, Dominique (ed). Behnisch & Partners : 50 Years of Architecture (New York: John Wiley & Son Ltd, 1998).

Jacobs, Steven; Robbrecht, Paul; Moussavi, Farshid; Munoz, Juan; Daem, Hilda. Paul Robbrecht & Hilda Daem: Works in Architecture (London: Ludion, 1998).

Koolhaas, Rem. S,M,L,Xl (New York: Penguin USA, 1998).

Koolhaas, Rem. Oma Rem Koolhaas Living, Vivre, Leben (Basel: Birkhäuser, 1999).

Linder, Mark (ed); Bergen, Ann; Kipnis, Jeff; Vidler, Anthony. Scogin Elam and Bray: Critical Architecture/ Architectural Criticism (New York: Rizzoli, 1992).

Maas, Winy, van Rijs, Jacob and Koek, Richard (eds). FARMAX (Rotterdam, 1998).

Mack, Gerhard. Herzog & De Meuron 1978–1988: The Complete Works (Basel: Birkhäuser, 1997).

Ons Erfeel Foundation. The Low Countries: Arts and Society in Flanders and The Netherlands (1998).

Pawley, Martin. Norman Foster: A Global Architecture (New York: Universe Publishing, 1999).

Salazar, Jaime (ed). MVRDV at VPRO (Actar, 1998).

Williams, Tod; Tsien, Billie; and Carter, Brian; W LeCuyer. Annette (eds). MAP 5: Tod Williams Billie Tsien (The Michigan Architecture Papers. University of Michigan College of Architecture, 1998).

Photographic Acknowledgements

All illustrations supplied by the architects, unless otherwise specified. Photographic sources are listed where possible, but the publisher will endeavour to rectify any inadvertent omissions.

Archivio Senosiain: p25cr; p40; p41tr, c, cl, b; p42.
©Peter Barber: p76; p77; p78; p79; p80; p81.
Behnisch & Partner, Stuttgart/Christian Kandzia: p27; p29; p30; p31.
©Reiner Blunck: p22; p24tl, cl; p33; p34; p35tr, c, cl; p36tl, cl, bl; p37; pp38/9; p39t; p39tc; p44tl, tc; p45; p46tl, cl, bl; p47tl, tr, c, cr, br; p48; p49; pp50/1; p66; p87tl.
©Anthony Browell/Oki-Doki: p151; pp152/3; pp154/5; p156br; p157.
©Martin Charles: p5tl.
©Peter Cook/VIEW: p10tl; p19; p174cl.
©Ross Coombes: p111br.
©Stéphane Couturier/ARCHIPRESS: p159tl, tr, b; p160; p161; p162tl; p163.
Photographs by Grey Crawford, as seen in Metropolitan Home, May/June 2000: p144; 149.
©Kristien Daem: p70; p71; pp72/3; p74.
The Daily Mail: p219cl,cr.
©Richard Davies: p172; p209, p210; p212/3; p214.
Daniel Dobers: p84tr; p85t, cl, bl.
James Dow: p177tl, cl; p179tl, cl, bl; p180; p181tc, c, tr.
Pierre d'Avoine Architects: p216; p225tr; p226; p227.
First Garden City Heritage Museum, Letchworth Garden City: p118tl.
©Dennis Gilbert/VIEW: p102tl; p103; 104tl; p105t; p106; p107tr, cl, bl.
©Stephen Goodenough: p109; p110.

p111tr; pp112/113; p114t; p115t.
David Grandorge: p224; p225tl, cl.
Thomas Heinser: p69tr; p82tc; p83; p85cr; p86tl, br; p87tr, c.
Lucien Hervé: p68tl.
Hochschule für Architektur und Bauwesen: p8tl.
Dieter E. Hoppe/AKG London: p7tr.
©Timothy Hursley: p88; p90tl, tr; p91c; p92; p93; p182; p183cl; p185; pp186/7; p188; p189tl, tc.
Jones, Partners: Architecture: p230; p231.
Vasant Kamath: p120b; p121; p123tl, tc, tr, bl; p124tl.
© Nicholas Kane 1999: p164; p165cl; p166tl, tc; p169cl; p170; p171.
©KNTA: p105ucr,lcr,b; p107tl.
Nelson Kon: p25tl, cl; p53; p54b; p56; p57.
LA Aerial Photography Inc: p147.
©Christophe Lab: p159cr.
Kyna Leski: p220; p221; p222; p223.
Mies van der Rohe Archive: p68cl.
Mitchell Library, State Library of New South Wales: p35bl.
©Michael Moran: p116; p132tl, tc; p133; p134tl, tc, tr, c; p136; p137.
Mario Mutschlechner: p25br; p41tl; p43.
Paul Ockrassa: p5cr.
Open University: p9tr.
©Frank den Oudsten: p14tr; p15b.
Stuart Parker: p13tr.
Patkau Architects: p177tr; p178r; p179tr; p181bl.
Erik Pawassar: p86bl.
©Alberto Piovano: p202c, cr; p203t; pp204/5; p206b, cr; p207.
©Undine Pröhl: p176; p177c; p179br; p181cl.
Range/Bettman/UPI: p18tl.
©Philippe Ruault: p69cr; p96t; p98bl; p175; p191; p192; p194tl, c, cr; p195.

Scala Fotografico: p174tr.
©Shinkenchiku-sha: p138; p139; p140; p142/3.
Sandip Singh: p123c.
The Daily Mail: p219br.
©Margherita Spiluttini: p126tl; p127; p128; p129b; p130; p131br.
Bill Timmerman: p196br; p197; p199; p200; p201.
Bernard Tschumi Architects: p228; p229.
Venturi, Scott Brown & Associates: p6tl, cl;
Philip Vile: p219tr.
Hans Werlemann, Hectic Pictures: p94; p96b; p97; 98t, c; p99; p100tl; p101.
Copyright ©1994, 2000 The Frank Lloyd Wright Foundation, Scottsdale AZ: p218tl.
©Nigel Young/Foster and Partners: p2; p58; p60tl, tc, br; pp62/3; p64tl, c, cr, br; p65.

Author's Acknowledgements

I am indebted to the editorial and picture research team at Phaidon for being so helpful, sympathetic and efficient in their collaboration with me on the realization of this book. Many thanks to: commissioning editor Vivian Constantinopoulos, project editor Hannah Barnes-Murphy, picture researcher Miranda Snow, picture research manager Sophia Gibb, and production controller Karen Farquhar.

Thanks are also due to Christine Garcia for help with translation; Chris Tilley, who kindly read the text; the Department of Anthropology, University College, London, for the Master of Arts in Material Culture which has helped me to develop my ideas; and, above all, Pierre d'Avoine for providing endless inspiration, advice and support.

It is my great pleasure to dedicate this book to Pierre and Ivan.

Phaidon Press Limited
Regent's Wharf
All Saints Street
London N1 9PA

First published 2000
© 2000 Phaidon Press Limited

ISBN 0 7148 3987 6

A CIP catalogue record for this book is
available from the British Library

Designed by Karl Shanahan

Printed in Hong Kong

Jacket illustrations: front, House near
Bordeaux, Rem Koolhaas, Office for
Metropolitan Architecture, 1994–8; back,
Suburban House, Wes Jones, 2000

Frontis: Crescent House, Ken
Shuttleworth, Foster and Partners, 1997